Better Homes and Gardens ®

GARDEN FRESH
Meals

Better Homes and Gardens®

GARDEN FRESH
Meals

More than 200 delicious recipes for
enjoying produce at its just-picked peak

WILEY

John Wiley & Sons, Inc.

Better Homes and Gardens® *Garden Fresh Meals*

Editor: Jan Miller

Project Editor: Lisa Kingsley, Waterbury Publications, Inc.

Contributing Editors: Tricia Laning, Mary Williams, Waterbury Publications, Inc.

Contributing Writer: Deborah Vickers Wagman

Recipe Development and Testing: *Better Homes and Gardens* Test Kitchen

Contributing Photographers: Quentin Bacon, Jason Donnelly, Scott Little, Kritsada Panichgul, Jay Wilde

Contributing Stylists: Sue Mitchell, Annie Peterson, Jennifer Peterson, Charles Worthington

John Wiley & Sons, Inc.

Publisher: Natalie Chapman

Associate Publisher: Jessica Goodman

Executive Editor: Anne Ficklen

Editor: Charleen Barila

Production Director: Diana Cisek

Senior Production Editor: Amy Zarkos

Manufacturing Manager: Tom Hyland

Design Director: Ken Carlson, Waterbury Publications, Inc.

Associate Design Director: Doug Samuelson, Waterbury Publications, Inc.

Production Assistants: Kim Hopkins, Mindy Samuelson, Waterbury Publications, Inc.

Recipes on pages 220 and 242 courtesy of Hugo Matheson, The Kitchen, Boulder, Colorado.

Our seal assures you that every recipe in Better Homes and Gardens® *Garden Fresh Meals* has been tested in the Better Homes and Gardens® Test Kitchen. This means that each recipe is practical and reliable and meets our high standards of taste appeal. We guarantee your satisfaction with this book for as long as you own it.

Contents

Eat Fresh!

Anyone whose interest is piqued by eating more healthfully, locally, and sustainably will use this book as a go-to guide to accomplish all these objectives—and do so deliciously.

Garden Fresh Meals offers more than 200 recipes that call for fresh fruits and vegetables at the height of their fresh, in-season peak, plus it provides a buying guide for finding bountiful foods—fresh, fabulous, flavorful, and ready to transform everyday meals into seasonal celebrations.

Whether you grow fruits and vegetables in your own backyard; forage at farmers' markets, supermarkets, and roadside stands; pick them in farmers' fields; or receive weekly boxes of handpicked produce from Community Supported Agriculture programs, this book shows you how to make recipes with the freshest, best-tasting, and most nutritious fruits and vegetables.

Just Picked

SEASONAL PRODUCE GUIDE

Whether you pick your produce from your own garden, a farmers' market, or supermarket, here's how to get the best that each season has to offer— and how to keep it as fresh as possible.

To add extra crispness to lettuces and salad greens—or to refresh those that have wilted—tear greens into bite-size pieces and soak in lukewarm water for 30 minutes. Drain greens in a colander, roll in a clean terry cloth towel, and refrigerate about 2 hours.

Lettuces and Salad Greens

PEAK SEASON FROM MARCH TO APRIL

Not long ago, iceberg lettuce ruled the lettuce world. Today lettuce textures range from butter-tender to crisp and crunchy, and the pale leaves have been painted over with deep, verdant shades of green, crimson, and aubergine.

HEAD LETTUCES As these lettuces grow, leaves clasp together to form heads. Buttery texture and loosely clasped leaves characterize butterhead lettuces—such as Boston, Bibb, and Buttercrunch. The crisphead family—fathered by iceberg lettuce—is known for its crisp, cold, and clean personality.

ROMAINE Sturdy romaine grows in tall, loosely packed heads. The ribs contain a milky fluid that lends the greens a refreshing yet bitter herb flavor.

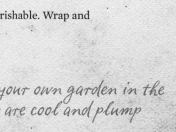

LOOSELEAF Like its ancestors, this family of greens develops in leaves. Each boasts refreshing flavor with a hint of bitterness.

- **ARUGULA** Peppery and slightly bitter.
- **BELGIAN ENDIVE** A chicory, with crunchy, slightly bitter leaves.
- **CRESS** Possesses a potent, peppery punch.
- **CURLY ENDIVE** Also called frisée, it is crisp and quite bitter.
- **ESCAROLE** Use its sturdy leaves in salads when they are young.
- **LEAF LETTUCE** Mild and pliable, the leaves have ruffled surfaces that add layers of texture to salads.
- **MÂCHE** Also known as "corn salad" or "lamb's tongue," the miniature leaves have tender texture and milk flavor.
- **MESCLUN** A mix of various young salad greens.
- **MIZUNA** Popular in Japanese cuisine, it has tender leaves that are pleasantly peppery.
- **OAKLEAF** Delicate and tender.
- **RADICCHIO** Enlivens with color and slightly bitter notes.
- **RED MUSTARD** Pungent, peppery, and zippy.
- **TAT SOI** Little leaves have burly texture and peppery flavor.
- **WINTER PURSLANE** Succulent, crisp, and slightly salty on the tongue.

PICKING Choose heads or leaves with deep color and crisp texture. Avoid wilt, rust, brown edges, and flabby texture.

STORING Lettuces and salad greens are delicate and highly perishable. Wrap and refrigerate—unwashed—for only a day or two.

Harvest lettuce from your own garden in the morning, when leaves are cool and plump with moisture.

Peas PEAK SEASON FROM MARCH TO MAY

These climbers—among the first garden vegetables to welcome spring—root their toes in cold, damp soil while their tendrils twist toward the warming sun.

The hardiness of peas, however, is short-lived. Plump, sweet-tempered pods wither quickly once picked. They are best immediately upon harvest.

GARDEN PEA Because garden—or English—peas begin to convert sugars to starch the second they are plucked from the vine, this vegetable is seldom available in supermarkets. To enjoy these peas at the height of perfection, grow them in your garden or purchase them at farmers' markets, then shell and cook them right away.

SNOW PEA Eat the slender, translucent, and delicately sweet pods whole.

SNAP PEA A hybrid with characteristics of both the garden pea and snow pea, these rotund, glossy peas are a mange-tout—or "eat-it-all—variety. Of the three pea sisters, snap peas have the longest shelf life.

PICKING The freshest, most flavorful are glossy and bright green, with fresh-looking ends. Look closely at snow pea pods—you should be able to see flat peas within. Give snap peas a shake. If peas rattle inside, pass them by. For both varieties, smallness indicates sweetness. Avoid dull, faded, yellowish, limp, or overgrown pods.

STORING Serve peas—raw or cooked—as quickly as possible. Keep peas, unwashed and unshelled, in the refrigerator for 1 or 2 days. Or blanch the peas in boiling water for 2 minutes and freeze.

KITCHEN TIP
Pea tendrils and leaves are also edible. Add them to salads or wrap them in rice paper with other spring roll fillings.

1 pound of garden peas yields 5 ounces of edible peas.

Young carrots—harvested from backyard gardens or farmers markets—seldom need peeling. Just scrub with a stiff brush.

Carrots PEAK SEASON FROM MARCH TO MAY

Beneath the ground, under a canopy of feathery, umbrella-like greens, grows the humble carrot. Second only in popularity to potatoes, these thick, fleshy, and deeply colored roots snap with crispness and minty, aromatic flavor.

Although orange is the color most associated with this hale and hardy root vegetable, more than 100 varieties make up the carrot family. Venture beyond your supermarket to discover carrots with shapes that vary from golf ball-size orbs to long, slender cones. Some wear coats of deep indigo, icy white, sunny yellow, Cabernet-red, and black.

PICKING Bigger is not necessarily better. Look for carrots that are less than 8 inches long, with plump, crisp, smooth, shiny roots. Avoid carrots that have spidery white roots. These are over the hill. Carrots purchased with fresh, perky foliage attached will be the freshest and most flavorful.

STORING When foliage is intact, cut it off. Attached greens pull moisture from the roots. Carrots are great keepers. Store them up to a month in the refrigerator in vented plastic bags.

Spinach PEAK SEASON FROM MARCH TO MAY

Spinach germinates in the coldest soil, pushing succulent, lush leaves out of still-snowy ground. The earliest of leafy greens, spinach sprints from sandy garden soil to the table in as few as 37 days—a welcome and green relief from the chill gray of winter.

Renowned for its Popeye-esque strength-enhancing benefits, spinach has a healthful reputation. The leafy vegetable is touted for its nutrient-dense healthfulness, year-round availability, and versatility.

PICKING Whether purchasing the crinkly leaved Savoy variety of spinach or its smooth-leaf cousin, look for crisp, dark green leaves with no sign of wilting. Loose-leaf spinach sold in small bunches—rosettes—will remain fresh longer than bagged varieties.

STORING Spinach prefers sandy soil and tends to retain sand in its crinkly leaves. Wash leaves meticulously, then spin and towel dry. Spinach keeps for 3 to 4 days, tightly bagged and refrigerated.

For longer storage, steam spinach in its own moisture for 2 to 3 minutes, wrap tightly, and freeze up to 8 months.

KITCHEN TIP
To clean fresh spinach, rinse the leaves in a basin of cool water. Sand and dirt will settle to the bottom of the basin. Several changes of water may be necessary. Immerse leaves in warm water on the final rinse—warmth relaxes the spinach crinkles and releases any remaining sand.

To keep cauliflower pristine white while cooking, add a tablespoon of lemon juice to the cooking water.

Cauliflower and Broccoli PEAK SEASON FROM APRIL TO JUNE

Broccoli and cauliflower—big-bone sisters of the garden—are hardly glamorous vegetables. What this hearty duo lacks in delicacy and refinement, both more than make up for with robust flavor and heavy nutritional payload.

The two vegetables are nearly identical botanically, with thick flower stalks containing masses of tightly closed buds that are harvested and eaten before they open.

When Mark Twain described cauliflower as "nothing but cabbage with a college education," he was fairly accurate. Cauliflower is a member of the cabbage, or cruciferous, family. Although cauliflower was originally only white, horticulturalists have developed amazing color variants of cheddar-orange, chartreuse, and deep violet.

Broccoli—another cabbage incarnation—is named for its Italian ancestors. Its dense heads are vibrant green except when grown in especially cold weather, when the heads—or "curds" in horticultural nomenclature—take on a bluish cast.

Two foreigners form part of the broccoli family tree—Chinese gai lan and Italian rapini, also known as broccoli rabe. Gai lan has an abundance of thick, glossy leaves and miniature heads that bloom with vestigial white flowers. The flavor is more bitter than other broccoli. Rapini stalks branch with dull, spiked leaves surrounding quarter-size open curds upon which tiny yellow flowers bloom. Nutty, bitter, and pungent describe its flavor.

PICKING BROCCOLI For best quality, choose broccoli with 4- to 6-inch-wide stalks and firm, rounded heads. Buds should be no larger than a matchhead. Avoid loose, yellowing heads and open buds.

PICKING CAULIFOWER Select solid, heavy heads of cauliflower surrounded by fresh green leaves. Avoid flabby, yellowing heads and rust spots.

STORING Both cauliflower and broccoli keep well for 3 or 4 days when tightly wrapped and stored in the refrigerator. For long-term storage, blanch and freeze. Both vegetables freeze well.

BROCCOLI AT ITS BEST

To minimize the sometimes off-putting aroma of cooking broccoli, cook it briefly. Overcooking increases its aroma, dulls its color, and leaches its nutrients.

Artichokes

PEAK SEASON FROM MARCH TO MAY

The curiously unusual flavor and bizarre morphology are only part of the magic of an artichoke. These green globes alter the chemistry of taste buds, making anything that is eaten immediately following them taste sweet. Artichokes are one of the few foods that do not pair with wine.

The three sizes of this edible thistle do not correspond to plant maturation, but rather to where it sprouts on the plant. Jumbo artichokes grow atop the center stalk, medium-size artichokes are harvested from side shoots, and miniature artichokes are pinched from the base of the stem. Gourmands prize the leaves and hearts of these tightly closed buds wherever they grow.

Many artichoke cultivars are grown in Europe. A few, including a thornless version and a beautiful new purple variety, grow in California. The most common artichoke in supermarkets is the Globe artichoke.

PICKING Look for firm, heavy, deep green globes with tight heads. Those with spreading leaves are past their prime. Squeeze an artichoke: If it squeaks, it is fresh. Do not pass up squeaky, tightly headed artichokes with bronze-color leaf tips—those have been kissed by frost and may have the best flavor of all.

STORAGE Artichokes boast excellent keeping qualities and may be stored in a humid drawer in the refrigerator up to 2 weeks. Canning or freezing artichokes is time-consuming and labor-intensive. Leave the task to commercial processors.

To prevent discoloration, cut artichokes with a stainless-steel knife. Artichokes may stain hands. Wear kitchen gloves when preparing them.

Radishes

PEAK SEASON FROM APRIL TO MAY

Radishes—an instant-gratification vegetable—mature in as little as 3 weeks, which makes them a reliable choice for children's first gardens. Their taste—sharp, with a potent and peppery bite—is guaranteed to wake up the palate.

SUMMER RADISHES Summer radishes, including the supermarket standard fuchsia and white variety, are most often eaten raw. Specialty cultivars vary in shape from small and round to elongated, carrotlike shapes. Easter egg bunches, comprised of light pink, dark crimson, and pale purple radishes, may be available in specialty markets.

WINTER RADISHES These cooking radishes arrive in the kitchen dressed in black, white, and white streaked with stripes of lime green. A few are turnip-shape, some are slender, some are fat, and others grow up to be as much as a yard long. Use these pungent radishes sparingly in stir-fries, grilling, baking, boiling, and broiling.

PICKING Top-quality radishes will be brightly colored, well formed, smooth, firm, and crisp. Avoid spongy, wilted radishes.

STORING Radishes with leaves attached may be stored in the refrigerator for 3 to 5 days, while those with greenery removed keep, refrigerated, for 2 to 4 weeks. Radishes do not freeze well, but they are delicious when pickled.

Leeks and Scallions   PEAK SEASON FROM MARCH TO MAY

The *Allium* family—to which onions, shallots, leeks, scallions, garlic, and chives belong—abides by the rules of a firmly entrenched hierarchy. At the top is the leek, a true gustatory aristocrat that requires nearly 6 months to reach its full potential. At the opposite end are scallions, brazen teenyboppers that leap out of the ground early in their lives.

LEEKS

In most parts of the country, leeks carry a fancy price tag that perhaps reflects short supply—a sad state of affairs for one of the sweetest, most subtle members of the onion family. Cooking transforms the hot, bitter bite of raw leeks into creamy, velvety, almost buttery luxuriousness.

Unleashing this beguiling flavor requires careful attention. As leeks grow, they are blanketed with sandy soil so the roots blanch or remain alabaster white. As a result, the symmetrical, herringbone-like plant is always filled with dirt and sand. They must be attentively cleaned.

Scallions, however, have few liabilities. These fast-growing onions—also called spring or green onions—are ready to harvest within a few weeks of planting. Mild but zesty scallions are most often eaten raw; they also enhance quick-cooked dishes with spunky vitality.

PICKING LEEKS   Slender leeks possess the best flavor. Look for small- to medium-size leeks with long white stems.

STORING LEEKS   Refrigerate leeks, unwashed, for a few days. To freeze leeks, cut into ½-inch-thick slices and bag tightly. Add frozen leeks directly to soups and stews—do not thaw first.

PICKING SCALLIONS   Dark green leaves and bright white, smooth, and crisp roots tell you that scallions are fresh. Avoid limp or discolored plants.

STORING SCALLIONS   Scallions keep in a refrigerator produce drawer up to 1 week. To keep them nice and crisp, wrap them in a damp towel. Because scallions are readily available year-round, they are seldom preserved by freezing or canning.

GET WILD
If you ever have the opportunity to pick or purchase ramps—or wild leeks—do so. These small, glossy-leaved leeks resemble lilies of the valley plants and grow in shaded woodland settings nationwide. They have a strong garlicky aroma and a pronounced onion flavor.

Asparagus

PEAK SEASON FROM MARCH TO JUNE

This short-lived vegetable makes two hefty and contradictory demands for growing and harvesting. Growers must be patient. This herbaceous flowering perennial requires 3 years to become mature enough to harvest.

Second, asparagus must be harvested at its tender best; spears quickly peek out of cool soil and form shoots in a matter of a days. If that window is missed, the crop becomes a useless, although beautiful, mass of feathery, fernlike fronds.

Asparagus—harvested between April and June— may be the vegetable most associated with the arrival of spring. Best rushed from field to table before sugars turn to starches, it is indeed one of the greatest glories of the fresh new season.

Lauded for its elegant shape and succulent green stalks, asparagus is best eaten young.

PICKING Select asparagus spears when bright green, straight, firm, and brittle. Choose stalks with tight, compact, pointed tips. Open, wilted, or shriveled tips indicate stalks that are past prime and that will be tough and stringy.

STORING For best quality, store asparagus, bases down, in cool water. Cut ½ inch from the bottom of the stalks, place in a dish containing about 1 inch of water, and refrigerate up to 3 days.

To trim woody bottoms from asparagus spears, hold the tip and the base in different hands and bend. The woody portion of the stalk will snap off from the tender shoot.

Rhubarb PEAK SEASON FROM APRIL TO MAY

Spring may come in like a lamb, but rhubarb—one of spring's first gifts that leaps into the season with a rosy-red flourish—comes in like a lion.

The season's most celebrated leaf stem—botanically classified as a vegetable but commonly referred to as a fruit—possesses the garden's most aggressive flavor, a taste with mouth-puckering, bracing tartness.

Although rhubarb—aptly known as "pie plant"—is most often combined with a large amount of sugar to make desserts and sweet-tart sauces, stalks also melt magnificently into savory recipes, where they punctuate dishes with brightness in the way that a squirt of lemon juice or a measure of vinegar does.

Rhubarb can be cultivated in hot houses, resulting in smooth, tender stalks, or be field grown, which engenders deep stalk color and greater acidity.

Whether field or greenhouse grown and whether used in sweet or savory applications, rhubarb's tough, stringy stalks melt into a sensationally satiny softness when cooked.

PICKING Fresh rhubarb should be as crisp and brittle as celery. Slender stalks are often sweeter than stockier ones. Avoid rhubarb that's wilted or blemished.

STORING Rhubarb, wrapped and stored in the refrigerator, will last for several days. Take advantage of rhubarb in abundance by slicing the stalks into ½-inch pieces, bag tightly, and freeze. No blanching is necessary. Frozen rhubarb remains delicious up to 10 months.

LEAVE THE LEAVES ALONE

Unless you grow your own rhubarb or visit farmers who do, you will seldom see rhubarb with its crinkly, elephantine leaves attached. The leaves contain oxalic acid, a corrosive substance that may upset stomachs. Rhubarb leaves, however, make a fine cleaner for pots and pans and will restore even the dullest aluminum pans to a glossy shine.

BITE OF HISTORY
Heirloom tomatoes are the antithesis of commercially grown shipping tomatoes. Unlike hybrids, heritage tomatoes need long growing seasons and yield only a few tomatoes per plant. Many varieties— ranging from small irregular- shape fruit to large, smooth fruits in nearly every color—are more than 100 years old. To choose from the most comprehensive collection of heirloom tomato seeds, visit Seedsavers Exchange (seedsavers.org).

Tomatoes PEAK SEASON FROM JULY TO SEPTEMBER

Decades ago, large industrial growers of tomatoes replaced juicy, drip-down-the-chin tomatoes with varieties that shipped well. The tomatoes were picked brick-hard and green—then packed and shipped with the hope that they would ripen along the way.

Then, in the mid-1990s, a tomato renaissance blazed through the country, again bringing locally grown tomatoes to the forefront of American cuisine, a reminder that tomatoes allowed to ripen fully on the vine have astounding flavor and aroma.

VARIETIES Tomatoes grow in many shapes, forms, and colors—including black, brown, green, purple, pink, orange, and yellow.

- **CURRANT TOMATOES** Rare pea-size tomatoes.
- **CHERRY TOMATOES** 1 to 2 inches in diameter, in shades of red, orange, and yellow.
- **GRAPE TOMATOES** Developed in Asia and fairly new to the American market, these elongated cherry-size tomatoes quickly became popular.
- **ROUND RIBBED TOMATOES** In most colors, these large tomatoes have large lobes separated by tight ribbing.
- **ROUND SMOOTH** The typical tomato.
- **BEEFSTEAK** Jumbo-size red tomatoes; great slicers.
- **PEAR AND PLUM TOMATOES** Elongated and especially meaty, these are the best sauce-making tomatoes. These beauties are yellow, orange, and red.

PICKING Serving freshly harvested, locally grown tomatoes is the best way to bring true tomato goodness to your table. Choose barely firm, plump tomatoes, aromatic with tomato fragrance. Avoid soft spots, bruises, and large growth cracks.

STORING Always store tomatoes at room temperature—flavor suffers greatly with refrigeration. Enjoy within a day or two of harvest for fullest flavor.

Tomatoes lend themselves to home canning, such as stewed tomatoes, salsa, ketchup, chutney, and sauces.

Gardeners with an abundance of tomatoes often bag and freeze the fruits whole to toss into soups and sauces.

KITCHEN TIP
Caprese salad—simply sliced fresh tomatoes, fresh mozzarella cheese, and leaves of fresh basil drizzled with olive oil and balsamic vinegar—is one sure way to celebrate the glory of tomatoes.

Natural herbal companions for tomatoes include basil, oregano, dill, thyme, parsley, and garlic.

Beans PEAK SEASON FROM JULY TO AUGUST

Beans settle into summer with relaxed productivity and a preference for sun, the very sort of proclivities one would expect from an indigenous South American row crop.

Which is your favorite—red, yellow, green, purple, brown, pink, black, or white? Beans come from a large family, with a vast majority of them, such as black beans and pintos, cultivated for their seeds.

Edible-pod beans—including green beans, yellow wax beans, French beans (also called haricots verts), and Italian flat beans (also called Romanos)—are summer staples.

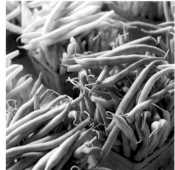

PICKING Choose beans with velvety, even color and a healthy snap. Avoid beans that show signs of shrivel or mold and those with swollen seeds, which are overmature.

STORING Store fresh beans in the refrigerator for no longer than 3 days. Beans make excellent candidates for canning and freezing.

GARDEN TIP
Yellow wax beans, which taste like green beans, are sometimes smaller and more tender. Unfortunately yellow beans are inferior to green beans in nutritional value.

Summer Squash PEAK SEASON FROM JULY TO AUGUST

Summer squash are the sweet innocents of the squash family. Unlike their older siblings—which are allowed to mature on the vine until the skins become tough enough for storage, these tender-skinned toddlers are plucked from the vine young and tender.

VARIETIES Although they may be different in appearance, all summer squash are tender in texture and mild in flavor.
- **PATTYPAN SQUASH** These diminutive squash resemble little pincushions with scalloped edges. They may be white, green, or yellow. (Pictured at left.)
- **SPAGHETTI SQUASH** Elongated and lemony yellow, with creamy golden strands of flesh that scoop out like strands of spaghetti.
- **ZUCCHINI** Unrivaled in culinary versatility and renowned for rapid growth, it is the most popular summer squash. Some fruits are yellow; most are dark green.
- **GOOSENECK YELLOW SQUASH** Similar in taste and texture to zucchini, but characterized by a bent stem end.

PICKING Select summer squash that are very young, crisp, and unblemished. Summer squash are especially susceptible to rot, so avoid bruises, dents, and cuts in the flesh.

STORING Summer squash are highly perishable and will have the best, most flavorful quality when refrigerated no longer than a day or two. Although summer squashes are not good for canning, they are excellent for pickles and relishes. Grated, frozen summer squash are excellent for making muffins and quick breads.

The leaves of crinkly-leaved chard tend to harbor sand and garden soil. To clean them, swish stalks vigorously in a basin of cool water.

Swiss Chard PEAK SEASON FROM JUNE TO OCTOBER

Swiss chard, a leafy member of the beet family, is regularly tossed into the categorical bin with herbs or greens, such as kale and collards, and it does not belong there. The glossy, crisp leaves and fleshy leaf stalks of chard are mild and delicate, with a sweet, earthy flavor—quite different from the assertive flavors of kale and collards.

PICKING The most commonly marketed chard is dark green with reddish ribs. Other colors range from pale celadon to vivid scarlet. Leaves may be smooth or crinkly. Choose crisp bunches of chard with firm, bright leaves.

STORING Chard keeps, refrigerated, for several days. To extend its freshness, wrap bunches in a damp towel. Freezing chard is a simple task: Simply blanch the stalks in boiling water for 30 seconds, plunge into a bowl of ice water, drain, bag, and label.

Eggplant PEAK SEASON FROM JULY TO OCTOBER

In spite of its royal purple cloak, eggplant has had a long, slow struggle for acceptance as a nutritious food. Years ago the vegetable was called *mala insana*—or insane apple—because eating it was thought to cause mental illness.

Fortunately that theory is not true. Shiny as patent leather shoes, these fruits vary in hues from purple to white and yellow to gray. Although most are elongated, others are round and flat. Meaty and satisfying, eggplant is distinctive enough to enjoy on its own yet mild enough to carry other flavors.

PICKING Small eggplants are better than larger ones. Choose eggplants that feel plump, firm, and heavy for their size. Caps should be green and fresh, not shriveled and dry.

STORING Because eggplants tend to become bitter when stored, refrigerate the fruit immediately after picking or purchase and use it within a day or two. Eggplants do not freeze or can well, but they may be combined with other vegetables and herbs to make relishes.

IT'S IN THE DIMPLES

An old maxim says that the quality of an eggplant can be determined by checking the shape of a dimple on the blossom end. If the dimple is oval, rather than round, the eggplant will have fewer seeds and meatier flesh. This tale is most often true.

KITCHEN TIP
The age-old technique of salting sliced eggplant to remove excess moisture and bitterness is seldom necessary. Improved varieties of the vegetable are much sweeter than they used to be.

Sweet Peppers and Chiles

PEAK SEASON FROM JULY TO SEPTEMBER

In most families, children's temperaments vary. There are usually a few perfect, gentle, well-mannered children plus one or two kids who give their mothers gray hair. It is no different in the *Capsicum* family, whose members include not only gently flavored sweet peppers, but also a few rambunctious, hotheaded ones—the chiles.

Together, the fruits underscore the maxim, "Don't judge a book by its cover." Anyone who judges the sweetness or spiciness of a pepper by its color or shape is in for a surprise.

Sweet peppers— or bell peppers—skip to the palate with refreshing, crisp flavors. For decades the common pepper color was green, but in recent years white, yellow, orange, and purple peppers are more popular. Red sweet peppers—green peppers allowed to ripen—possess a softer version of green pepper taste. White, yellow, and orange sweet peppers are surprisingly sweet and extraordinarily crispy. Purple peppers, which are lime green inside, have snappy, full-bodied character.

Chiles—for centuries an integral ingredient in the fiery cuisines of Mexico, South America, and Asia—are now frequently grown by home gardeners and are readily available in both indoor and outdoor markets.

Peppers and chiles are rated on the Scoville Scale, which measures the amount of capsaicin—the chemical responsible for firing up human nerve receptors. Between sweet peppers, which measure 0, and law enforcement-grade pepper spray, which measures at 5 million, peppers and chiles vary widely in ferociousness.

KITCHEN TIP
The natural oils found in chiles can cause an unpleasant burning sensation to eyes and skin. Try to avoid handling them too much, wear gloves if possible, and be sure not to touch your face or eyes during preparation.

VARIETIES   In general, the smaller the chile, the hotter it is.
- **ANAHEIM CHILES** Mildly incendiary, these 8-inch-long chiles rate 500 on the Scoville Scale.
- **HABANERO CHILES** These small, usually orange lantern-shape chiles score 100,000 Scoville units.
- **JALAPEÑOS** Blunt-tipped and petite, these chiles pack a lot of power for their size—2,500 on the Scoville Scale.
- **POBLANO CHILES** Known as the chief ingredient in Chiles Rellenos, these mild, dark green chiles rate a tame 500 units.
- **SERRANO CHILES** The flesh of these smooth, sleek chiles provides an intense, lasting burn that merits 10,000 units on the Scoville Scale.

PICKING   When shopping for sweet peppers or chiles, look for those that are firm, crisp, and unblemished.

STORING   Peppers and chiles tolerate lengthy storage times. Loosely wrapped and refrigerated, they will last as long as 2 weeks.

Chiles may be dehydrated for long-term storage. Sweet peppers may be roasted, skinned, and frozen or canned.

Complementary flavor companions for cucumbers include dill, parsley, and mustard.

Cucumbers PEAK SEASON FROM JUNE TO AUGUST

Cucumbers are cool. Literally. No other food has the power to so remarkably and quickly take the swelter out of summer. These elongated green members of the gourd family are a true summer crop—ripening only when days are long and temperatures high. The vegetable's thick, ruddy skin capably protects the crisp flesh and cool liquid within.

VARIETIES From long and elegant to short, squat pickle cukes, each type of cucumber has its best use.

- **ENGLISH OR HOTHOUSE CUCUMBERS** Long, slender, and expensive, these nearly seedless beauties are touted as burpless and are available year-round.
- **SHORT THICK SLICERS** The variety most often grown in home gardens, they are especially liquid and have large white seeds.
- **SMALL ROUND PICKLERS** Of the annual U.S. cucumber crop, 70 percent are destined for the pickle jar. Varieties include gherkins—no larger than a baby's pinky finger—to large dill size.

PICKING Cucumbers should be firm, fresh, bright, well shaped, and vivid green.

STORING Cucumbers, best the day they are harvested, will keep, tightly wrapped, in the refrigerator for 2 to 3 days. Cucumbers do not freeze well; they do, however, star in canned pickles and relishes.

Sweet Corn PEAK SEASON FROM JULY TO SEPTEMBER

The plated confluence of juicy corn, melted butter, and barely dissolved crystals of salt is the making of many happy summertime memories. Eating corn on the cob is a treasured rite of summer and requires only one tool—a good set of teeth. Sweet corn, the only cereal crop indigenous to North America, engenders drip-down-the-chin gustatory pleasure.

PICKING When choosing sweet corn, look for creamy-color cobs of kernels wrapped in fresh, moist green leaves. If you can, pull back the husk and puncture a kernel with your fingernail. If the corn is fresh, it will exude a milky liquid.

STORING The advice that sweet corn should be cooked only minutes after harvest to prevent the kernels' sugar from turning starchy has been amended. In recent decades plant geneticists have more than doubled the sugar content in sweet corn—making the vegetable taste sweet for a longer post-harvest time. Nevertheless, for the best corn experience, rush the cobs from stalk to pot as quickly as possible.

GARDEN TIP
Ears of corn with ample amounts of silk have more kernels on the cobs. Although it may be more challenging to shuck silky ears, the sweet reward is greater.

Herbs PEAK SEASON FROM JUNE TO JULY

An astonishing variety of herbs inhabits gardens worldwide. Their roots burrow into the multitextured topography of every temperate continent, and their bright bouquets waft across every nation on the globe. Each culture has its favorites, based on which herbs thrive well, and these preferences have woven themselves so deeply into cultures that certain herbs have come to denote specific culinary traditions.

VARIETIES Herbs are divided into two types—soft-stemmed and woody-stemmed herbs. Basil is an example of a soft-stemmed herb, while rosemary is woody-stemmed.

- **BASIL** This tender, low-growing herb, prominent in Italian and Asian cuisines, is strong and sweet, with an enticing hint of anise.
- **CORIANDER** Also called Chinese parsley or cilantro, coriander is an essential ingredient in Latin American and Asian cuisines. It contributes pungent flavor.
- **DILL** This herb's familiar feathery leaves are prized in Scandinavian and Eastern European cookery for enlivening vegetables and seafood.
- **MARJORAM** This herb's warm Mediterranean flavor is similar to oregano. Like oregano, it is used to enhance poultry, eggs, salads, and vegetables.
- **MINT** The many varieties of this perennial possess a fresh, cool quality with flavors from sweet to peppery.
- **OREGANO** Pungent oregano lends its essence to seafood, poultry, and tomatoes.
- **ROSEMARY** The sappy blue-gray needles of the rosemary plant enhance foods with piney, lemony personality.
- **SAGE** Often used to flavor poultry and fatty meats, this rugged, woody perennial has velvety leaves often used in poultry stuffing.
- **TARRAGON** Favored by the French, this potent herb infuses sauces, butters, eggs, and seafood with its assertive licorice flavor.
- **THYME** The tiny leaves of minty, lemony thyme are common in dishes throughout the world.

PICKING Look for perfectly fresh leaves and the clean scent characteristic of each herb. Avoid herbs that have begun to brown around the edges of their leaves and those that look bruised or marred by spots of rust or yellow.

STORING Wrap herbs in a damp paper towel and refrigerate for a day or two, or place stems in 1 inch of water in a glass, cover loosely with a plastic bag, and refrigerate up to 1 week. (Basil is the one exception to this rule; place stems in 1 inch of water in a glass and store at room temperature. If you change the water daily, the basil will stay fresh for several days.) Most herbs may be dried, made into aromatic pastes and frozen, or infused into syrups and vinegars.

KITCHEN TIP
To heighten the vibrant tastes of fresh herbs, add them fresh while cooking, then add more at the finish to introduce a burst of fresh flavor to your dish.

Strawberries

PEAK SEASON FROM LATE MAY TO JULY

In early times Greeks would not eat red foods—including strawberries—because they believed that they possessed suspiciously great powers. Anyone fortunate enough to have had the opportunity to stand in a strawberry patch—devouring the crimson fruits while they are still warm from the sun—knows that the Greeks were correct: Strawberries have the power to condense all of the joys of early summer into one luscious, juicy bite.

Unfortunately modern shipping and merchandising techniques require extra-firm berries that will travel well and keep on market shelves. For these jet-setting berries, flavor is a fleeting thought that rarely comes to fruition. The best berries are those acquired locally at farmers' markets, pick-them-yourself berry farms, or plucked from your own patch.

PICKING Strawberries should be unblemished, deeply colored, slightly soft, and quite fragrant. Avoid those with green or white tips or shoulders—these have not had enough sun to allow them to develop full sweetness. When purchasing strawberries in baskets, be sure to check the bottom for signs of bleeding or moisture.

STORING Sort berries immediately after you get them home, discarding any bruised or damaged fruit. Refrigerate and then enjoy them as soon as possible. Do not wash strawberries until right before you eat them.

Because strawberries heighten the flavor and appeal of cereal, salads, soufflés, muffins, shortcake, and ice cream, long-term storage is seldom a consideration. The berries freeze nicely and are ripe with potential for making jams, jellies, and preserves.

Raspberries and Blackberries

PEAK SEASON FROM JUNE TO SEPTEMBER

The raspberry is the Miss Congeniality of the bramble world—an amiable berry of the rose family, with a diversity of colors and a repertoire of rich, exotic, spice-laden, and wholly intoxicating tastes.

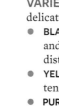

Of all of the raspberries, the red raspberry is the most known and beloved. This cherished plant, which grows on long, arching canes, is an obliging shrub with far fewer prickles than other berries in its species. Even its leaves point to raspberries' sweet nature—they are heart-shape at the base and their undersides are as soft as eider down.

GARDEN TIP

If raspberries are the most congenial of the berry clan, blackberries are the gnarly, challenging members. Raven black, yet formed by innocent pink or white flowers, their thorns pierce, but their berries entice.

VARIETIES A beautiful rainbow of this delicate berry exists in nature.

- **BLACK RASPBERRIES** Somewhat smaller and seedier than red raspberries, but distinctively aromatic.
- **YELLOW RASPBERRIES** Especially sweet, tender, and juicy and often found in the wild, particularly in Maryland.
- **PURPLE RASPBERRIES** A hybrid between red and black raspberries, with qualities of both.

PICKING Choose bright, clean, and uniformly colored raspberries and blackberries. Always check the bottom of the container to make sure that it is not stained from crushed fruit. Handle delicate berries as little as possible—they are highly perishable, and even a rinsing in water washes off some of their sweet perfume.

STORING Raspberries and blackberries are best when enjoyed fresh, but raspberries will keep, wrapped and refrigerated, in the refrigerator for a day or two. Blackberries, whose drupelets are more substantial, should keep, refrigerated, for up to 4 days. In either case, do not wash berries until right before eating.

Both berries freeze well. To freeze, arrange berries in a single layer on a baking sheet and freeze overnight. Once frozen, transfer berries to bags and place back in the freezer. This method of individual freezing is a great way to keep out-of-season berries available for topping cereal and oatmeal year-round.

Raspberries are fruit-producing powerhouses. Mature red raspberry plants can produce from 1 to 2 pounds of fruit; purple and black raspberries are even more prolific.

Blueberries top most "best foods" lists because they are high in antioxidants. More good news is that they are delicious.

Blueberries   PEAK SEASON FROM MAY TO AUGUST

Smooth, perfectly round, and indigo blue with a slight frosty cast, blueberries have become especially prominent recently. They have considerable health-enhancing benefits—especially cancer-fighting abilities.

These sweet, wholesome berries may be harvested from early, midseason, and late-bearing bushes, producing frequently enough to keep blueberry fans satiated all summer.

PICKING   Choose blueberries that are plump, clean, dry, deep blue in color, and with a white, powdery "bloom" on their skins. Overripe blueberries will look dull and soft. Be sure to check the bottom of the container for stains or leaking.

STORING   Blueberries remain juicy and flavorful up to 7 days when refrigerated. They are excellent for freezing, jams, chutneys, and for both dessert and savory sauces.

KITCHEN TIP Toss blueberries with salad greens or add them to a fruit salad to add lovely dots and dashes of color. Or toss freshly washed blueberries into a bowl of warm oatmeal and drizzle with maple syrup.

Cherries   PEAK SEASON FROM JUNE TO AUGUST

Wouldn't it be wonderful if life were just a bowl of cherries—sweet, juicy, and delicious? Of course, cherries may also be extraordinarily tart, juicy, and delicious, which makes life—and cherries—even more interesting.

These cheerful ambassadors of summer sweetness roll to market in three varieties—sweet, sour, and sweet-sour hybrids—and range in color from yellow to blushed yellow to pink, red, and black. Sweet cherries—the kind eaten out of hand—are most plentiful and most likely to cause celebration when they first arrive in market bins.

PICKING   Look for glossy-skinned, chubby cherries with deep color. Avoid mushy, dull, or shriveled cherries; discard those that have cracked or split skin.

STORING   Loosely wrap and refrigerate for a day or two.

CHOOSE YOUR CHERRIES
Cherries are either sweet or sour. Sweet cherries such as Bing and the decadently sweet Rainier can be eaten right off the tree. Their tart cousins, the sour cherry (also called tart cherries) include Nanking and Montmorency and are excellent for baking as long as sugar sweetens them.

Peaches and Nectarines

PEAK SEASON FROM JULY TO SEPTEMBER

Peaches and nectarines signal summer. Syrupy, sensuous, and tantalizingly aromatic, tree-ripened peaches—and their cousins, nectarines—drip nectar with each bite.

If they have any fault, it is their exceedingly delicate nature. Once summer heat puts its sweet finishing touch on these stone fruits, they are easily bruised. Unless each round fruit is cradled in its own soft bassinette, it will not survive shipping or even market display.

VARIETIES Peaches and nectarines can be used interchangeably in most recipes.

- **CLINGSTONE PEACHES AND NECTARINES** So named because the flesh clings to the pit, these are the first to arrive in summer. They tend to be juicier and sweeter than freestones, but are less convenient to prepare.
- **FREESTONE PEACHES AND NECTARINES** These arrive in late July and last through September. Valued for out-of-hand eating because they can be split in half by hand and their stone easily removed.

PICKING Peaches should be firm and blemish-free, yet yield to light pressure at their stem ends. Your nose will direct you to the best peaches—they will wave a warm, fragrant aroma. Select nectarines with slightly firmer flesh, soft seams, and lovely aroma.

Tree-ripened peaches and nectarines, available locally at farmers' markets or from orchard stands, will be incomparably better than commercial varieties. Avoid peaches and nectarines that exhibit any greenness—these were picked before ripe and will disappoint.

STORING Peaches and nectarines are best eaten quickly, but will keep, refrigerated, for 2 to 3 days. They may also be canned and dried.

Pit peaches easily by cutting along the seam all the way around and through the fruit to the pit. Then twist each half in opposite directions.

Plums PEAK SEASON FROM JUNE TO AUGUST

In spring—when the amethyst leaves of plums unfurl and orchards drift with blossoms of blushing pink and snowy white—the ambitiousness of the plum tree is in full display. More than half of plum blossoms pollinate for an abundant harvest.

These drupe fruits (fruits that have a pit or shell surrounded by juicy flesh) grow on every continent but Antarctica, sharing juicy plumpness with people the world over. Ripe plum flavor, a luscious balance of sweet and tart, distinguishes the plum as one of summer's finest fruits wherever it grows.

VARIETIES Plums are divided into two broad categories—Japanese plums and European plums. Japanese plums are generally the larger of the two and have juicier flesh. European plums are delicious eaten out of hand but are also well suited to drying and cooking. Some common varieties:

- **ITALIAN PRUNE PLUM** As its name suggests, when dried this European plum is called a prune.
- **DAMSON** A small European plum that is oval shape with deep blue skin and tart yellow-green flesh.
- **SATSUMA** This Japanese plum has dark red skin and sweet red flesh.
- **SANTA ROSA** One of the most common varieties, this Japanese plum is large and dark purple with yellow flesh.

PICKING Plums vary in shape and, according to variety, may be purple or shades of yellow, green, red, or black. Plums look shiny when not fully ripened then become dull matte when ripe. Top-quality plums are chubby, clean, and fresh looking with no signs of shriveling or splitting. Mature but not fully ripened plums will become fragrant and soft when allowed to stand at room temperature for a few days.

STORING Plums are moderately good keepers and fare well when stored in the refrigerator for 4 or 5 days. Plums do not freeze well, but they may be canned, pickled, and dried with great success.

Cantaloupe and Honeydew Melons

PEAK SEASON FROM JULY TO SEPTEMBER

Native to Persia, melons are members of the cucumber family. With exotic lushness and intoxicating perfume, cantaloupes and honeydews stride into the last half of summer, providing fans with two of the final flavors of the growing season.

These buxom beauties take forever to get ready for the party, most requiring at least 3 months on the vine. Once they show up, all eyes are on them.

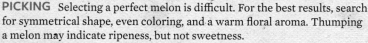

CANTALOUPE

VARIETIES Although there are many different cultivars of muskmelon, the two most common are canteloupe and honeydew melons.

- **CANTALOUPE** This fruit is a netted cultivar of muskmelon. When ripe, this melon has intensely orange flesh.
- **HONEYDEW** A variety of muskmelon, the honeydew has pale green flesh that is considered the sweetest of all melons. It was once believed to be a sacred food by the Egyptians.

PICKING Selecting a perfect melon is difficult. For the best results, search for symmetrical shape, even coloring, and a warm floral aroma. Thumping a melon may indicate ripeness, but not sweetness.

The ripest, sweetest cantaloupes—or muskmelons—have no stem. Instead, they have a smooth, shallow basin where the stem was attached. The netting will be even, thick, and corky, with a buff skin color under the netting.

Honeydews should have a pale, creamy-color skin with the slightest greenish cast. The fruits will give slightly when pressed at the stem end, and the ripest picks will feel a little sticky to the fingers.

STORING Melons taste best at room temperature and lose flavor when refrigerated. If you must, store melons in the refrigerator for no longer than a day or two.

HONEYDEW

A perfectly ripe melon is intensely sweet. An interesting way to balance and even enhance its sweetness is to sprinkle a slice with a little bit of sea salt.

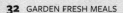

Watermelon PEAK SEASON FROM JULY TO SEPTEMBER

There is nothing dainty about watermelons. Unlike their melon brethren, toted to market in well-cushioned flats or boxes, watermelons are so heavy that they are transported with skid loaders.

But inside of these torpedo-shape melons—hidden beneath thick, striped green rinds—is an intricate cellular structure that miraculously suspends an abundance of cool, refreshing water. And that is only one of its attractions. Watermelons also have impeccable timing—reaching juicy perfection just when long, sultry summer days make them most appreciated.

VARIETIES The hefty varieties of watermelons are now accompanied by smaller, sometimes seedless hybrids.

- **PICNIC WATERMELONS** These weigh between 15 and 50 pounds but have been known to tip the scales at more than 300 pounds.
- **ICEBOX VARIETIES** So named because they fit in a refrigerator, these melons weigh between 5 and 15 pounds.
- **PERSONAL WATERMELONS** A small seedless variety, these weigh between 2 and 3 pounds—or just enough for a meal.

PICKING On the subject of choosing watermelons, opinions abound. Field growers themselves practice the best method: Give it a good thump. If the sound is hollow, the melon is ripe. Another indicator is color. Look for a melon that has a smooth, creamy-color underside.

STORING Whole watermelons will keep, refrigerated, for up to a week. Once sliced, eat them within a few days. Watermelons do not freeze or can well, but the rinds can be made into delicious sweet pickles, and the seeds, toasted, make an unusual snack.

STEALTH HEALTH

While watermelon has long been considered a treat equating to candy or dessert, it does have nutritional contributions. It is an excellent source of both vitamin A and vitamin C—two of the most important antioxidants.

Beets

PEAK SEASON FROM SEPTEMBER TO OCTOBER

To many a mother's chagrin, a spoonful of beets provides a baby with means by which she can express her first food preference—or in the case of beets, distaste. This is a strange phenomenon because beets are by far the sweetest of all the vegetables.

Beets are humble but honest vegetables. Inexpensive and simple to grow, these ruby-red roots hold a wealth of sweetened earth flavor that is difficult to describe. Perhaps that they are a vegetable of choice on high-end restaurant menus gives them their due.

PICKING Garden beets, depending on variety, may be magenta, golden yellow, or—as with the trendy Italian Chiogga beet—sliced open to reveal concentric striations of pinkish red and white. Whatever their color, the best-tasting beets will be the size of a golf ball or smaller and have smooth, firm flesh, with twinelike tap roots still attached. Avoid oversized beets that have scars or scabrous circles on the leaf ends—these have remained in the soil too long and will be woody-textured and woody-tasting.

STORING If beets will be stored for longer than a few days, remove the greens, which sap moisture and nutrients from the roots, before wrapping and refrigerating.

Slices of deep garnet beets are excellent for canning and pickling, but they do not freeze well.

Cabbage and Brussels Sprouts

PEAK SEASON FROM SEPTEMBER TO NOVEMBER

Both cabbage and Brussels sprouts, its diminutive cruciferous cousin, are culinary treasures when cooked properly—a true treat of fall.

Cabbage, a cool-climate crop that is an inexpensive, vitamin-rich vegetable, has many terrific uses beyond coleslaw. Raw, the heads are gentle and delicate-tasting. It is only by overcooking that the vegetable becomes strong and waterlogged. Likewise, there is good news for those whose only memories of Brussels sprouts are of malodorous mush. When lightly cooked to retain their bright green color and crisp centers, they are positively delicious. In the simplest manner, roast them—trimmed and halved and drizzled with good-quality olive oil and a sprinkling of coarse salt and freshly ground pepper—for about 30 minutes in a 400°F oven.

BRUSSELS SPROUTS

CABBAGE VARIETIES Of the many varieties, these are the most common:

- **DANISH CABBAGE** This late-season cabbage, with tight compact heads, is a good keeper.
- **DOMESTIC CABBAGE** With loose heads and brittle leaves, it does not keep well. Most often used to make sauerkraut.
- **RED CABBAGE** A purple-pigmented Danish cabbage, its leaves are a bit tough, but its keeping qualities are good.
- **SAVOY CABBAGE** An Italian varietal, it is super-tender and sweet. It is easily distinguished by its yellow-green crinkly leaves.

PICKING Look for cabbages with heavy, solid heads and flawless outer leaves. The best Brussels sprouts will be fresh, green, and even in size.

STORING Tightly wrapped and refrigerated, cabbages remain in good condition for 2 weeks or more, and Brussels sprouts up to a week.

Fennel PEAK SEASON FROM NOVEMBER TO DECEMBER

Fennel is one of the generous products of the late-summer garden. A single plant provides cooks five way to infuse foods with refreshing crispness and subtle aniselike flavor. Its thick, bulbous stem base and celerylike stalks may be used raw, chopped into salads, or cooked. Its feathery leaves may be used as an herb or fresh garnish. The licorice-tasting seeds—tiny but potent—imbue Italian sausage with distinctive taste. Even the pollen—shaken from its flower heads—becomes a magical fairy dust to use in Italian cooking.

Although fennel is indigenous to the Mediterranean, it is now widely cultivated around the world. Most of the fennel in American supermarkets is grown in California. Although few home gardeners attempt to cultivate it, it is easy to grow and does surprisingly well—even in containers with as little as 8 inches of soil. From seed to harvest, it takes 8 to 10 weeks.

PICKING Look for round white bulbs with fresh green stems and leaves.

STORING Refrigerate, wrapped, for no longer than 2 or 3 days.

KITCHEN TIP
Most recipes that feature fennel call for the bulb—whether tossed with fresh orange segments and olive oil in a salad or stirred into a soup. Don't throw away the leafy fronds, though. Store them in a tightly sealed container in the refrigerator and use as a garnish.

Kohlrabi PEAK SEASON FROM SEPTEMBER TO NOVEMBER

Kohlrabi, like other members of the cabbage family, gets little respect, perhaps due to its odd-looking appearance and globular swollen stem, or because few people know what a magical vegetable it is. Although one would expect this *Brassica* to taste like cabbage, it doesn't mimic the flavor of its big brother at all. Instead, it is full of surprises. Raw, it tastes like a radish; cooked, it tastes more like a turnip.

Kohrabi has two varieties—purple and apple-green. Both varieties have pale green—almost ivory-color—flesh. The purple-skinned variety tends to be a little sweeter. Because of its appearance, kohlrabi is often mistaken for a root vegetable, when, in fact, it grows right above the ground, forming a turnip-shape swelling at the base of the stem.

PICKING Plant tops are the best indicator of quality—they should be young and green.

STORING Kohlrabi is a good keeper and will not show signs of wilting from as long as 2 weeks in the refrigerator.

American food writer James Beard believed parsnips to be one of the most neglected vegetables—but he preferred them to sweet potatoes for Thanksgiving.

Root Vegetables PEAK SEASON FROM SEPTEMBER TO NOVEMBER

Homely and rustic root vegetables—parsnips, turnips, and rutabagas—are often relegated to the background. In modern produce departments, they're only found in the smallest, out-of-the way bins.

But with proper treatment in the hands of an able home cook, these gnarly, virtually ignored veggies can bring earthy, sweet flavors to the dinner table. They've been around long enough to have been treated all kinds of ways in the kitchen—and they're surprisingly delicious braised, roasted, mashed, grilled, gratinéed—even turned into crispy chips and fries.

RUTABAGAS
PARSNIPS

TURNIPS

VARIETIES Though parsnips, rutabagas, and turnips have slightly different provenances, they often get lumped together under the term "root vegetables."

- **PARSNIP** This denizen of the deep earth looks like an anemic carrot, which reveals its family tree. It is the most nourishing root of the carrot family and tastes exceptionally sweet and nutty.
- **RUTABAGA** A Swiss botanist crossed cabbage and turnips to come up with this sweet old guy. Larger than a turnip and mild, the root has texture that makes it very good at absorbing other flavors, such as the aromatics used in braises.
- **TURNIP** This root will win no beauty contests, but its starchy goodness has nourished the poor for centuries. The flavor of the turnip, a member of the cabbage clan, is similar to that of the rutabaga.

PICKING When shopping for any of these vegetables, choose roots of small to medium size—extra-large specimens may be tough and pithy. Avoid roots that feel light for their size or show signs of softness or shriveling. The stem and root ends of turnips should be intact—flavor is lost when they are trimmed. To extend their shelf life, these root vegetables are usually dipped in a thick coat of paraffin, so they should always be peeled before use.

STORING Root vegetables, cellared through winters in the old days, keep for a long time. Store, covered or bagged, in the refrigerator for up to a month.

COOKING ROOTS

- Like potatoes, parsnips will turn brown quickly when peeled. Either hold off until right before cooking to peel them or hold them in a pan of cool water and a little bit of lemon juice.
- Older turnips can release a strong smell when boiled. Add a teaspoon of sugar to the water to lessen this.

KITCHEN TIP
Roasting works magic on humble root vegetables. Simply scrub, peel, and cut into large chunks. Toss with good-quality olive oil and season with salt and freshly ground pepper. Spread in a single layer on a shallow baking sheet and roast in a 400°F oven for 30 minutes or until golden and crispy—delicious!

Potatoes

PEAK SEASON FROM SEPTEMBER TO NOVEMBER

Truly one of nature's most perfect foods, potatoes are incredibly versatile. They're equally delicious seasoned and buttered and mashed, roasted, steamed, pan-fried, or deep-fried—or simply baked whole in a hot oven.

VARIETIES Each type of potato has its most perfect use—and some are good for more than one type of cooking method.

- **RUSSETS** Named for its netted, reddish-brown skin, this tater is the most commonly used in the United States. Its high starch content makes it the best choice for baking, mashing, frying, and roasting.
- **WHITES** This tuber, with smooth off-white skin, bright white flesh, and shallow eyes, contains less starch than the russet and lends itself to several preparation methods, including boiling, steaming, mashing, and roasting, and appears in soup, salads, and casseroles.
- **REDS** Round, smooth, and waxy, these potatoes may be as small as an inch in diameter and as large as a baseball. Firm and low in starch, this variety shines most brightly when boiled, roasted, or steamed.
- **YELLOWS** These golden potatoes are enjoying a great deal of contemporary popularity, thanks to dense, creamy texture and buttery flavor. Yellows are perfect for baking, broiling, and frying.
- **SWEET POTATOES** Although called potatoes, these orange-flesh tubers do not belong to the potato family at all. Highly nutritious and syrupy sweet, this variety is delicious roasted, boiled, steamed, mashed, or baked in gratins and is especially wonderful when baked in its own jacket.

The best potatoes will be plump, firm, and regularly shaped. Skins of mature potatoes should be clean and thin, while the skin of baby, or new, potatoes should be glossy. Avoid cuts, bruises, shrivel, and sprouted eyes.

Store potatoes in a cool, dry place with good air circulation up to a month.

Onions PEAK SEASON FROM SEPTEMBER TO OCTOBER

Many a tear has been shed over this innocuous-looking root vegetable, whose sulfuric compounds delight the palate, infuse kitchens with homey aromas, and cause even happy cooks to weep.

The benefits of onions greatly outweigh its liabilities, however, and it has the reputation as the most universally eaten vegetable and an indispensable staple.

VARIETIES The pungent-sweet flavor of common onion types is similar yet varies in intensity.

- **WHITE ONIONS** These are the strongest, most pungently flavored variety.
- **YELLOW ONIONS** Milder and sweeter than white onions, these onions are a bit smaller.
- **RED ONIONS** These are the sweetest of all.

PICKING Look for onions that are firm and heavy, with dry, papery skins. Avoid signs of softness, mildew, and sprouting.

STORING All onion types are lengthy keepers when stored in a cool, dry place with good ventilation. Do not refrigerate!

Garlic PEAK SEASON FROM SEPTEMBER TO OCTOBER

For such a diminutive bulb, garlic has a gargantuan reputation. Beneath its papery white skin, this delightful herb contains medicine so powerful that it's purported to cure everything from the plague to the common cold, to repel vampires, and to make nearly every dish it graces something wonderful.

Garlic flavors range from warm and sweet to hot and heady, depending on the cooking method. Whole cloves possess the mildest flavor, but once minced, they become pungent. When simmered, garlic melts into sweet subtlety. When sautéed, it becomes domineering and assertive.

PICKING When selecting garlic, look for bulbs that are firm and heavy, with dry, papery skins. Avoid signs of softness, mildew, and sprouting.

STORING Garlic is generally a good keeper when stored in a cool, dry place with good ventilation. As with onions, do not store garlic in the refrigerator.

GO GREEN

Green garlic, also called garlic scapes, often appears in early spring in farmers' markets. If you are ever fortunate enough to spy a pile of vivid green scapes, their loopy stems cascading from market stands, buy a bunch. Their fresh, clean, and mildly garlicky flavor enhances soups and stir-fries like no other ingredient can.

Butternut Squash PEAK SEASON FROM SEPTEMBER TO NOVEMBER

Mother Nature is known for some pretty fantastic feats of engineering, but the butternut squash may be her greatest pride. Both models—one with a stocky linebacker's physique and the other with an awkward flared blossom end topped with a gangly neck—surprise. Beneath the dull color skin of butternut, its flesh radiates a ravishing deep marigold hue.

As astonishing as its color is its texture. Unlike other winter squash, which tends to be stringy and fibrous, butternut squash boasts sweet-tasting, finely grained pulp that provides a superb, sensationally silky mouth feel—one that eases the transition from summer to fall.

Butternut squash is highly adaptable—it can be cooked into both sweet and savory dishes. It has a firm enough texture to hold its own, chopped and stirred into a risotto. It also makes a fabulously creamy and smooth soup.

PICKING Choose sturdy, heavy fruits with unblemished skin.

STORING Butternut squash will keep for a month or even more if stored in a cool, dry, dark, and well-ventilated place.

KITCHEN TIP

The best butternut flavor is in the moist, webby strands that hold the seeds. Rather than scooping out this mass cleanly as you might with other varieties of squash, just pick the seeds out by hand and leave the strands intact.

Acorn Squash PEAK SEASON FROM SEPTEMBER TO NOVEMBER

These little fellows—with resolutely protective dark green skin, dense ochre-color flesh, and a hard shell—must be split with a whack of a sharp knife. Oven heat, however, quickly coaxes the sweet, nutty nature from these tough customers. Its autumnal flavor is a delectable complement to hearty fall meals.

Although acorn squash has all the characteristics of winter squash (and is considered to be a winter squash), it actually belongs to the same species as the summer squashes—zucchini and yellow crookneck squash.

PICKING Acorn squash should be sturdy, feel heavy, and have unmarred, shiny, and firmly ribbed skin.

STORING Acorn squash has great long-term storage potential and will keep, if stored in a cool, dry, well-ventilated place, for a month or more. If you'd like to freeze it, cook it first. Leave it in chunks or mash it, then store it in an airtight container and freeze it up to 12 months.

Pumpkins

PEAK SEASON FROM SEPTEMBER TO OCTOBER

When a bracing crispness is in the air, an army of orange-thumbed growers begins to harvest the most iconic harbinger of fall—pumpkins. After spending a long summer accumulating energy from the sun and soil, these portly orbs waddle to market, offering up unique, celebratory aroma and a deep musky, nutty flavor.

VARIETIES There is a distinct division in in the world of pumpkins. While one type looks pretty on the porch, the other is best for making pie.

- **DECORATIVE PUMPKINS** This type, which American children and patient parents carve just before Halloween, is grown with color, structural strength, a flat bottom, and a sturdy stem as their main attributes. The flesh tends to be bland, watery, and fibrous.
- **CULINARY PUMPKINS** Used to make pumpkin pie, pickles, preserves, and savory dishes, these pumpkins have firm flesh and sweet taste. There are many varieties of culinary pumpkins, and heirloom varieties are highly prized for taste and texture. Among the best are Small Sugar, Winter Luxury, Cheese, and Golden Cushaw.

PICKING Pumpkins should be sturdy, feel heavy, and have unmarred, shiny skin.

STORING These members of the gourd family have great long-term storage potential and will keep, stored in a cool, dry, well-ventilated place, for a month or more. Or they can be cooked into puree and frozen (see the recipe on page 85.)

Apples

PEAK SEASON FROM SEPTEMBER
TO NOVEMBER

So admired is the archetypal apple that throughout history, fruits and vegetables bearing even the slightest resemblance to the apple's round shape have been given its name. The French word for potato—*pomme de terre*—means "apple of the ground." Italians used the word pomidoro, or "golden apple," to describe the yellow tomatoes that first arrived on their shores from the New World. Even the pomegranate is one of apple's many namesakes.

Apples are customarily categorized according to their sweetness, with tart apples generally known as "baking apples" and sweet varieties referred to as "eating apples."

The fruit further distinguishes itself according to the side of the chronological and geographical track on which it is grown. Commercial apples—or varieties bred for long-distance shipping, such as Delicious, Granny Smith, Jonathan, and McIntosh, have their own qualities. Heritage breeds, such as Cortland, Gravenstein, and Wealthy, grow only in small, specific geographical areas.

PICKING   Apples should be bright-skinned, plump, and crisp-looking. Avoid bruised, shriveled fruits that feel light for their weight.

STORING   Store apples unwrapped up to 2 weeks in the refrigerator. Avoid enclosing apples in a closed produce drawer with other fruits—apples release a gas that causes other fruits to overripen.

There are more than 7,500 varieties of apples grown worldwide. A little more than a decade ago, Americans began to discover the fabulous flavors and textures of the world of apples—far beyond the iconic Red Delicious.

Pears PEAK SEASON FROM LATE AUGUST TO NOVEMBER

The elegantly seductive pear is the most subtle of all orchard fruits. Its cool and juicy, slightly grainy flesh—clean and fresh on the palate—is so tender that it has been called "butter fruit." The distinctive taste has been loved for centuries. Through the years, it has been baked, stewed, poached, and pickled—as well as tossed into salads, stirred into relishes, and chosen to elevate desserts to extraordinary heights.

Pears have one perfect day—a brief moment in the ripening process when they are at their most luscious. Because pears, unlike other fruits, ripen from the inside out, they quickly become overripe. Pear perfectionists can time that day to the moment.

VARIETIES Although the hourglass shape of the pear is similar among varieties, the texture, taste, size, and hue of the skins vary.

- **SECKEL** Tiny, spicy, crisp—and a perfect portion size for children.
- **BOSC** Rubenesque in shape, with ruddy skin and smooth, juicy flesh.
- **ANJOU** This gracefully rounded pear is spicy, sweet, and firm.
- **BARTLETT** Yellow or red, this finely grained pear is the most popular variety.
- **COMICE** The finest of pears, this heavily perfumed beauty melts in the mouth.

PICKING Purchase pears when they are firm but not rock hard. Ripen pears at home under a watchful eye.

STORING Store firm pears in the refrigerator for a day or two before ripening at room temperature or until the pear smells sweet and fruity and yields to gentle pressure.

PEEL OUT

Always peel pears before cooking. Their skin will darken and toughen when exposed to heat—which is in sharp and uncomplementary contrast to their buttery interior.

The Fresh-Produce Pantry

Unlike many foods that require huge supporting casts to make them the stars of the show, the inherently natural goodness of sun-ripened fruits and carefully cultivated vegetables needs little—if any—assistance to flaunt tasty attributes.

A select set of simple pantry products, however, can help coax the essences of fruits and vegetables—whether they are cooked or simply dressed and eaten raw.

BROTH A bath in simmering low-sodium broth, particularly chicken broth, is a wonderful way to bring out the sweetness of vegetables.

CITRUS FRUITS Zesty lemons, limes, and oranges, in both juice and grated peel forms, awaken flavors of vegetables from artichokes to zucchini. Combinations of citrus fruits with with berries, apples, and pears are sublime.

CHEESE Hard grating cheeses such as Asiago, Parmigiano-Reggiano, and Grana Padana have an affinity for potatoes, squash, and tomatoes, Kid-friendly cheddar is renowned for making healthful vegetables, such as broccoli, appealing to children.

DIJON-STYLE MUSTARD The assertive nature of French mustards, particularly whole-grain varieties, adds spark to root vegetables, including potatoes.

HERBS Every vegetable has its herb companion. Carrots love dill, tomatoes love basil, and green beans love marjoram. Be a matchmaker and experiment with herb and vegetable combos that please your palate.

HONEY This affable elixir complements almost any fruit or vegetable, either by accentuating its natural sweetness or by serving as a palate-awakening counterpoint.

OLIVE OIL Extra virgin olive oils lend a hand in making dressings and vinaigrettes that highlight, rather than obliterate, the unique tastes of veggies. Used to lightly coat vegetables to be roasted, these lovely lipids really shine.

NUTS When cooking softens the textures of fruits and vegetables, there is nothing else quite as good as a crunchy sprinkling of toasted nuts to spring texture into toothsome flavor.

SALT Salt has a way of grounding the flavor of vegetables and of bringing out unique characters. To elevate simple steamed vegetables to flavorful heights, sprinkle lightly with gray salt, pink salt, or other artisan-harvested sea salt.

SOY SAUCE No other flavor than soy sauce is as capable of bringing out the brightness in stir-fried or simply steamed carrots, cabbage, and spinach. Millions of Asians attest to its capabilities.

SPICES As with herbs, each fruit and vegetable has a partner of choice. Try a little nutmeg on sautéed spinach, cinnamon on sweet potatoes, ginger or cumin on carrots, fennel seeds or caraway on cabbage; and dill seeds on corn.

PEPPER Pepper has the power to jazz up any vegetable, as well as a few berries and fruits. The ground stuff in the shaker will do, but for fullest flavor, choose a premium peppercorn, such as Tellicherry, and grind it yourself.

VINEGARS All vinegars, but especially balsamic vinegar and sherry vinegar, expertly balance savory and sweet. Try a drizzle on freshly cooked vegetables.

Tossed & Composed

SEASONAL SALADS

Crisp lettuces wait to be snipped. Juicy strawberries drip from vines beneath
leafy bonnets. Tomatoes sun themselves under the summer sky. Ripe and ready,
these garden dwellers take no detours on their way from soil to supper. All they
need is a salad bowl and a gentle hand to toss them.

FOR INFORMATIONON ON SELECTING AND STORING RADISHES, SEE PAGE 16.

Chive Butter, Breadsticks, and Radishes

START TO FINISH: 15 MINUTES   MAKES: 8 TO 10 APPETIZERS

IF YOU DON'T HAVE FRESH CHIVES, THE FINELY MINCED STEMS OF
SCALLIONS WILL DO THE TRICK JUST AS WELL.

⅓ cup butter, softened

2 tablespoons snipped chives (with
blossoms, if desired)

8 to 10 breadsticks or one 12-ounce baguette

1 bunch (12 ounces) radishes with tops,
trimmed and root tips removed

¼ cup sea salt or kosher salt

1. For chive butter, in a small bowl stir together
butter and chives. Cut breadsticks lengthwise
in half. (Or cut baguette in half crosswise,
then cut halves lengthwise to make 8 to
10 breadsticks.)

2. Spread chive butter on cut sides of
breadsticks. Serve bread with radishes and salt
for dipping.

PER APPETIZER *233 cal., 10 g total fat (5 g sat. fat),
21 mg chol., 961 mg sodium, 31 g carbo., 2 g fiber,
5 g pro.*

SIMPLY RED
- To make radishes crisper, cover with ice water and refrigerate for 2 to 3 hours.
- Most radish heat is in the skin. For milder flavor, remove skin with a vegetable peeler.
- One pound of radishes yields 4 cups of sliced radishes.

Smoked Chicken Salad with Raspberry Vinaigrette

START TO FINISH: 20 MINUTES MAKES: 4 MAIN-DISH SERVINGS

THIS QUICK AND EASY SALAD CAN BE WHIPPED UP IN A SNAP WITH SMOKED CHICKEN FROM THE DELI, ASSORTED FRESH GREENS, AND FRESH RASPBERRIES.

⅓ cup balsamic vinegar

⅓ cup seedless raspberry jam

¼ cup extra virgin olive oil

12 ounces smoked chicken or turkey breast,* cut into thin strips

8 cups mixed salad greens

2 cups fresh raspberries

¼ cup sliced almonds, toasted

1. For raspberry vinaigrette, in a screw-top jar combine balsamic vinegar, jam, and olive oil; shake well.

2. In a large bowl toss chicken with about half of the dressing. Line a large platter with greens. Top with chicken mixture, raspberries, and almonds. Pass remaining dressing.

PER SERVING *457 cal., 30 g total fat (5 g sat. fat), 62 mg chol., 558 mg sodium, 31 g carbo., 4 g fiber, 18 g pro.*

*NOTE:

To smoke a chicken or turkey, soak 3 cups of wood chips in enough water to cover for at least 1 hour. Lightly brush 1 pound skinless, boneless chicken breast halves or turkey tenderloin with olive oil and sprinkle with salt and pepper. Arrange medium-hot coals around a drip pan. Test for medium heat above drip pan. Add 1 inch of water to drip pan. Drain wood chips. Sprinkle wood chips over hot coals. Place chicken on grill rack over the drip pan. Close grill hood. Grill chicken for 15 to 18 minutes (allow 25 to 30 minutes for turkey) or until tender and no longer pink (170°F). (For a gas grill, preheat grill. Reduce heat to medium. Adjust for indirect cooking. Add wood chips according to manufacturer's directions. Place chicken on grill rack over burner that is turned off. Grill as directed.)

FOR INFORMATION ON SELECTING AND STORING RASPBERRIES, SEE PAGE 28; FOR INFORMATION ON SALAD GREENS, SEE PAGE 11.

Chicken and Quinoa Salad with Roasted Chiles

PREP: 45 MINUTES ROAST: 20 MINUTES COOK: 25 MINUTES STAND: 45 MINUTES
OVEN: 425°F MAKES: 4 TO 5 MAIN-DISH SERVINGS

IF YOU LIKE, SUBSTITUTE 2 CUPS COOKED COUSCOUS FOR THE COOKED QUINOA.

8 ounces fresh Anaheim chile peppers, poblano chile peppers, banana chile peppers, and/or red sweet peppers (see tip, below)

1 cup quinoa

1 cup water

3 tablespoons lime juice

2 tablespoons extra virgin olive oil

2 cloves garlic, minced

¼ teaspoon salt

¼ teaspoon black pepper

8 ounces shredded cooked chicken or pork

⅓ cup pine nuts or slivered almonds, toasted

½ cup coarsely chopped fresh cilantro

½ cup chopped scallions (4)

Butterhead lettuce leaves

1. Preheat oven to 425°F. Halve whole peppers lengthwise. Remove stems, seeds, and membranes. Place pepper halves, cut sides down, on a foil-lined baking sheet. Roast for 20 to 25 minutes or until skins are blistered and dark. Carefully fold foil up and around pepper halves to enclose; let stand about 15 minutes. Use a sharp knife to loosen the edges of the skins; gently and slowly pull off the skin in strips. Cut peppers into bite-size strips. Set aside.

2. In a fine-mesh sieve thoroughly rinse the quinoa with cold water. In a medium saucepan combine quinoa and the 1 cup water. Bring to boiling; reduce heat. Simmer, covered, for 25 minutes. Remove from heat. Uncover; let stand about 30 minutes.

3. For dressing, in a small screw-top jar combine lime juice, olive oil, garlic, salt, and black pepper. Cover and shake well to combine; set aside.

4. In a large bowl combine cooked quinoa, roasted pepper strips, the dressing, chicken, pine nuts, cilantro, and scallions. Toss to mix. Line serving plates with lettuce. Top with quinoa mixture. Serve salad at room temperature.

PER SERVING *454 cal., 22 g total fat (3 g sat. fat), 50 mg chol., 220 mg sodium, 43 g carbo., 5 g fiber, 26 g pro.*

KITCHEN TIP

Because hot chile peppers contain volatile oils that can burn your skin and eyes, avoid direct contact with chiles as much as possible. When working with chile peppers, wear plastic or rubber gloves. If your bare hands do touch the chile peppers, wash your hands and nails well with soap and water.

FOR INFORMATION ON SELECTING AND STORING CHILES, SEE PAGE 24.

FOR INFORMATION ON SELECTING AND STORING SALAD GREENS, SEE PAGE 11.

Frisée with Bacon and Poached Egg

START TO FINISH: 20 MINUTES   MAKES: 6 MAIN-DISH SERVINGS

FRISÉE—OR CURLY ENDIVE—IS KNOWN FOR ITS PEPPERY PUNCH AND HINT OF BITTERNESS, BOTH OF WHICH MAKE IT AN INCREDIBLE ACCOMPANIMENT FOR RICHLY FLAVORED POACHED EGGS.

1 tablespoon white wine vinegar

¾ teaspoon Dijon-style mustard

½ teaspoon light mayonnaise

⅛ teaspoon salt

⅛ teaspoon black pepper

3 tablespoons extra virgin olive oil

5 slices turkey bacon

8 cups chopped frisée (2 large heads)

12 radishes, thinly sliced

6 eggs

1. For dressing, in a small bowl whisk together vinegar, mustard, mayonnaise, salt, and pepper. Slowly whisk in olive oil.

2. Cut turkey bacon crosswise into ½-inch pieces. In a large nonstick skillet cook turkey bacon over medium-high heat about 7 minutes or until crisp. Remove bacon from skillet; drain on paper towels.

3. In a large bowl combine frisée, radishes, and the bacon. Drizzle dressing over salad; toss to coat. Divide salad among plates.

4. To poach eggs, fill a large skillet three-fourths full with water. Bring water to boiling; reduce heat to simmering. Break an egg into a cup and slip egg into simmering water. Repeat with remaining eggs. Simmer, uncovered, for 3 to 5 minutes or until whites are completely set and yolks begin to thicken but are not hard. Remove eggs with a slotted spoon and place on individual servings.

PER SERVING *250 cal., 18 g total fat (4 g sat. fat), 235 mg chol., 544 mg sodium, 13 g carbo., 10 g fiber, 14 g pro.*

FAST FLAVOR

To use the last of a jar of mustard, for each tablespoon of mustard left in the jar, add ¼ cup of extra virgin olive oil, ¼ cup wine vinegar, 1 minced clove of garlic, and 1 teaspoon Italian seasoning. Shake vigorously and drizzle over greens right before tossing.

FOR INFORMATION ON SELECTING AND STORING WATERMELON, SEE PAGE 33; FOR INFORMATION ON CHILES, SEE PAGE 24.

Watermelon Wedges with Jalapeño Syrup

START TO FINISH: 15 MINUTES MAKES: 8 TO 10 SIDE-DISH SERVINGS

FOR A LESS SPICY GLAZE, SLICE THE JALAPEÑOS IN HALF LENGTHWISE AND REMOVE THE SEEDS AND FIBERS BEFORE CHOPPING.

¼ cup lemon juice

¼ cup lime juice

½ cup sugar

2 fresh jalapeño chile peppers, coarsely chopped (see tip, page 51)

1 1-inch piece fresh ginger, coarsely chopped

1 small watermelon, halved and cut into serving-size wedges

1. For jalapeño syrup, in a small saucepan combine lemon juice, lime juice, and sugar. Bring just to boiling. Cook and stir until sugar is dissolved. Reduce heat; add chile peppers and ginger. Simmer, uncovered, for 4 minutes. Remove from heat. Strain through a fine-mesh sieve; discard solids. Cool to room temperature.
2. To serve, drizzle syrup over watermelon wedges.
PER SERVING *167 cal., 1 g total fat (0 g sat. fat), 0 mg chol., 4 mg sodium, 43 g carbo., 2 g fiber, 2 g pro.*

Spiced Cantaloupe

START TO FINISH: 10 MINUTES MAKES: 4 SIDE-DISH SERVINGS

LIME JUICE GIVES THIS PERFECTLY SIMPLE DISH TERRIFIC TANGINESS WHILE NUTMEG INFUSES THE MELON WITH SWEET, WARM, AND SPICY NOTES.

2 cups cubed cantaloupe

2 tablespoons lime juice

1 tablespoon sugar

¼ teaspoon ground nutmeg

1. In a medium bowl combine cantaloupe, lime juice, sugar, and nutmeg; toss gently to combine. Spoon into serving dishes.
PER ½ CUP SERVING *41 cal., 0 g total fat, 0 mg chol., 13 mg sodium, 10 g carbo., 1 g fiber, 1 g pro.*

FOR INFORMATION ON SELECTING AND STORING CANTALOUPE, SEE PAGE 32.

Spicy Cucumber with Lime and Mint

PREP: 25 MINUTES CHILL: 45 MINUTES MAKES: 4 SIDE-DISH SERVINGS

JAPANESE CUCUMBERS—ALSO CALLED ENGLISH OR HOTHOUSE CUCUMBERS, ARE NEARLY SEEDLESS, WHICH MAKES THEM LESS LIKELY TO WEEP AND DILUTE THE STAND-UP-AND-GET-NOTICED FLAVORS OF THIS THAI-INSPIRED DRESSING.

¼ cup fresh lime juice

2 tablespoons fish sauce

1 tablespoon sugar

½ teaspoon salt

1 pound Japanese cucumbers, thinly sliced

½ cup thinly sliced scallions (4)

¼ cup torn fresh mint leaves

1½ teaspoons vegetable oil

¼ to ½ teaspoon very finely chopped Thai chile peppers (see tip, page 51)

1. For dressing, in a small bowl combine lime juice, fish sauce, sugar, and salt; set aside.

2. In a large bowl combine cucumbers, scallions, mint, oil, and chile peppers. Drizzle with dressing; toss to mix. Cover and chill for 45 minutes before serving.

PER 1 CUP *58 cal., 2 g total fat (0 g sat. fat), 0 mg chol., 992 mg sodium, 10 g carbo., 1 g fiber, 2 g pro.*

Sugar Snap Pea and Cantaloupe Salad

START TO FINISH: 35 MINUTES MAKES: 6 TO 8 SIDE-DISH SERVINGS

TO REMOVE THE STRINGS FROM SNAP PEAS, GENTLY GRASP THE STRING ON THE BLOSSOM, THEN PULL IT THE LENGTH OF THE POD.

½ cup bottled raspberry vinaigrette or poppyseed salad dressing

1 teaspoon snipped fresh tarragon

12 ounces sugar snap peas

1 small cantaloupe

2 cups watercress, tough stems removed

¼ cup sliced almonds, toasted

1. Stir together raspberry vinaigrette and tarragon; cover and chill until serving time.

2. Remove strings and tips from peas; halve peas diagonally. In a medium saucepan cook peas in boiling water for 1 minute; drain. Rinse with cold water; drain again.

3. Halve cantaloupe; remove seeds and peel. Using a mandoline, cut cantaloupe into thin slices. Arrange peas, cantaloupe, and watercress on a platter. Drizzle dressing over salad and sprinkle with almonds.

PER SERVING *117 cal., 6 g total fat (0 g sat. fat), 0 mg chol., 97 mg sodium, 15 g carbo., 3 g fiber, 3 g pro.*

FOR INFORMATION ON SELECTING AND STORING SUGAR SNAP PEAS, SEE PAGE 12; FOR INFORMATION ON CANTALOUPE, SEE PAGE 32.

Butter Lettuce Salad

START TO FINISH: 25 MINUTES MAKES: 6 TO 8 SIDE-DISH SERVINGS

VELVETY CRÈME FRAÎCHE ADDS A DELICATE TANG TO THE DRESSING. LOOK FOR IT IN SPECIALTY MARKETS OR LARGE SUPERMARKETS—OR MAKE YOUR OWN.

2 cloves garlic, minced

½ teaspoon salt

1 tablespoon lemon juice

¾ cup homemade or purchased crème fraîche or sour cream

2 tablespoons whipping cream

Salt and freshly ground black pepper

12 ounces fresh green beans, trimmed (3 cups)

3 or 4 large heads butterhead (Boston or Bibb) lettuce, torn (12 to 14 cups)

2 medium cucumbers, halved lengthwise, seeded, and thinly bias-sliced (1½ cups)*

3 to 4 tablespoons thinly sliced chives

1. For crème fraîche dressing, on a cutting board finely chop garlic. Sprinkle with a pinch of salt and rub with side of a knife to form a paste. Transfer paste to a small glass bowl. Stir in ½ teaspoon salt and lemon juice; let stand for 10 minutes. Whisk in crème fraîche and whipping cream. Season to taste with salt and pepper.

2. Add green beans to a large pan of rapidly boiling, lightly salted water. Cook, uncovered, for 5 to 7 minutes or just until tender. Drain beans and place in a bowl of lightly salted ice water to quickly chill. Let stand for 3 to 5 minutes or until cold; drain.

3. Arrange lettuce, green beans, and cucumbers on a platter. Season with salt and freshly ground black pepper. Drizzle with a little dressing; sprinkle with chives. Pass additional dressing.

PER SERVING *163 cal., 13 g total fat (8 g sat. fat), 47 mg chol., 336 mg sodium, 10 g carbo., 3 g fiber, 3 g pro.*

*TIP If cucumber peel is waxed or thick, peel before slicing.

HOMEMADE CRÈME FRAÎCHE
In a small glass bowl combine ½ cup whipping cream (not ultrapasteurized) and ½ cup sour cream. Cover with plastic wrap and let stand at room temperature for 2 to 5 hours or until thickened. Cover and chill for up to 48 hours.

FOR INFORMATION ON SELECTING AND STORING LETTUCES, SEE PAGE 11.

FOR INFORMATION ON SELECTING AND STORING FRESH HERBS, SEE PAGE 26; FOR INFORMATION ON LETTUCES AND SALAD GREENS, SEE PAGE 11.

Herb Salad with Creamy Lemon Dressing

START TO FINISH: 20 MINUTES MAKES: 6 TO 8 SIDE-DISH SERVINGS

FOR THE BEST FLAVOR, TAKE ADVANTAGE OF FRESH HERBS IN EARLY SUMMER, BEFORE THEY BOLT AND BECOME BITTER.

4 teaspoons finely shredded lemon peel

⅓ cup lemon juice

2 teaspoons Dijon-style mustard

3 cloves garlic, minced

¼ teaspoon salt

¼ teaspoon black pepper

½ cup extra virgin olive oil

½ cup sour cream

6 to 8 cups torn butterhead (Boston or Bibb) lettuce or mixed baby salad greens

1½ cups torn assorted fresh herbs, such as chives, basil, parley, or mint

12 to 16 radishes, thinly sliced

1. For dressing, in a small bowl combine lemon peel, lemon juice, mustard, garlic, salt, and pepper. Slowly whisk in olive oil until thickened. Whisk in sour cream.

2. In a large bowl toss together lettuce and herbs; transfer to a serving platter. Top with sliced radishes; pass dressing.

PER SERVING (3 TBSP. DRESSING) *215 cal., 22 g total fat (5 g sat. fat), 7 mg chol., 161 mg sodium, 5 g carbo., 1 g fiber, 2 g pro.*

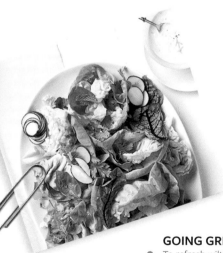

GOING GREEN

- To refresh wilting greens, place the leaves in ice water mixed with 1 tablespoon of lemon juice. Refrigerate for 1 hour, drain well, and wrap them in a clean kitchen towel. Refrigerate wrapped greens for 4 hours.
- To prevent salad from becoming soggy, dress it right before serving; present salad on chilled plates.
- Save cleanup time by mixing dressing right in the salad bowl. Then add greens and toss well.
- Make tossing simple by adding dressing directly into the lettuce storage bag. Close bag and shake to toss.

Baby Greens and Potato Salad with Red Pepper Dressing

PREP: 15 MINUTES   CHILL: 24 HOURS   BAKE: 30 MINUTES   OVEN: 400°F
MAKES: 4 MAIN-DISH OR 8 SIDE-DISH SERVINGS

BECAUSE BABY POTATOES AND BABY GREENS ARE OFTEN HARVESTED AT THE SAME TIME, THIS SENSATIONAL SALAD IS SUPER-SEASONAL.

1 7-ounce jar roasted red sweet peppers, drained

½ cup extra virgin olive oil

⅓ cup rice vinegar or white wine vinegar

1 teaspoon salt

Dash cayenne pepper

1 tablespoon snipped fresh thyme leaves

1 tablespoon olive oil

¼ teaspoon garlic salt

¼ teaspoon black pepper

10 to 12 ounces medium new potatoes (assorted colors) (about 12 potatoes), halved

8 to 10 cups mixed baby greens

4 hard-cooked eggs, peeled and sliced

Shaved Parmigiano-Reggiano cheese (optional)

1. Preheat oven to 400°F. In a blender or food processor combine peppers, ½ cup olive oil, vinegar, 1 teaspoon salt, and cayenne pepper; cover and blend or process until nearly smooth. Stir in thyme; cover and chill up to 24 hours.

2. In a small bowl combine 1 tablespoon olive oil, garlic salt, and black pepper. Place potatoes in a shallow baking pan; brush with oil mixture. Bake, uncovered, about 30 minutes or until tender and browned on edges, stirring once. (If desired, cover and chill up to 8 hours; reheat before serving.)

3. To serve, arrange greens on 4 dinner plates or 8 salad plates. Top with eggs and potatoes. Drizzle with dressing. If desired, garnish with shaved cheese.

PER MAIN-DISH SERVING *435 cal., 36 g total fat (6 g sat. fat), 212 mg chol., 724 mg sodium, 19 g carbo., 4 g fiber, 9 g pro.*

FOR INFORMATION ON SELECTING AND STORING SALAD GREENS, SEE PAGE 11; FOR INFORMATION ON POTATOES, SEE PAGE 38.

FOR INFORMATION ON SELECTING AND STORING STRAWBERRIES, SEE PAGE 27.

Strawberry and Spring Onion Salad

START TO FINISH: 20 MINUTES MAKES: 4 TO 6 SIDE-DISH SERVINGS

JUICY-SWEET STRAWBERRIES MARRY HAPPILY WITH SAVORY SCALLIONS—AND THEY MAKE A HANDSOME COUPLE AS WELL.

1 tablespoon champagne or white wine vinegar

2 teaspoons snipped fresh chives

2 teaspoons Dijon-style mustard

¼ teaspoon snipped fresh dillweed

¼ teaspoon salt

⅛ teaspoon black pepper

3 tablespoons extra virgin olive oil

1 pound strawberries, hulled and sliced ¼ inch thick

2 bunches scallions, thinly sliced

1. For dressing, in a small bowl combine vinegar, chives, mustard, dill, salt, and pepper. Whisk in olive oil.
2. In a medium bowl combine strawberries and onions. Drizzle with dressing; toss to coat. Serve immediately.
PER ¾ CUP SERVING *149 cal., 11 g total fat (1 g sat. fat), 0 mg chol., 217 mg sodium, 13 g carbo., 4 g fiber, 2 g pro.*

Herbed Potato Salad

PREP: 40 MINUTES CHILL: 6 TO 24 HOURS MAKES: 8 TO 10 SIDE-DISH SERVINGS

THE BEST SALAD POTATOES ARE WAXY RED. GOLDEN AND YELLOW VARIETIES ALSO WORK WELL. AVOID RUSSET (BAKING) POTATOES—THE STARCHY TUBERS TEND TO DISINTEGRATE WHEN STIRRED INTO SALADS.

8 medium potatoes, peeled and chopped

1 cup light mayonnaise

⅓ cup milk

⅓ cup chopped scallions

¼ cup chopped onion

2 teaspoons snipped fresh rosemary

2 teaspoons snipped fresh lemon thyme

½ teaspoon salt

½ teaspoon black pepper

¼ teaspoon snipped fresh chives

Snipped Italian parsley (optional)

1. In a large covered saucepan cook potatoes in lightly salted boiling water for 7 to 8 minutes or just until tender. Drain in colander; transfer to a large bowl. Let cool completely.
2. For dressing, in a small bowl combine mayonnaise, milk, scallions, onion, rosemary, thyme, salt, pepper, and chives. Pour over potatoes; toss gently to coat. Cover and chill for 6 to 24 hours. If desired, sprinkle with snipped parsley before serving.
PER SERVING *169 cal., 2 g total fat (1 g sat. fat), 7 mg chol., 440 mg sodium, 34 g carbo., 3 g fiber, 4 g pro.*

FOR INFORMATION ON SELECTING AND STORING POTATOES, SEE PAGE 38.

Parsley Salad

START TO FINISH: 30 MINUTES OVEN: 375°F MAKES: 4 SIDE-DISH SERVINGS

THIS UNUSUAL SALAD IS SERVED ON TOASTED CRUSTY BREAD. USING A COMBINATION OF FLAT-LEAF AND CURLY PARSLEY ADDS EXTRA GREEN FLAVOR AND REFRESHING TASTE.

2 tablespoons sherry vinegar

1 clove garlic, minced

4 ½-inch slices round semolina or other crusty bread, toasted

4 tablespoons extra virgin olive oil

2 roma tomatoes, cut into 6 slices each

Salt and freshly ground black pepper

½ teaspoon salt

¼ teaspoon freshly ground black pepper

2 cups loosely packed Italian parsley leaves

2 cups loosely packed curly parsley leaves

½ cup finely shredded Parmesan cheese (2 ounces)

Shaved Parmesan cheese (optional)

Yellow and red cherry tomatoes (optional)

1. In a large bowl combine vinegar and garlic. Let stand for 30 minutes.

2. Meanwhile, preheat oven to 375°F. Brush both sides of bread slices with 1 tablespoon of the olive oil. Place bread on baking sheet; toast in oven for 12 to 15 minutes or until golden, turning once. Place each slice of toast on a salad plate. Arrange 3 tomato slices on each bread slice; season with salt and pepper.

3. Add the remaining 3 tablespoons oil, ½ teaspoon salt, and ¼ teaspoon pepper to the vinegar mixture. Whisk to mix. Add Italian parsley, curly parsley, and finely shredded cheese; toss to mix. Spoon parsley mixture onto bread slices. If desired, garnish with shaved Parmesan cheese and cherry tomatoes.

PER SERVING *273 cal., 18 g total fat (4 g sat. fat), 7 mg chol., 817 mg sodium, 21 g carbo., 9 g pro.*

PRETTY PARSLEY

- To perk up limp parsley, snip ¼ inch from the base of the stems and place, stem ends down, in a glass of water for 30 minutes.
- To coarsely chop fresh parsley, stuff leaves into a glass measuring cup, insert scissors into the cup, and snip away.
- Don't discard parsley stems—use them to add wonderful flavor to homemade stock and broth.

Tabbouleh

PREP: 20 MINUTES STAND: 1 HOUR CHILL: 4 HOURS MAKES: 6 TO 8 SERVINGS

BULGUR IS KERNELS OF WHEAT THAT HAVE BEEN BOILED, ALLOWED TO DRY, AND THEN CRUSHED. IT REQUIRES NO TRUE COOKING; IT SIMPLY REHYDRATES WHILE STANDING IN BOILING WATER.

2 cups boiling water

1 cup bulgur

¼ cup lemon juice

¼ cup extra virgin olive oil

½ teaspoon salt

1 cup chopped, seeded tomatoes (2 medium)

1 cup chopped fresh parsley

½ cup sliced scallions (4)

¼ cup snipped fresh mint

Fresh parsley (optional)

1. In a medium bowl combine boiling water and bulgur. Cover and let stand for 1 hour.
2. Meanwhile, for dressing, in a screw-top jar combine lemon juice, olive oil, and salt. Cover and shake well to mix; set aside.
3. Drain bulgur in a fine-mesh sieve, squeezing out excess water using the back of a spoon. Transfer bulgur to a serving bowl; fluff with a fork. Stir in tomatoes, 1 cup parsley, scallions, and mint; stir in dressing. Cover and chill up to 4 hours. If desired, garnish with parsley before serving.

PER SERVING *176 cal., 9 g total fat (1 g sat. fat), 0 mg chol., 210 mg sodium, 22 g carbo., 6 g fiber, 4 g pro.*

FAST FLAVOR

To turn tonight's tabbouleh into tomorrow's brown bag treasure, stir in some chunks of well-drained albacore tuna, sprinkle in a little chopped fresh dill if you have it, and roll up the mixture in a whole grain wrap.

FOR INFORMATION ON SELECTING AND STORING TOMATOES, SEE PAGE 21.

Orange-Beet Salad

PREP: 15 MINUTES **COOK:** 40 MINUTES **CHILL:** 2 HOURS **MAKES:** 4 SIDE-DISH SERVINGS

IN ADDITION TO REFRESHING ORANGE, THIS SALAD GETS A FLAVOR BOOST FROM TOASTED WALNUTS AND WALNUT OIL. LOOK FOR THE OIL AT SPECIALTY SHOPS AND LARGE SUPERMARKETS.

3 medium beets (about 12 ounces)

3 tablespoons walnut oil or salad oil

1 teaspoon finely shredded orange peel

2 tablespoons orange juice

1 tablespoon white wine vinegar or white vinegar

3 tablespoons crumbled feta cheese

2 tablespoons broken walnuts, toasted

¼ teaspoon coarsely ground black pepper

1. To cook beets, cut off all but 1 inch of stems and roots; wash. Do not peel. In a covered large saucepan cook beets in boiling salted water for 40 to 50 minutes or until tender. Drain; cool slightly. Slip skins off beets. Cut beets into wedges and place in a medium bowl.

2. Meanwhile, for dressing, in a screw-top jar combine walnut oil, orange peel, orange juice, and vinegar. Cover and shake well. Drizzle dressing over beets; toss gently to coat. Cover and chill for 2 to 24 hours.

3. To serve, let mixture come to room temperature. Sprinkle with feta cheese, nuts, and pepper. Serve with a slotted spoon.

PER SERVING *149 cal., 14 g total fat (2 g sat. fat), 4 mg chol., 83 mg sodium, 6 g carbo., 2 g pro.*

FAST FLAVOR

To get the best flavor from beets, roast them in the oven as you would baking potatoes. First remove the greens, wrap the unpeeled roots in foil packets, and place the packets on a baking sheet. Roast at 400°F until the beets are tender enough to pierce easily with a paring knife. Set aside until they're cool enough to handle. The skins will slip right off. Peel or quarter the beets and toss them with a little oil and vinegar, salt, and pepper. You may blanch the tops and mix those in as well.

FOR INFORMATION ON SELECTING AND STORING BEETS, SEE PAGE 34.

FOR INFORMATION ON SELECTING AND STORING CUCUMBERS, SEE PAGE 25; FOR INFORMATION ON RADISHES, SEE PAGE 16.

Curly Cukes and Radish Salad

START TO FINISH: 20 MINUTES   MAKES: 6 SIDE-DISH SERVINGS

THIS SIMPLE SALAD IS SENSATIONAL MADE WITH CUCUMBERS AND RADISHES PLUCKED FROM YOUR OWN GARDEN.

10 radishes

2 medium seedless cucumbers

1 fresh jalapeño chile pepper, seeded and sliced into rings (see tip, page 51)

2 tablespoons snipped fresh basil or sorrel

½ teaspoon sugar

¼ teaspoon salt

1 tablespoon extra virgin olive oil

1 tablespoon white wine vinegar

1. Set aside 1 whole radish for garnish. Thinly slice 5 of the remaining radishes. Cut the remaining 4 radishes into halves or quarters.
2. Using a vegetable peeler, cut thin lengthwise slices from cucumbers, discarding first slice. (You should have about 2 cups.)
3. In a bowl combine radish slices and halves; cucumber ribbons; chile pepper; basil; sugar; and salt. Drizzle with olive oil and white wine vinegar. Toss gently to coat. Garnish with reserved whole radish.

PER SERVING *36 cal., 2 g total fat (0 g sat. fat), 0 mg chol., 93 mg sodium, 4 g carbo., 1 g fiber, 1 g pro.*

CUCUMBER COOL

● To seed cucumbers, cut cukes in half lengthwise. Starting at one end, scrape out seeds and pulpy flesh along the length of the cucumber.

● To make pretty cucumber slices, trim ends of a whole cucumber, then press the tines of a fork from top to bottom of the cucumber, pressing firmly to score the skin before slicing.

Assorted Greens with Roasted Garlic

PREP: 40 MINUTES OVEN: 425°F MAKES: 8 TO 10 SIDE-DISH SERVINGS

IF YOUR FAMILY IS NOT FOND OF GOAT'S MILK CHEESES, SUBSTITUTE CRUMBLED QUESO FRESCO OR FARMER'S CHEESE FOR THE CHÈVRE IN THIS RECIPE.

1 recipe Roasted Garlic Paste

12 cups mixed salad greens greens

1 cup pear-shape cherry tomatoes, halved

1 cup watermelon radishes or radishes, sliced

⅓ cup red wine vinegar

⅓ cup fresh basil leaves, lightly packed

1½ teaspoons packed brown sugar

1½ teaspoons Dijon-style mustard

1½ teaspoon salt

¼ to ½ teaspoon black pepper

1 to 1¼ cups extra virgin olive oil

⅔ cup chèvre (soft goat cheese)

8 to 10 crusty Italian bread slices

1. Prepare Roasted Garlic Paste; set aside. In an extra-large salad bowl combine greens, tomatoes, and radishes; set aside.

2. For vinaigrette, in a food processor or blender combine vinegar, basil, brown sugar, mustard, salt, pepper, and Roasted Garlic Paste. Cover and process or blend until combined. With the blender or food processor running, slowly add the olive oil until combined.

3. Spread chèvre over toasted bread. Drizzle dressing over greens; toss to coat. Serve salad with bread.

ROASTED GARLIC PASTE: Preheat oven to 425°F. Peel away the dry outer layers of skin from 1 large head of garlic, leaving skins and cloves intact. Cut off the pointed top portion (about ¼ inch), leaving the bulb intact but exposing individual cloves. Place the garlic head, cut side up, in a custard cup. Drizzle with a little olive oil. Cover with foil and bake for 25 to 35 minutes or until the cloves feel soft when pressed. Set aside just until cool enough to handle. Squeeze out the garlic paste from individual cloves (you should have about 1 tablespoon).

PER SERVING *407 cal., 33 g total fat (7 g sat. fat), 9 mg chol., 723 mg sodium, 21 g carbo., 2 g fiber, g pro.*

GARDEN TIP
When harvesting lettuce from your own garden, do so early in the morning, when leaves are cool and plump with moisture.

FOR INFORMATION ON SELECTING AND STORING SALAD GREENS, SEE PAGE 11; FOR INFORMATION ON GARLIC, SEE PAGE 39.

FOR INFORMATION ON SELECTING AND STORING FENNEL, SEE PAGE 36; FOR INFORMATION ON FRESH HERBS, SEE PAGE 26.

Fennel and Parsley Salad with Meyer Lemon

PREP: 20 MINUTES   MAKES: 4 TO 6 SIDE-DISH SERVINGS

MEYER LEMONS ADD DISTINCTIVE FRAGRANCE AND FLAVOR TO FENNEL; BUT WHEN THEY'RE NOT AVAILABLE, USE REGULAR LEMONS, TANGERINES, OR ORANGES.

2 medium fennel bulbs

½ cup snipped fresh Italian parsley

2 teaspoons finely shredded Meyer lemon peel

2 tablespoons Meyer lemon juice

2 tablespoons extra virgin olive oil

¼ teaspoon salt

⅛ teaspoon black pepper

1. Cut off and discard fennel stalks. Remove any wilted outer layers; cut a thin slice from the base of each bulb. Cut the fennel in half lengthwise. Cut out the core. Using a mandoline or sharp knife, thinly slice the fennel crosswise.

2. In a medium bowl combine fennel slices, parsley, lemon peel, lemon juice, olive oil, salt, and pepper; toss gently to mix. Serve immediately or chill up to 1 hour.

PER SERVING *101 cal., 7 g total fat (1 g sat. fat), 0 mg chol., 211 mg sodium, 10 g carbo., 4 g fiber, 2 g pro.*

Kohlrabi Coleslaw

PREP: 30 MINUTES   CHILL: 2 TO 24 HOURS   MAKES: 12 SERVINGS

IF YOU HAVE A FOOD PROCESSOR, USE THE SHREDDING BLADE TO QUICKLY SHRED THE CABBAGE, CARROTS, AND KOHLRABI.

¾ cup mayonnaise

¼ cup white vinegar

2 tablespoon sugar

2 teaspoon celery seeds (optional)

½ teaspoon salt

¼ teaspoon black pepper

9 cups chopped or finely shredded green cabbage (1 pound)

1 cup finely shredded carrots (2 medium)

1 cup shredded kohlrabi, jicama, or radishes

1 cup snipped Italian parsley

1. For dressing, in a small bowl stir together mayonnaise, vinegar, sugar, celery seeds (if desired), salt, and pepper. Set aside.

2. In an extra-large bowl combine cabbage, carrots, kohlrabi, and parsley. Stir in the dressing; mix well. Cover and chill for 2 to 24 hours. Serve with a slotted spoon.

PER SERVING *124 cal., 11 g total fat (2 g sat. fat), 5 mg chol., 209 mg sodium, 7 g carbo., 2 g fiber, 1 g pro.*

KITCHEN TIP

Instead of the cabbage and carrots, substitute one 16-ounce package of shredded cabbage with carrot (coleslaw mix).

FOR INFORMATION ON SELECTING AND STORING KOHLRABI, SEE PAGE 36.

FENNEL AND PARSLEY SALAD WITH MEYER LEMON

FOR INFORMATION ON SELECTING AND STORING APPLES, SEE PAGE 42;
FOR INFORMATION ON FENNEL, SEE PAGE 36.

Apple-Fennel Salad

START TO FINISH: 40 MINUTES MAKES: 8 TO 10 SIDE-DISH SERVINGS

AT HOLIDAY TIME, MANY LARGE SUPERMARKETS SELL PLASTIC CONTAINERS FULL OF READY-TO-USE POMEGRANATE SEEDS.

1 pomegranate

3 lemons

3 to 4 tart crisp green and/or red apples

2 medium fennel bulbs

6 tablespoons canola oil

2 tablespoons mayonnaise

3 to 4 tablespoons snipped fresh Italian parsley

Coarse salt and freshly ground black pepper

1. Remove seeds from pomegranate; set aside. Squeeze the juice from 1 of the lemons into a large salad bowl. Leave the skin on the apples; halve and core them. Thinly slice the apples and toss with the lemon juice in the bowl; set aside.

2. Cut off fennel stalks. Discard stalks, reserving fronds. Remove any wilted outer layers on bulbs; cut thin slices from the bases. Cut bulbs into quarters lengthwise. Core and thinly slice each quarter. Add the fennel slices to the apples. Toss to combine; set aside. Coarsely chop some of the reserved fennel fronds (about ¼ cup); set aside.

3. For dressing, finely shred the yellow portion of peel from the 2 remaining lemons into a small bowl. Squeeze the juice from the 2 remaining lemons and add juice to peel. Whisk the oil into the juice and the peel. Whisk in the mayonnaise and parsley. Season with salt and pepper.

4. To serve, drain apples and fennel; return to bowl. Add dressing, pomegranate seeds, and reserved fennel fronds; toss to coat.

PER SERVING *182 cal., 13 g total fat (1 g sat. fat), 1 mg chol., 174 mg sodium, 19 g carbo., 5 g fiber, 2 g pro.*

MAKE-AHEAD DIRECTIONS
Prepare as above, except do not add the pomegranate seeds. Cover and chill up to 24 hours. Stir in the seeds just before serving.

Arugula, Corn, and Tomato Salad with Ricotta Salata

START TO FINISH: 25 MINUTES MAKES: 8 SIDE-DISH SERVINGS

RICOTTA SALATA—A FRESH ITALIAN CHEESE WITH BRINY TASTE AND GRAINY-BUT-SLICEABLE TEXTURE—IS MADE FROM WHEY RATHER THAN MILK.

6 cups fresh arugula

1½ cups fresh basil leaves, torn

1½ cups fresh or frozen corn kernels, thawed

1 cup halved cherry tomatoes

3 tablespoons extra virgin olive oil

2 tablespoons lemon juice

¼ teaspoon salt

⅛ teaspoon black pepper

2½ ounces ricotta salata

1. In a large bowl combine arugula, basil, corn, and tomatoes.

2. For dressing, in a small bowl whisk together olive oil, lemon juice, salt, and pepper. Drizzle dressing over arugula mixture; toss to coat. Divide among salad plates. Crumble cheese over each salad.

PER SERVING *107 cal., 7 g total fat (1 g sat. fat), 8 mg chol., 229 mg sodium, 8 g carbo., 1 g fiber, 3 g pro.*

FAST FLAVOR
To add a peppery bite to homemade potato salad—or even deli-purchased potato salad—toss in a bunch of coarsely chopped fresh arugula.

FOR INFORMATION ON SELECTING AND STORING SALAD GREENS, SEE PAGE 11; FOR INFORMATION ON SWEET CORN, SEE PAGE 25; FOR INFORMATION ON TOMATOES, SEE PAGE 21.

Carrot Ribbon Salad

PREP: 20 MINUTES   CHILL: 2 TO 4 HOURS   MAKES: 12 SIDE-DISH SERVINGS

THIS PRETTY AND PLEASING SALAD IS A COLORFUL SIDE DISH. TO SERVE IT ANOTHER WAY, PILE THE RIBBONS AND PEAS ON PASTA SALAD AS A GORGEOUS GARNISH.

2 cups shelled fresh peas or one 10-ounce package frozen peas

1 pound large carrots

1 cup thinly sliced scallions (8)

½ cup honey

¼ cup white wine vinegar

½ teaspoon salt

¼ teaspoon black pepper

1. In a medium saucepan cook peas in a small amount of boiling water for 2 to 3 minutes or just until crisp-tender. Drain and rinse with cold running water until cool. Peel carrots. Using a vegetable peeler, peel carrots lengthwise into thin strips. In a large bowl combine cooked peas, carrot strips, and scallions.

2. For dressing, in a small bowl combine honey, vinegar, salt, and black pepper. Drizzle dressing over vegetables and toss gently. Cover and chill for 2 to 4 hours. Serve with a slotted spoon.

PER SERVING *80 cal., 0 g total fat, 0 mg chol., 124 mg sodium, 19 g carbo., 2 g fiber, 2 g pro.*

KITCHEN TIP

For 2 cups shelled peas, start with 2 pounds of peas in shells.

FOR INFORMATION ON SELECTING AND STORING CARROTS, SEE PAGE 13; FOR INFORMATION ON GARDEN PEAS, SEE PAGE 12.

FOR INFORMATION SELECTING AND STORING TOMATOES, SEE PAGE 21;
FOR INFORMATION ON ZUCCHINI, SEE PAGE 22.

Tomato and Zucchini Platter with Blue Cheese

PREP: 25 MINUTES   CHILL: 4 HOURS   STAND: 30 MINUTES   MAKES: 6 TO 8 SIDE-DISH SERVINGS

IF YOU'RE LOOKING FOR A GORGEOUS SALAD TO TOTE TO A SUMMER POTLUCK, LOOK NO FURTHER—
THIS STUNNER IS SUPERLATIVE.

1½ pounds heirloom tomatoes (such as Lime Green, Cherokee Purple, Russian Rose, and/or Box Car Willie), thickly sliced

½ of a large zucchini and/or yellow summer squash

½ cup kalamata olives, pitted

½ cup crumbled blue cheese (2 ounces)

1 tablespoon snipped fresh chives or sliced scallions

Sea salt and black pepper

1 recipe Sherry-Thyme Vinaigrette

1. For salad, arrange the tomatoes on a large platter. Using a vegetable peeler, thinly slice zucchini lengthwise into ribbons. Tuck zucchini ribbons under and around tomatoes. Top with olives, cheese, and chives. Cover and chill up to 4 hours.

2. To serve, sprinkle salad lightly with salt and pepper. Drizzle with Sherry-Thyme Vinaigrette. Cover and let stand for 30 minutes before serving.

PER SERVING *182 cal., 16 g total fat (3 g sat. fat), 7 mg chol., 385 mg sodium, 6 g carbo., 2 g fiber, 3 g pro.*

SHERRY-THYME VINAIGRETTE In a screw-top jar combine 2 tablespoons sherry wine vinegar; 1 clove garlic, minced; 2 teaspoons snipped fresh thyme; and 1 teaspoon Dijon-style mustard. Add ⅓ cup extra virgin olive oil. Cover and shake well. Season with sea salt and black pepper.

TOMATO TRICKS

- Never refrigerate a tomato! Temperatures below 55°F ruin texture and destroy flavor.
- To core a tomato, run a paring knife around the stem end to remove the inner white core.
- When using fresh tomatoes in cooked dishes, quarter the tomatoes and give them a squeeze to remove seeds and gelatinous pulp.
- To ripen green tomatoes, place them stem sides down in a cardboard box between layers of newspaper. Check often and remove tomatoes when ripe.

Heirloom Insalata Caprese

PREP: 20 MINUTES   CHILL: 6 HOURS   MAKES: 12 SIDE-DISH SERVINGS

THIS ITALIAN CLASSIC IS MEMORABLE WITH VINE-RIPENED, HERITAGE TOMATOES AS ITS FOUNDATION. WHEN FARMERS' MARKET TABLES TUMBLE WITH TOMATOES, TRY THEM ALL TO DISCOVER YOUR FAVORITES.

½ cup extra virgin olive oil

¼ cup balsamic vinegar

3 cloves garlic, minced

¼ teaspoon salt

Dash black pepper

3½ pounds assorted heirloom tomatoes (such as Brandywine, Soldacki, and/or Nyagous), cored and cut into wedges

½ pound pear-shape tomatoes, halved if large

1 pound fresh mozzarella bocconcini or fresh mozzarella cheese, sliced ½ inch thick and slices halved

¼ cup loosely packed fresh basil shreds

Whole basil leaves

1. For dressing, in a screw-top jar combine olive oil, vinegar, garlic, salt, and pepper. Cover and chill up to 1 week. Shake before using.

2. Arrange tomato wedges on a large platter with rim. Top wedges with the pear tomatoes and mozzarella. Cover and chill up to 6 hours. Just before serving, sprinkle platter with the shredded basil and drizzle with dressing. Top with whole basil leaves.

PER SERVING *211 cal., 17 g total fat (6 g sat. fat), 28 mg chol., 201 mg sodium, 7 g carbo., 2 g fiber, 9 g pro.*

KITCHEN TIP
Bocconcini are small nuggets of fresh mozzarella packaged in whey or water.

FOR INFORMATION ON SELECTING AND STORING TOMATOES, SEE PAGE 21.

Stirred

SOUPS, RISOTTO, SAUCES & STIR-FRIES

Assisted by wooden spoons and willing hands, fresh vegetables and fruits take a turn around soup pots, saucepans, and skillets—mingling with meats, herbs, and seasonings and transforming into melanges of goodness.

Corn and Chicken Chowder

PREP: 30 MINUTES COOK: 20 MINUTES MAKES: 4 MAIN-DISH SERVINGS (5½ CUPS)

HEARTY AND FILLING, THIS CHUNKY CHOWDER IS A DELIGHTFUL ONE-DISH DINNER. TO CUT KERNELS FROM EARS OF CORN, HOLD THE COB TIP UP, THEN CAREFULLY CUT DOWN THE EAR AND THROUGH THE KERNELS WITH A GENTLE SAWING MOTION.

6 fresh ears of corn or 3 cups frozen whole kernel corn

1 tablespoon vegetable oil

¾ cup chopped onion

¾ cup chopped green and/or red sweet pepper

1 14-ounce can chicken broth

1 cup cubed, peeled potato (1 medium)

1 cup half-and-half, light cream, or milk

2 tablespoons all-purpose flour

2 teaspoons snipped fresh thyme

¼ teaspoon salt

¼ teaspoon black pepper

1¼ cups chopped cooked chicken (about 6 ounces)

2 slices bacon, crisp-cooked, drained, and crumbled

Fresh thyme sprigs (optional)

1. If using fresh corn, use a sharp knife to cut corn kernels off the cob; set aside. In a large saucepan heat oil over medium heat. Add onion and sweet pepper; cook until tender but not brown. Stir in broth, potato, and corn. Bring to boiling; reduce heat. Simmer, covered, about 20 minutes or until potato is tender, stirring occasionally.

2. In a small bowl combine half-and-half, flour, 2 teaspoons thyme, salt, and black pepper; stir into corn mixture. Cook and stir until mixture is thickened and bubbly; cook and stir for 1 minute more. Add chicken and bacon; cook and stir until heated through. If desired, garnish with thyme sprigs.

PER SERVING *410 cal., 18 g total fat (7 g sat. fat), 65 mg chol., 612 mg sodium, 43 g carbo., 6 g fiber, 24 g pro.*

FAST FLAVOR
To make corn even more flavorful—for this recipe or any other—roast it! To roast, cut kernels from the cob and spread them in a single layer on a rimmed baking sheet. Broil until golden brown and caramelized, about 4 to 5 minutes. Watch carefully so the corn doesn't burn!

FOR INFORMATION ON SELECTING AND STORING SWEET CORN, SEE PAGE 25.

FOR INFORMATION ON SELECTING AND STORING CAULIFLOWER, SEE PAGE 14.

Roasted Cauliflower Soup

PREP: 15 MINUTES COOK: 20 MINUTES OVEN: 400°F ROAST: 30 MINUTES
OVEN: 400°F MAKES: 8 SIDE-DISH SERVINGS

THIS PLEASING POTAGE BEGINS WITH OVEN-ROASTED CAULIFLOWER FLORETS. ROASTING CARAMELIZES THE CREAMY WHITE VEGETABLE'S NATURAL SUGARS, RESULTING IN LUXURIOUS FLAVOR.

1 large head cauliflower (3 pounds), cut into florets (10 cups)

1 large onion, sliced

2 cloves garlic, halved

2 tablespoons olive oil

2 14-ounce cans chicken broth

1 cup water

1 bay leaf

1 teaspoon snipped fresh thyme

1 cup half-and-half or light cream

1 teaspoon salt

⅛ teaspoon black pepper

1. Preheat oven to 400°F. In a large roasting pan toss cauliflower, onion, and garlic with olive oil. Roast, uncovered, for 30 minutes, stirring once after 15 minutes.

2. In a large saucepan combine the roasted cauliflower and onion, broth, the water, bay leaf, and thyme. Bring to boiling; reduce heat. Simmer, covered, for 20 minutes.

3. Discard bay leaf. Working in batches, transfer soup to a food processor or blender; process or blend soup until smooth. Return soup to saucepan. Stir in half-and-half, salt, and pepper. Heat through (do not boil).

PER SERVING *98 cal., 9 g total fat (3 g sat. fat), 13 mg chol., 741 mg sodium, 4 g carbo., 1 g fiber, 2 g pro.*

Broccoli-Cheddar Soup

PREP: 10 MINUTES COOK: 25 MINUTES MAKES: 6 SIDE-DISH SERVINGS

THE RICE IN THIS RECIPE IS A THICKENER. WHEN THE SOUP IS BLENDED, RICE GIVES THE MIXTURE RICH AND SUBSTANTIAL BODY AND HELPS IT FREEZE BEAUTIFULLY.

5 cups water

1 bunch broccoli (about 1½ pounds)

1 cup chopped onion (1 large)

⅓ cup long grain white rice

2 cups milk

1 teaspoon salt

¼ teaspoon black pepper

2 cups shredded cheddar cheese (8 ounces)

2 tablespoons spicy brown mustard

1. In a large saucepan bring the water to boiling. For garnish, cut 6 broccoli florets into quarters. Add quartered florets to boiling water; cook for 4 minutes. Remove and set aside.

2. Cut the stems off remaining broccoli; peel with a vegetable peeler. Coarsely chop broccoli. Add broccoli to water in saucepan. Add onion, rice, milk, salt, and pepper. Bring to boiling; reduce heat. Simmer, covered, about 20 minutes or until vegetables are tender.

3. Working in batches, remove vegetables and some of the liquid to a food processor or blender. Process or blend until smooth. Return mixture to saucepan. Add cheese and mustard. If necessary, stir in additional milk. Gently reheat over low heat; do not boil. Garnish with reserved broccoli.

PER 1⅓-CUP SERVING *269 cal., 14 g total fat (9 g sat. fat), 46 mg chol., 765 mg sodium, 20 g carbo., 2 g fiber, 15 g pro.*

BETTER BROCCOLI

- To minimize the strong odor of broccoli while it cooks, cook it only briefly. Overcooking increases its aroma, dulls its color, and leaches its nutrients.
- Once broccoli florets are removed, peel the stems and cut them into thin coins for later use in stir-fries and salads.
- To prevent cooked broccoli from cooking further, drain it immediately and rinse in cold water.
- To save time, cook broccoli along with pasta. Simply add the florets to the cooking water 3 minutes before the pasta is done. Drain in a colander.

FOR INFORMATION ON SELECTING AND STORING BROCCOLI, SEE PAGE 14.

Thai-Style Pumpkin Soup

PREP: 20 MINUTES COOK: 30 MINUTES MAKES: 6 APPETIZER OR SIDE-DISH SERVINGS

THAI CUISINE MASTERFULLY COMBINES SEEMINGLY INCOMPATIBLE INGREDIENTS—SUCH AS PUMPKIN, PEANUT BUTTER, AND MANGO NECTAR. THESE INGREDIENTS, HOWEVER, MELD INTO A MOST FLAVORFUL SOUP.

1¾ cups Pumpkin Puree or one 15-ounce can pumpkin

1 14-ounce can vegetable broth

1½ cups mango or apricot nectar

1 tablespoon grated fresh ginger

2 cloves garlic, minced

1 5-ounce can (⅔ cup) evaporated milk or ⅔ cup unsweetened coconut milk

¼ cup creamy peanut butter

2 tablespoons rice vinegar

Several dashes bottled hot pepper sauce or ¼ teaspoon crushed red pepper

¼ cup snipped fresh cilantro

Sour cream or plain yogurt (optional)

Dried Thai chile peppers (optional)

1. In a large saucepan combine pumpkin, broth, nectar, ginger, and garlic. Bring to boiling; reduce heat. Simmer, uncovered, for 30 minutes, stirring occasionally.

2. Whisk in milk, peanut butter, vinegar, and hot sauce until smooth. Stir in cilantro. Ladle soup into bowls. If desired, top with sour cream and garnish with Thai chile peppers.

PER SERVING *236 cal., 14 g total fat (4 g sat. fat), 7 mg chol., 402 mg sodium, 23 g carbo., 4 g fiber, 9 g pro.*

PUMPKIN PUREE Preheat oven to 375°F. Wash one 2- to 3-pound sugar pumpkin with a vegetable brush. Halve the pumpkin and remove seeds and strings. Place, cut sides down, on a foil-lined baking sheet. Roast about 1 hour or until a sharp knife inserted in the pumpkin offers little resistance. Let pumpkin stand until cool enough to handle. The flesh should easily peel away from the skin. Place flesh in a blender or food processor and blend or process pulp until smooth. Place puree in a fine-mesh sieve lined with 100%-cotton cheesecloth. Let stand for 1 hour to drain. Press lightly to remove any additional liquid. Discard liquid. Cover; chill for up to 3 days or freeze up to 6 months. Makes 1½ to 2 cups Pumpkin Puree.

KITCHEN TIP

To remove the stringy strands from pumpkin flesh, instead of removing strings before cooking, cook pumpkin with strings intact. Beat the cooked pumpkin with an electric mixer. The strings will attach to the beaters and will rinse off when beaters are removed and washed under running water.

FOR INFORMATION ON SELECTING AND STORING PUMPKINS, SEE PAGE 41.

FOR INFORMATION ON SELECTING AND STORING BUTTERNUT SQUASH, SEE PAGE 40.

Roasted Butternut Squash Soup

PREP: 35 MINUTES   **ROAST:** 50 MINUTES   **COOK:** 55 MINUTES   **OVEN:** 350°F   **MAKES:** 10 SIDE-DISH SERVINGS

WITHIN ITS RATHER HOMELY BUFF-COLOR SKIN AND BENEATH ITS AWKWARD SHAPE, THE VIBRANT ORANGE FLESH OF BUTTERNUT SQUASH BURSTS WITH SWEET, EARTHY FLAVOR.

2 medium butternut squash (1½ pounds each)

4 tablespoons butter, softened

Salt and freshly ground black pepper

4 ounces peppered bacon or hickory-smoked bacon

2 large onions, sliced

4 cloves garlic, minced

1 cup dry white wine

7 to 8 cups vegetable or chicken broth

2 teaspoons Worcestershire sauce

½ to 1 teaspoon bottled hot pepper sauce

Sour cream (optional)

1. Preheat oven to 350°F. Cut squash in half lengthwise. Remove and discard seeds and strings. Score the cut surfaces of the squash; rub with 3 tablespoons of the butter. Season with salt and black pepper. Place squash, cut sides down, in a large shallow roasting pan. Roast, uncovered, for 30 minutes. Turn squash halves cut sides up; roast, uncovered, for 20 to 30 minutes more or until tender and slightly caramelized. Let squash cool. Use a spoon to remove squash pulp from shells (should have about 3½ cups); set aside.

2. Meanwhile, in an 8-quart pot or kettle cook bacon over medium heat until crisp. Drain bacon on paper towels, reserving drippings in pot. Crumble bacon and reserve for garnish. Reduce heat to medium-low. Add the remaining 1 tablespoon butter and the onions to the bacon drippings. Cook, uncovered, for 25 to 30 minutes or until onions are golden brown and caramelized, stirring occasionally.

3. Add garlic and wine to pot; bring to boiling. Cook over medium-high heat for 5 to 6 minutes or until liquid is almost evaporated. Add the squash and 7 cups broth. Bring to boiling; reduce heat. Simmer, uncovered, for 25 minutes. Working in batches, transfer soup to a food processor or blender; process or blend until smooth. Return soup to pot. Stir in Worcestershire sauce and hot pepper sauce. If necessary, stir in additional broth to reach desired consistency. Heat through. Season with salt and freshly ground black pepper.

4. To serve, ladle soup into serving bowls. Crumble bacon; sprinkle over soup. If desired, top servings with sour cream.

PER SERVING *205 cal., 10 g total fat (5 g sat. fat), 24 mg chol., 950 mg sodium, 19 g carbo., 3 g fiber, 5 g pro.*

FAST FLAVOR

To dress up simple baked butternut squash, drizzle it with Sage Browned Butter. To prepare, melt 4 tablespoons butter in a heavy skillet; cook butter until fragrant and barely browned. Add leaves of fresh sage, remove from heat, and use immediately.

Curried Pumpkin Soup

PREP: 30 MINUTES BAKE: 1 HOUR 10 MINUTES COOK: 20 MINUTES OVEN: 375°F
MAKES: 8 SIDE-DISH SERVINGS (8 CUPS)

BEFORE YOU BAKE THIS SUPERLATIVE SOUP IN ITS GOLDEN, FLUTED SERVING BOWL, YOU MUST FIRST PICK THE PERFECT PUMPKIN. SELECT ONE WITHOUT BLEMISHES OR CRACKS, WITH A ROUND SHAPE, AND WITH A FLAT BOTTOM TO STAND STEADY AS YOU SERVE.

1 7- to 8-pound pumpkin

3 14-ounce cans chicken broth

2 apples (such as Cortland), peeled, cored, and coarsely chopped

½ cup chopped carrot (1 medium)

2 teaspoons grated fresh ginger

1 teaspoon curry powder

½ teaspoon ground cumin

6 slices turkey bacon

¼ cup chopped onion

2 tablespoons sugar

1 cup croutons

1. Preheat oven to 375°F. Using a large sharp knife, slice off the top fourth of the pumpkin; set aside. Scoop out seeds and stringy pulp. Replace top on pumpkin. Place pumpkin on a 15×10×1-inch baking pan. Bake for 50 to 60 minutes or until flesh can be scooped out easily. (Pumpkin will not be tender at this point.) Cool slightly for easier handling. Scoop out and reserve pumpkin flesh, leaving about a ¾-inch thickness of flesh on pumpkin walls. Cut flesh into chunks (you should have about 4 cups). Do not remove any flesh from bottom of shell. Discard pumpkin top.

2. In a large pot combine the 4 cups pumpkin chunks, the broth, apples, carrot, ginger, curry powder, and cumin. Bring to boiling; reduce heat. Simmer, covered, for 10 to 12 minutes or until vegetables are tender. In a food processor or blender, process or blend mixture, a third at a time, until smooth. Place pumpkin shell in a 3-quart casserole. Pour soup into shell. Bake, uncovered, for 20 minutes.

3. Meanwhile, in a skillet cook bacon until crisp. Remove bacon, reserving 1 tablespoon drippings in skillet. Drain bacon on paper towels. Cook onion and sugar in reserved drippings until onion is tender, about 10 minutes. Finely crumble bacon. Stir bacon and croutons into skillet. Sprinkle bacon mixture over soup in pumpkin.

PER SERVING *118 cal., 4 g total fat (1 g sat. fat), 7 mg chol., 678 mg sodium, 17 g carbo., 2 g fiber, 7 g pro.*

MAKE-AHEAD TIP If desired, discard pumpkin shell. Cover and chill precooked pumpkin up to 24 hours. Continue as above, except do not bake in shell.

FAST FLAVOR

Toasted squash seeds are a crunchy, flavorful garnish for soups and stews. Simply combine 1 cup of seeds with 1 tablespoon of oil, spread evenly on a baking sheet, sprinkle with coarse salt, and roast in a 275°F oven for 15 minutes or until seeds begin to pop.

FOR INFORMATION ON SELECTING AND STORING PUMPKINS, SEE PAGE 41.

Roasted Carrot Soup

PREP: 30 MINUTES   ROAST: 15 MINUTES   OVEN: 425°F   MAKES: 4 SIDE-DISH SERVINGS (6 CUPS)

THIS GORGEOUS MIXTURE IS THE COLOR OF AUTUMN. MAKE IT IN LATE SUMMER OR EARLY FALL, WHEN FRESHLY HARVESTED CARROTS ARE ULTRASWEET.

8 medium carrots, peeled and cut into 1-inch pieces

2 medium parsnips

1 cup coarsely chopped onion (1 large)

1 tablespoon olive oil

2 14-ounce cans chicken broth

1 teaspoon smoked paprika

1 teaspoon lemon juice

Salt and black pepper

Microgreens or mesclun (optional)

1. Preheat oven to 425°F. Toss carrots, parsnips, and onion with olive oil to coat. Spread vegetables in a single layer in a shallow baking pan. Roast for 15 to 20 minutes or until tender.

2. In a large saucepan combine roasted vegetables, broth, and paprika. Bring to boiling. Cool slightly.

3. Transfer half the vegetable mixture at a time to a blender or food processor. Blend or process until smooth. Return mixture to saucepan. Add lemon juice. Heat through. Season with salt and pepper. If desired, top each serving with greens.

PER SERVING *135 cal., 4 g total fat (1 g sat. fat), 0 mg chol., 971 mg sodium, 22 g carbo., 6 g fiber, 4 g pro.*

DIGGING CARROTS

- Spring-harvested carrots are mild in flavor.
- Summer-harvested carrots have more intense flavor.
- The very sweetest carrots are harvested in autumn, when cold weather causes the carrots' starches to convert to sugar.
- Spring- and summer-harvested carrots seldom need peeling. A good scrub with a stiff brush is all they need.

FOR INFORMATION ON SELECTING AND STORING CARROTS, SEE PAGE 13.

Honey-Lime Gazpacho

START TO FINISH: 20 MINUTES MAKES: 4 SIDE-DISH SERVINGS

THE SPANISH CHILLED SOUP, GAZPACHO, EPITOMIZES THE GLORY OF THE LATE-SUMMER GARDEN BOUNTY. HONEY, LIME, AND FRESH GINGER INFUSE THIS VERSION WITH COOL, REFRESHING CHARACTER.

3 large ripe red tomatoes, cored, seeded, and cut up

2 medium cucumbers, seeded and cut up

2 medium orange sweet peppers, seeded and cut up

1 jalapeño chile pepper, seeded and cut up (see tip, page 51)

1 clove garlic, minced

⅓ cup lime juice

2 tablespoons honey

2 tablespoons fresh cilantro leaves

1½ teaspoons grated fresh ginger

¼ teaspoon sea salt

Sea salt (optional)

Ice cubes

Lime wedges and scallions (optional)

1. In a large bowl combine tomatoes, cucumbers, sweet peppers, chile pepper, and garlic. Place half the tomato mixture in a food processor; process with several on/off turns to large chunks. Repeat with remaining tomato mixture. Return all of the mixture to the food processor. Add lime juice, honey, cilantro, ginger, and ¼ teaspoon sea salt. Cover and process with several on/off turns until the mixture is just a little chunky. If desired, season to taste with additional sea salt.

2. To serve, place 2 to 3 ice cubes in each of 4 shallow bowls or glasses; ladle soup over ice. If desired, serve with lime wedges and scallions.

PER 1¼-CUP SERVING *114 cal., 1 g total fat (0 g sat. fat), 0 mg chol., 114 mg sodium, 28 g carbo., 4 g fiber, 3 g pro.*

KITCHEN TIP

When red and yellow peppers are plentiful, freeze them. Place stemmed and seeded pepper pieces on a baking sheet and freeze until solid. Transfer frozen pieces to freezer bags and freeze up to 6 months. Pepper texture will be softer yet flavorful in cooked dishes such as casseroles and soups.

Cucumber-Yogurt-Mint Soup

PREP: 10 MINUTES   CHILL: 2 HOURS   MAKES: 4 SIDE-DISH SERVINGS

THE COMBINATION OF INGREDIENTS IN THIS CHILLED SOUP IS A FRESH-TASTING MEDITERRANEAN MAINSTAY THAT SHOWS UP IN SOUPS, SALADS, AND SAUCES.

1 large cucumber

1 6-ounce carton plain low-fat yogurt

1 tablespoon lime juice

1 teaspoon honey

½ teaspoon ground cumin

¼ teaspoon salt

2 tablespoons milk (optional)

⅓ cup snipped fresh mint

Snipped fresh mint

1. Peel the cucumber; cut in half lengthwise. Scoop out seeds and discard. Cut cucumber into ½-inch slices.

2. In a food processor or blender combine the cucumber, yogurt, lime juice, honey, cumin, and salt. Cover and process or blend until smooth. If necessary, stir in additional milk to reach desired consistency. Stir in ⅓ cup mint. Cover and chill for 2 to 24 hours. Stir before serving. If desired, sprinkle servings with additional snipped mint.

PER SERVING *56 cal., 1 g total fat (1 g sat. fat), 3 mg chol., 176 mg sodium, 8 g carbo., 1 g fiber, 4 g pro.*

FAST FLAVOR
Another time, call on this cool soup to serve as a sauce for grilled chicken.

FOR INFORMATION ON SELECTING AND STORING CUCUMBERS, SEE PAGE 25.

Fresh Pea Risotto

START TO FINISH: 35 MINUTES MAKES: 6 SERVINGS

FRESH PEAS HAVE BECOME A RARE TREAT, PERHAPS BECAUSE IT TAKES NEARLY A POUND OF WHOLE PEAS IN THE POD TO YIELD ONE CUP OF SHELLED PEAS. IF YOU GROW THEM YOURSELF, OR KNOW SOMEONE WHO DOES, YOU ARE LUCKY INDEED.

8 cups chicken broth

2 tablespoons butter

2 medium shallots, thinly sliced

1 clove garlic, minced

½ teaspoon fennel seeds, crushed

2 cups arborio rice

1½ cups shelled fresh peas or frozen peas

½ cup finely shredded Parmesan or Asiago cheese

2 ounces prosciutto, cut into thin strips

½ teaspoon finely shredded lemon peel

⅛ teaspoon black pepper

2 tablespoons sliced almonds, toasted

1. In a large saucepan bring broth to boiling; reduce heat. Cover; keep warm.

2. In a Dutch oven melt butter over medium heat. Add shallots, garlic, and fennel seeds; cook about 4 minutes or until tender. Stir in rice. Cook and stir for 2 to 3 minutes or until rice begins to brown.

3. Slowly add 1 cup of the chicken broth to the rice mixture, stirring constantly. Continue to cook and stir over medium heat until liquid is absorbed. Add another cup of the broth to the rice mixture, stirring constantly. Continue to cook and stir until the liquid is absorbed. Add 2 more cups of broth, 1 cup at a time, stirring constantly until the liquid is absorbed. Stir in fresh peas (if using). Add remaining broth, 1 cup at a time, stirring constantly until the broth has been absorbed. (This should take 15 to 20 minutes.)

4. Stir in frozen peas (if using), cheese, prosciutto, lemon peel, and pepper. Top each serving with almonds.

PER SERVING *308 cal., 10 g total fat (4 g sat. fat), 19 mg chol., 1,616 mg sodium, 43 g carbo., 2 g fiber, 12 g pro.*

KITCHEN TIP

If you're using frozen peas, add them at the end of cooking along with the cheese, prosciutto, lemon peel, and pepper.

FOR INFORMATION ON SELECTING AND STORING GARDEN PEAS, SEE PAGE 12.

Rosy Beet Risotto

PREP: 15 MINUTES ROAST: 1 HOUR 15 MINUTES COOL: 30 MINUTES COOK: 25 MINUTES OVEN: 350°F
MAKES: 8 SIDE-DISH SERVINGS

FOR A QUICKER VERSION OF THIS EARTHY RISOTTO, SUBSTITUTE ONE 15-OUNCE CAN OF BEETS FOR THE ROASTED BEETS. RESERVE THE LIQUID FROM THE CANNED BEETS TO USE IN MAKING THE BROTH.

2 medium beets (about 6 ounces each)

3 tablespoons olive oil

½ cup chopped red onion (1 medium)

1½ cups arborio or short grain rice

2 14-ounce cans reduced-sodium chicken broth

½ cup crumbled blue cheese (2 ounces)

2 tablespoons snipped fresh basil

Salt and freshly ground black pepper

Fresh basil leaves (optional)

1. Preheat oven to 350°F. Place beets in the center of an 18-inch square of heavy foil. Drizzle with 1 tablespoon of the olive oil. Fold together opposite edges of foil in double folds, allowing room for steam to build. Roast about 75 minutes or until tender. Cool for 30 minutes. Carefully open packet. Remove beets; gently transfer liquid to measuring cup; add water to equal ½ cup. Pour liquid into a medium saucepan. Cut beets in wedges.

2. In a large saucepan heat the remaining 2 tablespoons olive oil over medium heat. Add onion; cook until tender. Add rice; cook and stir for 5 minutes.

3. Meanwhile, add broth to beet liquid in saucepan. Bring to boiling. Reduce heat to maintain simmer. Carefully stir 1 cup of hot broth mixture into rice mixture. Cook and stir over medium heat until all the the broth mixture is absorbed. Continue adding broth mixture, ½ cup broth at a time, stirring constantly until broth is absorbed. (This should take about 20 minutes.)

4. Add beets; heat through. Remove saucepan from heat; stir in half the cheese and the snipped basil. Season with salt and pepper. Sprinkle with the remaining cheese and, if desired, basil leaves.

PER ¾-CUP SERVING *185 cal., 7 g total fat (2 g sat. fat), 5 mg chol., 441 mg sodium, 26 g carbo., 1 g fiber, 5 g pro.*

FAST FLAVOR
Take advantage of beets' affinity for blue cheese and walnuts by tossing the three ingredients into a green salad with a simple vinaigrette.

FOR INFORMATION ON SELECTING AND STORING BEETS, SEE PAGE 34.

20-Minute Tomato Sauce with Pasta

START TO FINISH: 20 MINUTES MAKES: 4 SIDE-DISH SERVINGS

THIS SUPER-QUICK RECIPE ALLOWS THE FANTASTIC FLAVOR OF FRESH VINE-RIPENED TOMATOES TO SHINE.

2 tablespoons olive oil

½ cup chopped onion (1 medium)

4 cloves garlic, minced

2 pounds ripe roma tomatoes or other tomatoes, seeded, if desired, and coarsely chopped

½ cup dry red wine

2 sprigs fresh rosemary

½ teaspoon sea salt

¼ to ½ teaspoon black pepper

2 tablespoons snipped fresh basil

6 ounces dried pasta or one 9-ounce package refrigerated pasta

Shredded Parmesan cheese (optional)

1. For sauce, in a large saucepan heat olive oil over medium heat. Add onion; cook about 4 minutes or until tender, stirring occasionally. Stir in garlic; cook and stir for 1 minute more.

2. Add tomatoes, wine, rosemary sprigs, salt, and pepper. Bring to boiling; reduce heat. Simmer, uncovered, about 8 minutes or until sauce is slightly thickened. Discard rosemary sprigs. Stir in basil.

3. Meanwhile, cook pasta according to package directions. Serve tomato sauce over pasta. If desired, top with shredded Parmesan cheese.

PER SERVING *291 cal., 8 g total fat (1 g sat. fat), 0 mg chol., 215 mg sodium, 43 g carbo., 4 g fiber, 8 g pro.*

KITCHEN TIP

If desired, add summer vegetables to the sauce. If you have a bumper crop of eggplant, chop 1 to 2 cups and add after cooking the onions, but before adding the tomatoes. Cook the eggplant until it softens slightly before adding the tomatoes. Fresh-cooked peas would also be nice tossed in at the end. Or, instead of the pasta, serve sauce over cooked zucchini strips (julienned lengthwise with a slicer or mandoline).

FOR INFORMATION ON SELECTING AND STORING TOMATOES, SEE PAGE 21S.

Indian-Style Cauliflower

START TO FINISH: 20 MINUTES   MAKES: 4 SIDE-DISH SERVINGS

A NONSTICK SKILLET OR WOK KEEPS COOKING OIL TO A MINIMUM WHEN STIR-FRYING VEGETABLES—
PLUS IT MAKES CLEANUP A SNAP.

½ teaspoon dry mustard

¼ teaspoon ground turmeric

¼ teaspoon ground cumin

⅛ teaspoon ground coriander

⅛ teaspoon cayenne pepper

1 tablespoon vegetable oil

4 cups cauliflower florets

1 small red or green sweet pepper, cut into 1-inch pieces

4 scallions, bias-sliced into 1-inch pieces

¼ cup chicken broth

1. In a small bowl combine mustard, turmeric, cumin, coriander, and cayenne pepper. Set aside.

2. In a wok or large skillet heat oil over medium-high heat. (Add more oil if necessary during cooking.) Add cauliflower; cook and stir for 3 minutes. Add sweet pepper and scallions; cook and stir for 1 to 1½ minutes. Reduce heat to medium. Add mustard mixture. Cook and stir for 30 seconds. Carefully stir in broth. Cook and stir about 1 minute more or until vegetables are heated through. Serve immediately.

PER SERVING *71 cal., 4 g total fat (1 g sat. fat), 0 mg chol., 58 mg sodium, 7 g carbo., 3 g pro.*

Kohlrabi Parmesan

START TO FINISH: 20 MINUTES MAKES: 4 SIDE-DISH SERVINGS

SHREDDED KOHLRABI IS COMBINED WITH SWEET PEPPER AND CARROT TO CREATE AN INVITING SIDE DISH. KOHLRABI IS USUALLY PALE GREEN ON THE OUTSIDE, ALTHOUGH PURPLE VARIETIES ARE AVAILABLE. BOTH VARIETIES HAVE WHITE FLESH.

3 tablespoons butter

3 cups shredded, peeled kohlrabi (4 small)

¾ cup chopped red or green sweet pepper (1 medium)

½ cup coarsely shredded carrot (1 medium)

¼ cup grated Parmesan or Romano cheese

2 teaspoons snipped fresh thyme

⅛ teaspoon salt

⅛ teaspoon cracked black pepper

Grated Parmesan or Romano cheese (optional)

Fresh thyme sprigs

1. In a large skillet melt butter over medium heat. Stir in kohlrabi, sweet pepper, and carrot. Cook and stir for 4 to 5 minutes or until vegetables are crisp-tender.

2. Stir in ¼ cup cheese, 2 teaspoons thyme, salt, and pepper. If desired, sprinkle with additional cheese and garnish with fresh thyme sprigs.

PER SERVING *145 cal., 11 g total fat (3 g sat. fat), 7 mg chol., 285 mg sodium, 10 g carbo., 5 g fiber, 4 g pro.*

FAST FLAVOR
Although kohlrabi bulbs may be the part of the plant most sought after, the leaves are delicious too. Sauté kohlrabi leaves in a bit of olive oil and minced garlic until crisp-tender and serve as a side dish to simple roast meats.

FOR INFORMATION ON SELECTING AND STORING KOHLRABI, SEE PAGE 36.

Broccoli-Beef Stir-Fry

START TO FINISH: 35 MINUTES   MAKES: 4 SERVINGS

TO MAKE IT EASY TO CUT THIN BITE-SIZE BEEF STRIPS, PLACE THE STEAKS IN THE FREEZER FOR 15 MINUTES BEFORE SLICING.

8 ounces Chinese egg noodles

1 tablespoon vegetable oil

1 pound boneless beef top loin steaks, cut into bite-size strips

1 medium onion, cut into thin wedges

1 medium carrot, thinly bias-sliced

1 tablespoon grated fresh ginger

2 cloves garlic, minced

3 cups broccoli florets

1 cup beef broth

1 tablespoon cornstarch

1 tablespoon soy sauce

1 teaspoon toasted sesame oil

¼ to ½ teaspoon crushed red pepper

½ cup cashew halves and pieces

1 tablespoon toasted sesame seeds

1. Cook noodles according to package directions. Drain and set aside.

2. In an extra-large skillet heat oil over medium-high heat. Add beef strips; cook and stir about 4 minutes or until browned. Remove beef from skillet.

3. Add onion, carrot, ginger, and garlic to skillet. Cook and stir for 2 to 3 minutes or until tender. Add broccoli to skillet. Cook and stir for 4 to 5 minutes or until crisp-tender.

4. For sauce, in a small bowl combine broth, cornstarch, soy sauce, sesame oil, and crushed red pepper. Add sauce to skillet. Cook and stir until thickened and bubbly. Add noodles, beef, and cashews to skillet; heat through. Sprinkle with toasted sesame seeds.

PER SERVING *684 cal., 34 g total fat (10 g sat. fat), 112 mg chol., 585 mg sodium, 58 g carbo., 6 g fiber, 38 g pro.*

FAST FLAVOR
Drizzle broccoli florets with olive oil and minced garlic; roast in a 425°F oven for 20 to 25 minutes. Sprinkle with finely grated lemon peel, pine nuts, julienned fresh basil leaves, and freshly grated Parmesan cheese.

FOR INFORMATION ON SELECTING AND STORING BROCCOLI, SEE PAGE 14.

Pork Rhubarb Skillet

START TO FINISH: 30 MINUTES MAKES: 4 MAIN-DISH SERVINGS

ALTHOUGH THE NICKNAME FOR RHUBARB IS "PIE PLANT," THE PLANT DOES MORE THAN FILL PIES, CRISPS, AND COBBLERS. ITS TART, ACIDIC STALKS LEND THEMSELVES TO SAVORY PREPARATIONS AS WELL—AND PAIR PERFECTLY WITH PORK.

1 tablespoon vegetable oil

1 pound lean boneless pork, cut into bite-size strips

1 medium onion, cut into thin wedges

1½ cups sliced fresh rhubarb or frozen unsweetened sliced rhubarb, thawed

1 medium cooking apple, cored and sliced

1 cup chicken broth

2 tablespoons brown sugar

1 tablespoon cornstarch

1 tablespoon snipped fresh sage

½ teaspoon salt

¼ teaspoon black pepper

2 cups hot cooked couscous

1. In an extra-large skillet heat oil over medium-high heat. Add pork to skillet. Cook and stir for 3 to 4 minutes or until browned. Remove pork from skillet.

2. Add onion to skillet. Cook and stir for 2 to 3 minutes or until tender. Add rhubarb and apple; cook for 3 to 4 minutes or until crisp-tender.

3. For sauce, in a small bowl combine broth, brown sugar, cornstarch, sage, salt, and pepper. Add to skillet; cook and stir until thickened and bubbly. Add pork to skillet; heat through. Serve over hot cooked couscous.

PER SERVING *373 cal., 11 g total fat (3 g sat. fat), 63 mg chol., 592 mg sodium, 38 g carbo., 4 g fiber, 29 g pro.*

RHUBARB TIPS

- Rhubarb leaves are mildly toxic and should always be discarded.
- If large rhubarb stalks are fibrous, remove the strings with a vegetable peeler.
- Halve rhubarb stalks more than 1½ inches wide before cooking.
- The redder the rhubarb, the sweeter it will be.

FOR INFORMATION ON SELECTING AND STORING RHUBARB, SEE PAGE 19.

Cajun Tri-Pepper Skillet

PREP: 30 MINUTES   COOK: 10 MINUTES   MAKES: 4 TO 6 MAIN-DISH SERVINGS

ANDOUILLE—PRONOUNCED *AN-DOO-EE*—IS A SPICY, HEAVILY SMOKED PORK SAUSAGE TRADITIONALLY USED IN CAJUN COOKING. IF YOU HAVE EXTRA, SLICE IT THINLY TO SERVE AS AN HORS D'OEUVRE—THE SAUSAGE IS DELICIOUS COLD.

1 tablespoon vegetable oil

1 pound cooked andouille sausage or spicy cooked smoked sausage, cut into ½-inch slices

1 large onion, cut into thin wedges

2 stalks celery, thinly bias-sliced

3 cloves garlic, minced

1 large green sweet pepper, cut into bite-size strips

1 large red sweet pepper, cut into bite-size strips

1 large yellow sweet pepper, cut into bite-size strips

2 cups chicken broth

2 tablespoons cornstarch

2 teaspoons brown sugar

2 teaspoons paprika

1 teaspoon snipped fresh thyme

½ teaspoon salt

¼ teaspoon cayenne pepper

2 to 3 cups hot cooked rice

Fresh thyme sprigs (optional)

1. In an extra-large skillet heat oil over medium-high heat. Add sausage; cook and stir about 3 minutes or until browned.

2. Add onion, celery, and garlic to skillet. Cook and stir for 2 to 3 minutes or until tender. Add sweet peppers to skillet. Cook and stir for 3 to 4 minutes or until crisp-tender.

3. For sauce, in a small bowl combine broth, cornstarch, brown sugar, paprika, snipped thyme, salt, and cayenne pepper. Add sauce to skillet; cook and stir until thickened and bubbly. Serve over hot cooked rice. If desired, garnish with fresh thyme sprigs.

PER SERVING *373 cal., 9 g total fat (2 g sat. fat), 95 mg chol., 1,622 mg sodium, 45 g carbo., 4 g fiber, 28 g pro.*

FOR INFORMATION ON SELECTING AND STORING SWEET PEPPERS, SEE PAGE 24.

Sautéed

SKILLET ENTRÉES & SIMPLE SIDES

When blessed with a quick hot kiss of butter or a tantalizing touch of olive oil in a piping-hot skillet, fruits and vegetables become sweeter as sizzling fat sears their sugars. A few shakes and tosses and garden goods are in and out of the pan and on the plate.

Pork Medallions with Cherry Sauce

START TO FINISH: 20 MINUTES MAKES: 4 MAIN-DISH SERVINGS

DURING AUTUMN, PORK IS OFTEN PREPARED WITH FRUIT SUCH AS PRUNES OR APPLES. THESE QUICK-SEARED MEDALLIONS, CLOAKED IN A DELIGHTFUL SWEET CHERRY SAUCE, PROVIDE ANOTHER GOOD REASON—AND SEASON—TO PAIR PORK WITH FRUIT.

1 pound pork tenderloin

Salt and freshly ground black pepper

Nonstick cooking spray

¾ cup cranberry, cherry, or apple juice

2 teaspoons spicy brown mustard

1 teaspoon cornstarch

1 cup fresh sweet cherries (such as Rainier or Bing), halved and pitted, or 1 cup frozen unsweetened pitted dark sweet cherries, thawed

Fresh parsley (optional)

1. Cut pork crosswise into 1-inch slices. Place each slice between 2 pieces of plastic wrap. Use the flat side of a meat mallet to lightly pound each slice into a ½-inch medallion. Discard plastic wrap. Sprinkle pork lightly with salt and freshly ground black pepper.

2. Coat a large nonstick skillet with cooking spray. Heat skillet over medium-high heat. Add pork; cook for 6 minutes or until pork is slightly pink in center and juices run clear, turning once. Transfer to a serving platter; cover with foil.

3. For cherry sauce, in a small bowl stir together cranberry juice, mustard, and cornstarch; add to skillet. Cook and stir until thickened and bubbly. Cook and stir for 2 minutes more. Stir in cherries. Serve cherry sauce over pork. If desired, garnish with fresh parsley.

PER SERVING *197 cal., 5 g total fat (2 g sat. fat), 81 mg chol., 127 mg sodium, 12 g carbo., 0 g fiber, 26 g pro.*

FAST FLAVOR
Marinate 1 cup halved, pitted cherries overnight in ½ cup orange juice and ½ teaspoon almond extract. Spoon marinated cherries over hot French toast or pancakes and top with vanilla yogurt.

FOR INFORMATION ON SELECTING AND STORING SWEET CHERRIES, SEE PAGE 29.

FOR INFORMATION ON SELECTING AND STORING PEARS, SEE PAGE 43.

Pork Chops with Gorgonzola and Pears

PREP: 10 MINUTES COOK: 20 MINUTES MAKES: 4 MAIN-DISH SERVINGS

RIB CHOPS ARE KNOWN FOR THEIR FLAVOR AND JUICINESS, AND THEY ARE EVEN BETTER IF YOU ARE ABLE TO BUY THEM ON THE BONE. CALL AHEAD—YOUR BUTCHER MAY BE ABLE TO HAVE BONE-IN RIB CHOPS READY FOR YOU.

4 pork rib chops, cut ¾ to 1 inch thick

Sea salt, kosher salt, or salt

2 tablespoons olive oil

2 medium ripe pears

2 tablespoons butter

¼ cup dry white wine or apple juice

¼ cup whipping cream

8 ounces creamy Gorgonzola or blue cheese, cut up

Freshly ground black pepper

Additional Gorgonzola cheese, cut into chunks (optional)

1. Sprinkle pork chops with salt. In an extra-large skillet heat oil over medium-high heat. Add pork chops; cook about 10 minutes or until browned and juices run clear (160°F), turning once halfway through cooking. Transfer chops to a serving platter; cover with foil. Drain fat from skillet.

2. Peel and core pears. Cut each pear into 8 wedges. Melt butter in the same skillet over medium-high heat. Add pear wedges; cook about 5 minutes or until browned, turning once. Add pears to platter.

3. For sauce, add wine and whipping cream to skillet. Bring to boiling; reduce heat. Boil gently, uncovered, for 1 to 2 minutes, or until slightly thickened. Add the 8 ounces Gorgonzola; whisk until cheese is almost melted. Remove from heat. Serve sauce with pork chops and pears. Sprinkle with pepper. If desired, serve with additional cheese.

PER SERVING *618 cal., 46 g total fat (24 g sat. fat), 147 mg chol., 1,105 mg sodium, 14 g carbo., 4 g fiber, 34 g pro.*

Sautéed Red Cabbage with Onions and Smoked Sausage

START TO FINISH: 40 MINUTES   MAKES: 6 MAIN-DISH SERVINGS

RED SWISS CHARD (ALSO CALLED RHUBARB CHARD) HAS DARK GREEN LEAVES AND REDDISH CELERYLIKE STALKS. ANY VARIETY WORKS IN THIS RECIPE.

2 tablespoons olive oil

1 pound kielbasa or smoked sausage, halved lengthwise and bias-sliced into 1½-inch pieces

2 cups chopped red onions (2 large)

2 teaspoons sugar

½ of a large head red cabbage, cut into 1-inch slices

1 teaspoon caraway seeds, crushed

1 pound red Swiss chard, trimmed and sliced crosswise into 1-inch pieces (about 6 cups)

¼ teaspoon salt

1. In an extra-large nonstick skillet heat 1 tablespoon of the olive oil over medium heat. Add kielbasa; cook about 5 minutes or until browned, stirring occasionally. Remove kielbasa from skillet and set aside.

2. Add onions and sugar to skillet. Cook and stir over medium heat about 5 minutes or until tender and caramelized. Remove onion mixture from skillet and set aside.

3. Add the remaining 1 tablespoon olive oil to skillet. Add cabbage and caraway seeds; cook and stir for 6 to 8 minutes or until cabbage is wilted. Stir in Swiss chard; cook and stir for 2 to 3 minutes more or until chard is slightly wilted.

4. Stir onion mixture and salt into cabbage mixture. Top with kielbasa. Heat through.

PER SERVING *337 cal., 27 g total fat (11 g sat. fat), 33 mg chol., 801 mg sodium, 13 g carbo., 2 g fiber, 11 g pro.*

GOOD AND GOOD FOR YOU

- Red and green cabbage have high levels of vitamin C.
- Savoy cabbage is rich in beta-carotene.
- Bok choy is rich in calciuim.
- Napa cabbage is a good source of Vitamin A, folic acid, and potassium.

FOR INFORMATION ON SELECTING AND STORING CABBAGE, SEE PAGE 35; FOR INFORMATION ON SWISS CHARD, SEE PAGE 23.

Pan-Roasted Chicken with Spinach and French Lentils

**PREP: 20 MINUTES BAKE: 20 MINUTES COOK: 20 MINUTES
OVEN: 450°F MAKES: 6 MAIN-DISH SERVINGS**

FIRM AND TOOTHSOME FRENCH LENTILS ARE WORTH SEEKING. OFTEN CALLED LENTILS DE PUY, THEY
ARE AVAILABLE IN SPECIALTY MARKETS, HEALTH FOOD STORES, AND ONLINE.

6 small bone-in chicken breast halves
(6 to 7 ounces each)

Kosher salt and freshly ground black pepper

¼ cup olive oil

1½ cups reduced-sodium chicken broth

½ cup dry French green lentils or other
petite green lentils, rinsed and drained

1 clove garlic, minced

1 shallot, chopped

1 tablespoon tarragon vinegar or balsamic
vinegar

12 ounces fresh baby spinach
(about 16 cups)

6 medium sweet potatoes, cooked and sliced

1 recipe Bacon and Tarragon Vinaigrette

1. Preheat oven to 450°F. Sprinkle chicken
with salt and pepper. In a 12-inch oven-going
skillet heat 1 tablespoon of the olive oil over
medium heat. Carefully place chicken breasts
in hot skillet, skin sides down. Cook for 4 to
5 minutes or until skin is golden brown. Turn
chicken skin sides up. Place skillet in oven.
Bake for 20 to 25 minutes or until chicken is no
longer pink (170°F).

2. Meanwhile, in a medium saucepan combine
chicken broth, lentils, and garlic. Bring to
boiling; reduce heat. Simmer, covered, for 15 to
20 minutes or until lentils are tender. Drain off
excess liquid. In a large skillet heat 1 tablespoon
olive oil over medium heat. Add shallot; cook
for 1 minute. Add cooked lentils and tarragon
vinegar. Season to taste with salt and pepper.

3. In a large pot heat the remaining 2 tablespoons
olive oil over medium heat. Add spinach and toss
gently just until spinach is wilted.

4. To serve, divide sweet potatoes and spinach
among 6 dinner plates or pasta bowls. Top
spinach with chicken breasts. Spoon lentil
mixture over chicken. Drizzle Bacon and
Tarragon Vinaigrette over all. Serve immediately.

BACON AND TARRAGON VINAIGRETTE: Cut up 1 slice
of bacon. In a small skillet cook bacon over
medium heat until crisp. Drain bacon on paper
towels. In a medium bowl combine cooked
bacon, 1 minced shallot, 2 tablespoons tarragon
or balsamic vinegar, 1 teaspoon Dijon-style
mustard, ½ teaspoon kosher salt, and ¼ teaspoon
freshly ground black pepper. Slowly whisk in
¼ cup olive oil. Makes ½ cup.

PER SERVING *598 cal., 31 g total fat (6 g sat. fat),
88 mg chol., 713 mg sodium, 41 g carbo., 10 g fiber,
37 g pro.*

FAST FLAVOR

Nutmeg and spinach are fast friends. Add freshly
grated nutmeg to spinach dishes at the beginning
of cooking time.

FOR INFORMATION ON SELECTING AND STORING GARLIC, SEE PAGE 39.

Aglio e Olio

START TO FINISH: 15 MINUTES   MAKES: 6 SIDE-DISH SERVINGS

AGLIO E OLIO, OR GARLIC AND OIL, IS THE RUSTIC DUO RESPONSIBLE FOR CREATING ITALY'S MOST SIMPLE, FULL-FLAVOR SAUCE. TOSSED WITH HOT COOKED PASTA—AND MAYBE STEAMED FRESH VEGETABLES—IT IS A MEAL IN ITSELF.

¼ cup olive oil

4 cloves garlic, minced

½ teaspoon crushed red pepper

8 ounces dried linguine, fettuccine, or malfalda pasta, cooked and drained

3 cups steamed asparagus pieces, broccoli florets, or cauliflower florets*

¼ cup finely shredded Pecorino Romano cheese (1 ounce)

2 tablespoons snipped fresh Italian parsley

¼ teaspoon freshly ground black pepper

Salt

1. In a small saucepan heat olive oil over medium heat. Add garlic and crushed red pepper; cook about 1 minute or until fragrant. Remove from heat.

2. In a large serving bowl toss together pasta and vegetables. Add garlic mixture; toss gently to coat. Add cheese, parsley, and black pepper; toss gently to combine. Season with salt.

PER SERVING *116 cal., 10 g total fat (2 g sat. fat), 5 mg chol., 102 mg sodium, 5 g carbo., 2 g fiber, 3 g pro.*

*TO STEAM VEGETABLES: Place a steamer basket in a saucepan. Add water to just below the bottom of the basket. Bring water to boiling. Add vegetables to the steamer basket. Cover and reduce heat. Steam until the vegetables are crisp-tender. For asparagus, allow 3 to 5 minutes; for cauliflower or broccoli, allow 8 to 10 minutes.

Brussels Sprouts with Crisp Prosciutto

START TO FINISH: 40 MINUTES MAKES: 12 SIDE-DISH SERVINGS

IF YOU BELIEVE THAT BACON MAKES ALMOST EVERYTHING BETTER, YOU'LL LOVE CRISPED PROSCIUTTO. SIZZLE PROSCIUTTO IN A HOT SKILLET UNTIL LIGHTLY BROWNED AND CRISPY. CRUMBLE LIKE BACON OVER COOKED VEGETABLES.

2½ pounds Brussels sprouts

1 tablespoon olive oil

4 ounces thinly sliced prosciutto

½ cup thinly sliced shallots or chopped onion

3 tablespoons butter

½ teaspoon salt

¼ teaspoon freshly ground black pepper

1 tablespoon red wine vinegar

1. Trim stems and remove any wilted outer leaves from Brussels sprouts; wash. Cut any large sprouts in half lengthwise.
2. In a covered large pot cook Brussels sprouts in enough boiling salted water to cover for 6 to 8 minutes or just until tender (centers should still be slightly firm); drain. Spread Brussels sprouts in a shallow baking pan.
3. In an extra-large skillet heat oil over medium-high heat. Cook prosciutto, half at a time, in the hot oil until crisp. Remove from skillet. Add shallots and butter to skillet. Cook and stir over medium heat about 2 minutes or until shallots start to soften.
4. Add Brussels sprouts, salt, and pepper to skillet. Cook and stir about 6 minutes or until Brussels sprouts are heated through. Drizzle with vinegar; toss gently to coat. Transfer to a serving bowl. Top with prosciutto.
PER SERVING *92 cal., 5 g total fat (2 g sat. fat), 15 mg chol., 391 mg sodium, 8 g carbo., 3 g fiber, 5 g pro.*
BRUSSELS SPROUTS WITH BACON: Prepare as directed, except substitute 4 slices bacon for the prosciutto and omit the olive oil. Cook bacon until crisp. Remove from skillet, discarding drippings. Drain bacon on paper towels; crumble bacon.

KITCHEN TIP
If desired, omit prosciutto and oil and substitute 4 slices chopped bacon. Cook bacon until crisp. Remove from skillet, discarding drippings.

Wilted Spinach with Portobello Mushrooms

PREP: 40 MINUTES BAKE: 20 MINUTES OVEN: 400°F MAKES: 4 SIDE-DISH SERVINGS

WILTED SALADS GAINED POPULARITY IN THE 1970S, WHEN THEY WERE USUALLY DROWNING IN BACON FAT. THIS UPDATED VERSION IS FABULOUSLY LIGHT AND HEALTHFUL.

8 ounces portobello mushrooms (2 to 3 caps with stems)

3 tablespoons garlic-flavor oil

¼ teaspoon salt

¼ teaspoon black pepper

1 medium red onion, thinly sliced

3 tablespoons white or balsamic vinegar

1 clove garlic, minced

½ teaspoon salt

⅛ teaspoon black pepper

8 cups lightly packed spinach leaves

3 cups torn escarole leaves

1 cup grape and/or cherry tomatoes

2 tablespoons pine nuts, toasted

1 tablespoon snipped fresh mint

¼ cup olive oil

1 ounce Parmesan cheese, sliced into shards (optional)

1. Preheat oven to 400°F. Remove the mushroom stems; wipe caps clean with a damp towel. Brush both sides of the mushrooms with garlic oil; sprinkle with ¼ teaspoon salt and ¼ teaspoon pepper. Place the mushrooms, gill sides up, on a baking sheet. Bake about 20 minutes or until tender, turning once halfway through baking. Set aside to cool.

2. Meanwhile, in a small bowl cover the onion slices with cold water; let stand for 10 to 15 minutes.

3. In an extra-large bowl combine vinegar, garlic, ½ teaspoon salt, and ⅛ teaspoon pepper. Thinly slice cooled mushrooms. Drain onions well. Add mushrooms, onions, spinach, escarole, tomatoes, pine nuts, and mint to vinegar mixture.

4. In a small skillet heat olive oil over high heat for 2 to 3 minutes or until hot. Drizzle hot olive oil over the salad; toss to coat. Serve immediately. If desired, top servings with Parmesan cheese.

PER SERVING *299 cal., 27 g total fat (4 g sat. fat), 0 mg chol., 500 mg sodium, 13 g carbo., 5 g fiber, 5 g pro.*

SIMPLE SPINACH SAUTÉES

- Sauté 1 pound fresh spinach leaves with 2 tablespoons chopped onion and 1 clove minced garlic in 2 tablespoons butter. Add salt and pepper to taste.
- Stir ¼ cup whipped vegetable-flavor cream cheese into above mixture.
- Stir ¼ cup plain yogurt, ⅓ teaspoon ground coriander, and ¼ teaspoon curry powder into above mixture.

Scallion-Potato Pancakes

PREP: 15 MINUTES COOK: 8 MINUTES PER BATCH MAKES: 12 PANCAKES

WHETHER SERVED AS AN APPETIZER OR SIDE DISH, THESE CRISPY TWO-POTATO PANCAKES WILL WIN RAVES.

5 scallions

1 large potato (12 ounces), peeled

1 medium sweet potato (8 ounces), peeled

2 eggs, lightly beaten

3 tablespoons all-purpose flour

1 tablespoon lemon juice

1 teaspoon snipped fresh tarragon

½ teaspoon salt

¼ teaspoon black pepper

1 cup vegetable oil

Sour cream (optional)

1. Cut off root ends and 2 inches from tops of scallions. Cut into 3-inch pieces. Cut the pieces lengthwise into thin julienne strips. Finely shred potato and sweet potato into a large bowl. Add scallions, eggs, flour, lemon juice, tarragon, salt, and pepper. Mix well.

2. In a large skillet heat oil over medium-high heat. For each pancake, drop ¼ cup potato mixture into hot oil; flatten each into a 4-inch pancake. Cook about 8 minutes or until golden and cooked through, turning once halfway through cooking. Adjust heat to prevent burning. Drain pancakes on paper towels; serve warm. If desired, serve with sour cream.

PER PANCAKE *88 cal., 5 g total fat (1 g sat. fat), 36 mg chol., 103 mg sodium, 8 g carbo., 1 g fiber, 2 g pro.*

FAST FLAVOR

Brush trimmed scallions lightly with olive oil. Grill over medium heat for about 3 minutes per side. Serve with grilled flank steak.

FOR INFORMATION ON SELECTING AND STORING SCALLIONS, SEE PAGE 17; FOR INFORMATION ON POTATOES, SEE PAGE 38.

Caramelized Carrots

PREP: 20 MINUTES **COOK:** 22 MINUTES **MAKES:** 8 SIDE-DISH SERVINGS

WHEN FRESH YOUNG CARROTS APPEAR ON MARKET STANDS, GRAB A BUNCH FOR THIS SWEET AND SAVORY SIDE DISH. MAKE IT WITH A PAINTERLY MIX OF ORANGE, YELLOW, AND RED CARROTS TO SERVE ON A PRETTY PLATTER.

1 tablespoon olive oil

1 pound whole small carrots with tops, peeled and halved lengthwise

⅛ teaspoon salt

2 cloves garlic, thinly sliced

⅓ cup whipping cream

Dash cayenne pepper

Snipped fresh Italian parsley

1. In a large skillet heat oil over medium heat. Add carrots, cut sides down; sprinkle with salt. Cook, covered, for 10 minutes; uncover. Turn carrots; add garlic. Cover and cook for 10 minutes more or until carrots are tender and both sides are golden brown. During cooking, gently shake skillet occasionally to prevent carrots from sticking. Transfer carrots to serving plate; cover and keep warm.

2. Add whipping cream and cayenne pepper to skillet. Bring to boiling. Reduce heat; boil gently, uncovered, for 2 to 4 minutes until cream is slightly thickened. Pour over carrots. Sprinkle with parsley. Serve immediately.

PER ½-CUP SERVING *146 cal., 11 g total fat (5 g sat. fat), 27 mg chol., 160 mg sodium, 12 g carbo., 3 g fiber, 2 g pro.*

Swiss Chard with Peppered Bacon

START TO FINISH: 20 MINUTES   MAKES: 4 SIDE-DISH SERVINGS

THIS QUICK DISH IS POPULAR IN NORTHERN CALIFORNIA WINE COUNTRY, WHERE A LARGE ITALIAN POPULATION IS DEVOTED TO DARK GREENS SUCH AS CHARD.

2 slices thick-sliced peppered bacon or regular bacon

½ cup chopped onion (1 medium)

8 cups coarsely chopped fresh Swiss chard leaves

½ teaspoon finely shredded lemon peel

Salt and black pepper

1. In an extra-large skillet cook bacon over medium heat until crisp. Remove bacon from skillet, reserving drippings in skillet; drain bacon on paper towels. Crumble bacon; set aside.

2. Cook onion in reserved drippings over medium heat about 5 minutes or until tender, stirring occasionally. Add Swiss chard. Cook about 5 minutes or just until tender, tossing occasionally. Stir in bacon and lemon peel. Season to taste with salt and pepper.

PER SERVING *45 cal., 2 g total fat (1 g sat. fat), 3 mg chol., 253 mg sodium, 5 g carbo., 2 g fiber, 3 g pro.*

FAST FLAVOR

Turn this enchanting chard into a full meal by spooning it onto a bowl of lentil soup. Top with several thick slices of grilled Merguez sausage, a spicy North African link made with lamb.

FOR INFORMATION SELECTING AND STORING SWISS CHARD, SEE PAGE 23.

Simmered

STOVETOP MAIN DISHES & SIDES

Just-picked veggies have the best, freshest flavor. Simmering—a kinder form of boiling—gently coaxes earthy sweetness from each and every tender piece of produce.

Minted Red Snapper with Summer Squash

START TO FINISH: 30 MINUTES MAKES: 4 MAIN-DISH SERVINGS

MINT INFUSES THE FISH AND VEGETABLE POACHING LIQUID FOR FRESH-FROM-THE-GARDEN FLAVOR.

4 5-ounce fresh or frozen red snapper, yellowtail snapper, or grouper fillets, 1 inch thick

1/8 teaspoon salt

1/8 teaspoon white pepper

2/3 cup Fish Stock or chicken broth

1/3 cup dry white wine

6 sprigs fresh mint

2 tablespoons olive oil

1 tablespoon butter

1 medium yellow summer squash (6 ounces), coarsely chopped

1 medium zucchini (6 ounces), coarsely chopped

4 lemon wedges

2 teaspoons snipped fresh mint

1. Thaw fish, if frozen. Rinse fish; pat dry. Sprinkle fish fillets with salt and white pepper. In an extra-large skillet combine Fish Stock, white wine, mint sprigs, olive oil, and butter. Bring to boiling; reduce heat. Add fish fillets; cover and simmer gently for 8 to 10 minutes or until fish flakes easily with a fork, adding the yellow squash and zucchini the last 2 to 3 minutes of cooking.

2. With a slotted spatula, transfer fillets, squash, and zucchini to soup plates; keep warm. Discard cooked mint.

3. Bring juices in skillet to boiling over high heat; cook about 6 minutes or until the sauce is thickened and reduced to 1/2 cup. Pour over the fillets. Squeeze a lemon wedge over each fillet. Sprinkle with 2 teaspoons snipped mint.

PER SERVING *263 cal., 12 g total fat (3 g sat. fat), 61 mg chol., 195 mg sodium, 5 g carbo., 2 g fiber, 31 g pro.*

FISH STOCK: In a large saucepan combine 2 pounds fish bones (including heads and tails, if you like) with enough cold water to cover (about 4 cups). Bring to boiling over high heat; reduce heat. Simmer, covered, for 45 minutes. Strain stock; cool. Store leftover stock in a covered container in the refrigerator for 1 day or freeze for up to 3 months. Makes 3 1/2 cups stock.

FAST FLAVOR

For a quick side dish, sauté 1/2-inch slices of zucchini with thinly sliced onion, slivered garlic, and a handful of halved cherry tomatoes just until the zucchini is crisp-tender.

FOR INFORMATION ON SELECTING AND STORING SUMMER SQUASH, SEE PAGE 22.

FOR INFORMATION ON SELECTING AND STORING GREEN BEANS, SEE PAGE 22; FOR INFORMATION ON LEEKS, SEE PAGE 17.

Pasta with Green Beans and Goat Cheese

PREP: 15 MINUTES   COOK: 13 MINUTES   MAKES: 6 SIDE-DISH SERVINGS

THYME AND MARJORAM HAVE A SPECIAL AFFINITY FOR GREEN BEANS, AND WHEN THE HERBS RUB SHOULDERS WITH MILD-MANNERED LEEKS, TANGY GOAT CHEESE, AND CRUNCHY WALNUTS, THE RESULT IS DELICIOUS.

12 cups water

½ teaspoon salt

8 ounces dried linguine

12 ounces fresh green beans, trimmed and cut into 1-inch pieces

2 tablespoons olive oil

1 tablespoon butter

2 medium leeks, thinly sliced (about ⅔ cup)

½ cup chopped walnuts

1 tablespoon snipped fresh thyme or marjoram

4 ounces semisoft goat cheese (chèvre), crumbled

Cracked black pepper

1. In a large pot bring water and salt to boiling. Add linguine and green beans; boil about 10 minutes or until linguine is tender but still firm and green beans are crisp-tender; drain in a colander.

2. In the same pot heat olive oil and butter over medium heat until butter melts. Add leeks and walnuts; cook for 3 to 4 minutes or until leeks are tender and walnuts are lightly toasted. Stir in thyme. Stir in drained linguine and green beans; heat through.

3. Transfer pasta mixture to a serving platter. Sprinkle with goat cheese and pepper. Serve immediately.

PER SERVING *351 cal., 19 g total fat (6 g sat. fat), 20 mg chol., 125 mg sodium, 35 g carbo., 3 g fiber, 11 g pro.*

Green Beans with Vermouth Butter

PREP: 20 MINUTES   CHILL: 1 HOUR   COOK: 10 MINUTES   MAKES: 6 SERVINGS

VERMOUTH IS A WHITE WINE FORTIFIED WITH AN AROMATIC COMBINATION OF BOTANICALS, INCLUDING HERBS, FLOWERS, AND SEEDS. THE FLAVOR OF DRY VERMOUTH QUICKLY DISSIPATES ONCE OPENED, SO BE SURE TO RECORK, REFRIGERATE IT, AND USE WITHIN 3 MONTHS.

2 tablespoons finely chopped shallots

2 teaspoons olive oil

½ cup butter, softened

2 tablespoons dry vermouth

1 pound fresh green beans

1. For vermouth butter, cook shallots in olive oil over medium-low heat for 10 to 12 minutes or until shallots are golden. Remove from heat; cool. Combine cooled shallot mixture with softened butter; stir in vermouth, 1 tablespoon at a time.

2. Transfer butter mixture onto a piece of plastic wrap. Shape into a 6-inch log by rolling the plastic wrap around the butter and rolling the wrapped butter back and forth between your hands. Twist ends of wrap tightly. Chill in the refrigerator at least 1 hour or freeze butter until ready to use. (For longer storage, wrap butter tightly in plastic wrap, then wrap in aluminum foil. Store in the refrigerator for up to 1 week or in the freezer for up to 1 month.)

3. Wash beans; remove ends and strings, if necessary. Leave whole or cut into 1-inch pieces. Cook, covered, in a small amount of boiling, salted water for 10 to 15 minutes or until crisp-tender; drain.

4. To serve, transfer hot beans to a serving bowl. Top with 3 tablespoons vermouth butter; toss lightly to coat.

PER SERVING *78 cal., 6 g total fat (3 g sat. fat), 15 mg chol., 60 mg sodium, 6 g carbo., 3 g fiber, 1 g pro.*

WHISKEY BUTTER: In a medium bowl combine ½ cup softened butter with 1 tablespoon dark brown sugar and 1 tablespoon bourbon whiskey. Mold and store butter as directed in Step 2.

JALAPEÑO-LIME BUTTER: In a medium bowl combine ½ cup softened butter with 2 teaspoons seeded and finely chopped fresh jalapeño pepper (see tip, page 51), 2 teaspoons finely shredded lime peel, and 1 clove garlic, minced. Mold and store butter as directed in Step 2.

FAST FLAVOR

To bring out the fullest flavor in green beans, add a pinch of sugar to the cooking water.

FOR INFORMATION ON SELECTING AND STORING GREEN BEANS, SEE PAGE 22.

Green Beans with Lemon and Walnuts

START TO FINISH: 20 MINUTES MAKES: 4 SIDE-DISH SERVINGS

FRESH BEANS SHOULD BE WASHED BEFORE YOU STORE THEM. REFRIGERATE THEM IN AIRTIGHT PLASTIC BAGS FOR 3 TO 4 DAYS.

12 ounces fresh green beans, trimmed

1 tablespoon butter

¼ cup chopped walnuts

1 teaspoon grated fresh ginger

¼ teaspoon finely shredded lemon peel

1 teaspoon lemon juice

1. In a medium saucepan cook beans, covered, in a small amount of boiling salted water for 5 to 10 minutes or until crisp-tender; drain.

2. Meanwhile, in a small saucepan melt butter over medium heat. Add walnuts and ginger; cook for 2 to 3 minutes or until nuts are toasted. Remove from heat; stir in lemon peel and lemon juice. Stir nut mixture into cooked beans.

PER SERVING *100 cal., 8 g total fat (2 g sat. fat), 8 mg chol., 35 mg sodium, 7 g carbo., 3 g fiber, 3 g pro.*

KITCHEN TIP
When purchasing beans, dig to the bottom of the bin, where the little ones tend to hide. Smaller beans tend to be sweeter and more tender. Hold a bean lengthwise between your thumb and index finger and squeeze—fresh beans snap under light pressure, while older beans just bend.

FOR INFORMATION ON SELECTING AND STORING GREEN BEANS, SEE PAGE 22.

FOR INFORMATION ON SELECTING AND STORING GREEN BEANS, SEE PAGE 22.

Green Beans with Sage and Shiitake Mushrooms

START TO FINISH: 30 MINUTES MAKES: 8 TO 10 SIDE-DISH SERVINGS

COOK THE BEANS AHEAD OF TIME, THEN CHILL THEM UNTIL JUST BEFORE SERVING. A FEW MINUTES IN THE SKILLET AND THIS DISH IS DONE.

2 pounds fresh green beans, trimmed

2 tablespoons olive oil

2 tablespoons butter

3 to 4 cloves garlic, thinly sliced

12 ounces fresh shiitake mushrooms, stemmed and halved

3 tablespoons snipped fresh sage

Coarse sea salt or kosher salt

Freshly ground black pepper

1. In a large saucepan cook green beans, covered, in a small amount of boiling salted water for 3 to 4 minutes or just until crisp-tender; drain. Immediately plunge beans into ice water; let stand for 3 minutes. Drain and set aside.

2. In an extra-large skillet heat oil and butter over medium heat. Add garlic; cook and stir just until golden brown. Add mushrooms; cook for 6 to 8 minutes or until tender, stirring occasionally. Add beans; cook for 5 to 8 minutes or until heated through, stirring occasionally. Remove from heat. Stir in sage. Season with salt and pepper.

PER SERVING *112 cal., 6 g total fat (2 g sat. fat), 8 mg chol., 150 mg sodium, 14 g carbo., 4 g fiber, 3 g pro.*

FAST FLAVOR

To infuse fresh green beans with Asian flavors, sauté the beans over medium-high heat along with a couple tablespoons of sesame oil, a bit of freshly grated ginger, and a clove or two of minced garlic. When beans are crisp-tender and vibrant green, add a drizzling of soy sauce and a sprinkling of sesame seeds. Toss well.

Marinated Dill Carrots

PREP: 20 MINUTES **COOK:** 10 MINUTES **MARINATE:** 4 HOURS **STAND:** 30 MINUTES
MAKES: 8 TO 10 SIDE-DISH SERVINGS

THESE PETITE ROOTS—BATHED IN DILL AND WHITE BALSAMIC—MAKE SENSATIONAL PICNIC FARE.

1 pound baby carrots, such as Romeo

4 ounces button mushrooms

¼ cup olive oil

¼ cup white balsamic vinegar

2 teaspoons snipped fresh dill

¼ teaspoon salt

¼ teaspoon freshly ground black pepper

½ cup jarred roasted red sweet peppers, drained and cut into strips (optional)

Fresh dill sprigs (optional)

1. If desired, trim tops from carrots. In a large saucepan cook carrots, covered, in a small amount of boiling lightly salted water for 4 minutes. Add mushrooms; cook, covered, for 4 to 6 minutes more or until carrots are tender. Drain; transfer carrots and mushrooms to a large bowl and cool slightly.

2. In a screw-top jar combine olive oil, vinegar, snipped dill, salt, and pepper. Cover and shake well. Pour over vegetables; toss gently to coat. Cover and chill for 4 to 24 hours.

3. Allow vegetables to stand at room temperature for 30 minutes before serving. If desired, add red pepper strips and garnish with fresh dill sprigs. Serve with a slotted spoon.

PER SERVING *56 cal., 3 g total fat (0 g sat. fat), 0 mg chol., 82 mg sodium, 6 g carbo., 2 g fiber, 1 g pro.*

CARROTS WITH CHARACTER

- Red carrots taste much like orange carrots. The pigment of red carrots contains lycopene, the health-enhancing substance found in tomatoes.
- Purple carrots are sweet, with appealing peppery notes. They have generous levels of the potent antioxidants also found in blueberries.
- Yellow and white carrots offer high levels of lutein—the substance that protects eyes from age-related macular degeneration.

FOR INFORMATION ON SELECTING AND STORING CARROTS, SEE PAGE 13.

Sweet Corn with Smoked Paprika Butter

PREP: 20 MINUTES CHILL: 1 HOUR COOK: 5 MINUTES MAKES: 12 SIDE-DISH SERVINGS

SMOKED PAPRIKA, GROUND FROM SMOKED AND DRIED PEPPERS, HAS A RICH, DEEP FLAVOR THAT ENHANCES FOODS WITH JUST A SPRINKLE. TRY IT ON BAKED POTATOES.

⅓ cup butter, softened

1 teaspoon lime juice

½ teaspoon smoked paprika

¼ teaspoon ground cumin

¼ teaspoon sea salt

12 ears of fresh sweet corn

1. For paprika butter, in a small bowl stir together butter, lime juice, smoked paprika, cumin, and salt. Transfer butter mixture to a piece of plastic wrap or parchment paper. Shape into a log by rolling the plastic wrap or parchment around the butter and rolling the wrapped butter back and forth between your hands. Twist ends of wrap tightly. Chill in the refrigerator at least 1 hour or freeze butter until ready to use. (For longer storage, wrap butter tightly in plastic wrap, then wrap in aluminum foil. Store in the refrigerator for up to 1 week or in the freezer for up to 1 month.)

2. Remove husks from fresh ears of corn. Scrub with a stiff brush to remove silks; rinse. Cook, covered, in enough boiling lightly salted water to cover for 5 to 7 minutes or until tender.

3. To serve, unwrap top of paprika butter and, holding on to wrapped sides, run butter over surface of each hot ear of corn.

PER 1-EAR SERVING *123 cal., 6 g total fat (3 g sat fat), 14 mg chol., 83 mg sodium, 17 g carbo., 2 g fiber, 3 g pro.*

KERNELS OF TRUTH

- Finding a worm in an ear of corn may be a good thing—a sign that the cornfield was not treated with pesticides.
- Remove the husk from corn right before cooking. Once the husk is removed, the kernels begin to dry out.
- Add stripped corncobs to vegetable broth. They will add intense corn flavor and sweetness to cooking liquids.
- To easily remove corn silk, rub the ears with a damp paper towel.

FOR INFORMATION ON SELECTING AND STORING SWEET CORN, SEE PAGE 25.

FOR INFORMATION ON SELECTING AND STORING GARDEN PEAS, SEE PAGE 12.

Dilled Peas and Almonds

PREP: 25 MINUTES   COOK: 10 MINUTES   MAKES: 4 SIDE-DISH SERVINGS

PEAS AND DILL—PERFECT PARTNERS—ARE MADE EVEN BETTER WITH A SPRINKLE OF TOASTED ALMONDS. FOR A PRETTY GARDEN GARNISH, ADD A PEA TENDRIL TO THE SERVING BOWL.

2 cups shelled fresh peas

¼ cup sliced onion

1 tablespoon butter

1½ teaspoons snipped fresh dill

¼ teaspoon salt

¼ teaspoon black pepper

3 tablespoons slivered almonds or broken walnuts, toasted

1. In a medium saucepan cook peas and onion, covered, in a small amount of boiling salted water for 10 to 12 minutes or until crisp-tender; drain. Stir in butter, dill, salt, and pepper; heat through. Sprinkle with almonds.

PER SERVING *127 cal., 7 g total fat (2 g sat. fat), 8 mg chol., 180 mg sodium, 12 g carbo., 4 g fiber, 5 g pro.*

FAST FLAVOR
Celebrate spring peas in the simplest style—cook in boiling salted water no longer than 1 minute. Drain and return to the pot with melted butter, coarse salt, and a bit of freshly ground black pepper.

Lemon-Tarragon Peas

PREP: 5 MINUTES COOK: 3 MINUTES MAKES: 6 SERVINGS

THIS TRIO OF PEAS ALSO MAKES A BEAUTIFUL, SPRING-FRESH SALAD. JUST USE OLIVE OIL INSTEAD OF BUTTER AND CHILL BEFORE SERVING.

3½ cups shelled fresh peas

1½ cups whole sugar snap and/or snow pea pods

1 tablespoon butter, softened

4 teaspoons snipped fresh tarragon

2 teaspoons finely shredded lemon peel

½ teaspoon freshly cracked black pepper

Lemon wedges (optional)

Tarragon sprigs (optional)

1. In a medium saucepan cook shelled sweet peas, covered, in ¼ cup lightly salted boiling water for 8 minutes. Add the whole sugar snap peas and cook for 3 to 4 minutes more or until just crisp tender; drain.

2. Add butter, snipped tarragon, lemon peel, and pepper to peas. Toss gently until butter melts. If desired, garnish with lemon wedges and tarragon sprigs. Serve immediately.

PER SERVING *91 cal., 2 g total fat (1 g sat. fat), 4 mg chol., 19 mg sodium, 14 g carbo., 5 g fiber, 5 g pro.*

GARDEN TIP
Harvest tarragon before its flowers bud. After the bush flowers, the herb's fragrance and flavor tend to become overpowering.

FOR INFORMATION ON SELECTING AND STORING PEAS, SEE PAGE 12.

FOR INFORMATION ON SELECTING AND STORING BEETS, SEE PAGE 34.

Wine-Poached Beets

PREP: 25 MINUTES   COOK: 45 MINUTES   MAKES: 8 TO 10 SIDE-DISH SERVINGS

USE A COMBINATION OF BEET VARIETIES—RED, WHITE, GOLDEN, EVEN CANDY-STRIPE—TO GIVE THIS DISH EYE-POPPING COLOR.

¾ cup dry red wine such as Merlot or Shiraz, or apple juice

½ cup water

1 tablespoon packed brown sugar

2½ pounds beets, peeled and cut into bite-size pieces

Salt and black pepper

Honey (optional)

1 tablespoon snipped fresh parsley

Lemon wedges (optional)

1. In a large saucepan combine ½ cup of the wine, the water, and brown sugar. Bring to boiling, stirring to dissolve sugar. Add beets. Return to boiling; reduce heat. Simmer, covered, about 45 minutes or until beets are tender and can be pierced with a fork, stirring occasionally. Drain.

2. Transfer beets to serving bowl. Sprinkle remaining wine over beets. Season to taste with salt and black pepper. If desired, drizzle with honey. Sprinkle with parsley. If desired, serve with lemon wedges.

PER ½-CUP SERVING *54 cal., 0 g total fat, 0 mg chol., 119 mg sodium, 9 g carbo., 2 g fiber, 1 g pro.*

KITCHEN TIP
You can avoid staining your hands with beet juice if you wear plastic gloves while peeling and cutting the beets. Trim beet tops or leave tops on.

FOR INFORMATION ON SELECTING AND STORING SWEET POTATOES, SEE PAGE 38.

Mashed Sweet Potatoes with Balsamic Vinegar

MAKES: 4 SERVINGS

BALSAMIC VINEGAR ADDS A MELLOW TANG TO BETA-CAROTENE-LOADED SWEET POTATOES.

1½ pounds sweet potatoes or yams

2 tablespoons fat-free dairy sour cream

1 tablespoon honey

2 teaspoons balsamic vinegar

¼ teaspoon ground cinnamon

Salt and black pepper

1. Wash and peel sweet potatoes. Cut off woody portions and ends. Cut into cubes. Cook, covered, in enough boiling salted water to cover for about 10 minutes or until tender. Mash potatoes with a potato masher or beat with an electric mixer on low. Beat in sour cream, honey, vinegar, and cinnamon. Add salt and pepper to taste. Serve immediately.

PER SERVING *132 cal., 0 g total fat, 1 mg chol., 220 mg sodium, 31 g carbo., 4 g fiber, 2 g pro.*

SWEET REWARDS

- For baking, choose potatoes of similar size so they bake evenly.
- To bake several sweet potatoes at the same time, stand the potatoes on end in a muffin pan. The pan makes it easy to move the potatoes in and out of the oven.
- To prevent flesh from darkening, place cut sweet potatoes in acidulated water—a teaspoon of lemon juice or vinegar per gallon—and store in the refrigerator for up to 24 hours.
- When slicing sweet potatoes, spray a knife with nonstick cooking spray—the spray will keep the potatoes from sticking to the knife.

New Potatoes with Lemon and Chives

START TO FINISH: 25 MINUTES MAKES: 4 SIDE-DISH SERVINGS

FOR A PRETTY PRESENTATION, USE A COMBINATION OF NEW ROUND RED POTATOES, NEW YELLOW POTATOES, AND ROUND WHITE POTATOES.

10 to 12 whole tiny new potatoes (1 pound)

2 tablespoons butter

1 tablespoon snipped fresh chives or green onion tops

1 tablespoon lemon juice

⅛ teaspoon salt

⅛ to ¼ teaspoon freshly ground black pepper

1. Scrub potatoes. Cut potatoes in halves or quarters. In a large saucepan cook potatoes in a small amount of boiling, lightly salted water for 15 to 20 minutes or until tender. Drain.

2. Add butter, chives, lemon juice, salt, and pepper to the potatoes. Toss gently to coat.

PER SERVING *162 cal., 6 g total fat (1 g sat. fat), 0 mg chol., 142 mg sodium, 25 g carbo.,1 g fiber, 3 g pro.*

FOR INFORMATION SELECTING AND STORING POTATOES, SEE PAGE 38.

Steamed

FRESH FISH & VEGETABLE DISHES

For spring vegetables such as artichokes, asparagus, and chard; summer crops of beans, broccoli, and cauliflower; and the latecomers fennel and leeks, a trip to the steamer is as invigorating as a trip to the spa. The quick burst of vapor intensifies their colors and garden-fresh flavors.

Mussels with Leeks and Pancetta

PREP: 20 MINUTES   COOK: 13 MINUTES   SOAK: 45 MINUTES   MAKES: 4 MAIN-DISH SERVINGS

TENDER LEEKS NEARLY MELT INTO THE COOKING LIQUID, GIVING THE SAUCE BODY AND SUBSTANCE—
AND MAKING IT AN ENTICING MIXTURE FOR DIPPING BREAD.

1 pound mussels in shells (about 30)

3 ounces pancetta, chopped

3 medium leeks, sliced (1 cup)

½ teaspoon finely shredded orange peel

½ cup orange juice

½ cup dry white wine

2 to 3 tablespoons snipped fresh chives

Crusty country bread (optional)

1. Scrub mussels under cold running water. Remove beards. In an 8-quart Dutch oven combine 4 quarts cold water and ⅓ cup salt; add mussels. Soak for 15 minutes; drain and rinse. Discard water. Repeat soaking, draining, and rinsing twice.

2. In a Dutch oven cook pancetta over medium heat until crisp. Using a slotted spoon, remove pancetta from Dutch oven; drain on paper towels. Drain fat from the Dutch oven, reserving 1 tablespoon. Return the 1 tablespoon fat to Dutch oven. Add leeks; cook and stir about 3 minutes or until tender.

3. Add orange peel, orange juice, and wine to Dutch oven. Bring to boiling. Add mussels to Dutch oven; reduce heat. Simmer, covered, for 5 to 7 minutes or until mussels open. Discard any mussels that do not open. Sprinkle with pancetta and chives. If desired, serve with crusty country bread.

PER SERVING *333 cal., 11 g total fat (3 g sat. fat), 47 mg chol., 905 mg sodium, 33 g carbo., 2 g fiber, 20 g pro.*

KITCHEN TIP

The accordian-like folds of leeks contain a lot of grit and dirt, so they need to be carefully cleaned before cooking. The best way to clean is to slice the white part in half horiztonally, then slice each half thinly. Swirl the sliced leeks in cold water. Rinse and repeat, then drain on paper towels and pat dry. If you have a salad spinner, clean them in that and then spin them dry.

FOR INFORMATION ON SELECTING AND STORING LEEKS, SEE PAGE 17.

Steamed Artichokes Stuffed with Lemony Crab Salad

PREP: 25 MINUTES COOK: 20 MINUTES MAKES: 4 MAIN-DISH SERVINGS

EVEN TOP-QUALITY CRABMEAT MAY CONTAIN SMALL BITS OF SHELL AND CARTILAGE. PICK THROUGH THE CRAB CAREFULLY—REMOVING ANY BITS OF FOREIGN MATTER—BEFORE MIXING THE MEAT INTO THIS REFRESHING, CITRUSY SALAD.

2 medium fresh artichokes

Lemon juice

1 cup cooked crabmeat or one 6-ounce can lump crabmeat, drained

⅓ cup sour cream

¼ cup mayonnaise

¼ cup finely chopped tomato

2 tablespoons finely chopped red onion

1 teaspoon finely shredded lemon peel

1 tablespoon lemon juice

1 tablespoon snipped Italian parsley

1 teaspoon Dijon-style mustard

⅛ teaspoon cayenne pepper

1. Wash artichokes; trim stems and remove loose outer leaves. Cut 1 inch off the top of each artichoke; snip off the sharp leaf tips. Brush the cut edges with a little lemon juice. Cut artichokes in half lengthwise. Scoop out and discard chokes.

2. Place a steamer basket in a large saucepan. Add water to just below the bottom of the basket. Bring water to boiling. Add artichoke halves to steamer basket. Cover and reduce heat. Steam for 20 to 25 minutes or until tender.

3. Meanwhile, for crab salad, in a medium bowl combine crabmeat, sour cream, mayonnaise, tomato, red onion, lemon peel, lemon juice, parsley, mustard, and cayenne pepper.

4. Spoon crab salad into artichoke halves to serve. If desired, sprinkle with additional snipped parsley and cayenne pepper.

PER SERVING *211 cal., 15 g total fat (4 g sat. fat), 56 mg chol., 297 mg sodium, 9 g carbo., 4 g fiber, 11 g pro.*

Steamed Salmon and Swiss Chard Stack

PREP: 30 MINUTES BAKE: 12 MINUTES COOK: 8 MINUTES OVEN: 350°F MAKES: 4 MAIN-DISH SERVINGS

STEAMING SALMON MAKES IT TASTE LIKE IT WAS JUST PULLED FROM CHILLY WATERS. BE SURE TO CHECK THAT YOUR STEAMER BASKET FITS IN YOUR SKILLET BEFORE YOU BEGIN.

10 sheets frozen phyllo dough (14×9-inch rectangles), thawed

10 teaspoons Meyer lemon olive oil, other lemon-infused olive oil, or other flavored oils such as garlic- or rosemary-Infused olive oil

2 tablespoons snipped fresh parsley

1½ teaspoons kosher salt

1 pound fresh or frozen skinless salmon fillet, ½ to ¾ inch thick

Freshly ground black pepper

2 medium lemons, very thinly sliced and seeds removed

4 cups packed torn Swiss chard leaves

1 tablespoon Meyer lemon olive oil, other lemon-infused olive oil, or other flavored oils such as garlic- or rosemary-infused olive oil

¼ cup very thinly sliced red onion slivers

1. Preheat oven to 350°F. To make phyllo squares, unroll dough sheets. Transfer 1 sheet to a large cutting board. (Cover remaining phyllo.) Brush phyllo with 1 teaspoon of the oil. Top with a phyllo sheet; brush again. Sprinkle with 1 teaspoon parsley and ½ teaspoon salt. Repeat layers twice. Place another phyllo sheet on top of phyllo stack. Brush with oil. Trim edges to make a 12×8 inch rectangle. Cut phyllo stack lengthwise into thirds. Cut each third into two squares, making twelve 4×4-inch squares. Repeat with remaining 5 sheets phyllo, 5 teaspoons oil, and remaining parsley and salt. Place phyllo squares on a large ungreased baking sheet. Bake for 12 to 14 minutes or until browned. Cool on baking sheet.

2. Thaw fish, if frozen. Cut fish into 8 pieces; set aside. Fill a large skillet with an inch of water. Bring to boiling, then reduce to simmer.

3. Place fish in bottom of a double-tiered bamboo steamer or steamer basket. Sprinkle with pepper and top with 1 of the sliced lemons. Layer remaining sliced lemon and Swiss chard in top basket of bamboo steamer or on top of salmon in steamer basket. Place over simmering water. Cover steamer or skillet. Steam for 8 to 12 minutes or until fish begins to flake when tested with a fork. To serve, place 1 square of phyllo on each of 4 plates. Divide half of the fish, chard, and lemon slices among phyllo squares on plates. Top each with another phyllo square and remaining fish, chard, and lemon slices. Crumble remaining phyllo squares over individual servings. Drizzle with additional oil and sprinkle with onion.

PER SERVING *401 cal., 25 g total fat (4 g sat. fat), 70 mg chol., 489 mg sodium, 20 g carbo., 4 g fiber, 27 g pro.*

KITCHEN TIP
If salmon is thicker than ¾ inch, slice it in half horizontally.

FOR INFORMATION ON SELECTING AND STORING SWISS CHARD, SEE PAGE 23.

Shrimp with Curried Lime Carrots

PREP: 20 MINUTES   **COOK:** 6 MINUTES   **MAKES:** 4 TO 6 MAIN-DISH SERVINGS

THIS VIBRANTLY COLORED COMBO IS A BIT SPICY AND A BIT SWEET FROM JUST A TOUCH OF HONEY
AND THE NATURAL SWEETNESS OF CARROTS.

1 pound fresh or frozen large shrimp in shells, peeled and deveined

½ teaspoon ground cumin

½ teaspoon ground turmeric

¼ teaspoon salt

⅛ teaspoon ground cardamom

⅛ teaspoon cayenne pepper

4 medium carrots, peeled and thinly bias-sliced

2 tablespoons chopped green onion (1)

2 tablespoons lime juice

1 tablespoon honey

½ teaspoon finely shredded lime peel

1. Thaw shrimp, if frozen. In a medium bowl combine cumin, turmeric, salt, cardamom, and cayenne pepper. Remove ¾ teaspoon of the mixture to another medium bowl. Add shrimp to 1 bowl and carrots to the second bowl with seasoning. Toss each to coat.

2. Place a steamer basket in a saucepan. Add water to just below the bottom of the basket. Bring water to boiling. Add carrots to steamer basket. Cover and reduce heat. Steam for 3 minutes. Add shrimp. Cover and steam for 3 to 5 minutes more or until shrimp are opaque and carrots are tender.

3. Transfer shrimp and carrots to a serving platter. Sprinkle with green onion. In a small bowl combine lime juice and honey. Drizzle over shrimp and carrots. Sprinkle with lime peel.

PER SERVING *167 cal., 2 g total fat (0 g sat. fat), 172 mg chol., 357 mg sodium, 12 g carbo., 2 g fiber, 24 g pro.*

KITCHEN TIP
To grate lime peel, be sure to remove only the very thin, outermost layer of skin. The spongy white membrane, or pith, between the flesh and peel is bitter.

FOR INFORMATION ON SELECTING AND STORING CARROTS, SEE PAGE 13.

FOR INFORMATION ON SELECTING AND STORING FENNEL, SEE PAGE 36.

Sea Bass with Fennel and Herbed Aïoli

PREP: 25 MINUTES   CHILL: 1 HOUR   COOK: 8 MINUTES   MAKES: 4 MAIN-DISH SERVINGS

AÏOLI IS A TRADITIONAL FRENCH GARLIC SAUCE OFTEN SERVED WITH FISH. THIS VERSION BEGINS WITH MAYONNAISE THAT IS INFUSED WITH SEAFOOD-FRIENDLY SEASONINGS SUCH AS TARRAGON, THYME, AND LEMON—PERFECT FOR DABBING ON BITES OF BEAUTIFUL WHITE FISH.

1 pound fresh or frozen sea bass fillets, 1 inch thick

⅓ cup mayonnaise

3 cloves garlic, minced

1 teaspoon snipped fresh tarragon

½ teaspoon snipped fresh thyme

½ teaspoon finely shredded lemon peel

1½ teaspoons lemon juice

⅛ teaspoon salt

¼ cup olive oil

1 large bulb fennel, cored and cut into thin wedges

1 medium shallot, thinly sliced

1 teaspoon ground coriander

½ teaspoon salt

¼ teaspoon black pepper

Snipped fresh fennel fronds

1. Thaw fish, if frozen. Cut fish into 4 serving-size portions.

2. For herbed aïoli, in a small bowl combine mayonnaise, garlic, tarragon, thyme, and lemon peel. Whisk in lemon juice and ⅛ teaspoon salt until smooth. Slowly whisk in olive oil until smooth. Cover and chill for at least 1 hour before serving.

3. Sprinkle fish, fennel, and shallot with coriander, ½ teaspoon salt, and pepper.

4. Place a steamer basket in an extra-large skillet with a lid. Add water to just below the bottom of the basket. Bring water to boiling. Add fish and vegetables to steamer basket. Cover and reduce heat. Steam for 8 to 12 minutes or until fish begins to flake when tested with a fork and fennel is tender. Sprinkle fish with fennel fronds. Serve fish and vegetables with herbed aïoli.

PER SERVING 395 cal., 31 g total fat (5 g sat. fat), 53 mg chol., 582 mg sodium, 8 g carbo., 3 g fiber, 22 g pro.

FAST FLAVOR
Finely chop lacy fennel fronds and scatter them in the bottom of a bread pan. Place bread dough on top, let rise, and bake as normal. The fronds will infuse homemade bread with enticing aroma and flavor.

Steamed Asparagus and Lobster Salad

START TO FINISH: 40 MINUTES MAKES: 4 TO 6 SERVINGS

THE TRIO OF LEMON, DILL, AND GARLIC IS DELIGHTFUL ON THIS ELEGANT CHILLED SALAD. TO SHAVE PARMESAN, LIGHTLY SCRAPE ROOM-TEMPERATURE CHEESE WITH A SUPER-SHARP VEGETABLE PEELER.

2 8-ounce fresh or frozen lobster tails

1 pound fresh asparagus spears

½ teaspoon finely shredded lemon peel

2 tablespoons lemon juice

2 tablespoons extra virgin olive oil

1 tablespoon minced shallot

2 teaspoons snipped fresh dillweed

2 teaspoons honey

¼ teaspoon salt

⅛ teaspoon black pepper

4 cups torn butterhead (Boston or Bibb) lettuce

¼ cup shaved Parmesan cheese

3 slices bacon, cooked, drained, and crumbled

1. Thaw lobster tails, if frozen. Butterfly lobster tails by using kitchen shears to cut lengthwise through centers of hard top shells and meat, cutting to but not through bottoms of shells. Spread halves of tails apart. Place a steamer basket in a saucepan. Add water to just below the bottom of the basket. Bring water to boiling. Add lobster tails to steamer basket. Cover and reduce heat. Steam for 8 minutes. Add asparagus; cover and steam for 3 to 5 minutes more or until lobster is opaque and asparagus is tender. When cool enough to handle, remove lobster from shells and coarsely chop. Bias-slice asparagus into 1½-inch pieces.

2. For vinaigrette, in a screw-top jar combine lemon peel, lemon juice, olive oil, shallot, dillweed, honey, salt, and pepper. Cover and shake well to combine.

3. Line a serving platter with lettuce. Arrange asparagus and lobster on lettuce. Drizzle with vinaigrette; sprinkle with cheese and bacon.

PER SERVING *250 cal., 12 g total fat (3 g sat. fat), 119 mg chol., 701 mg sodium, 8 g carbo., 2 g fiber, 28 g pro.*

KITCHEN TIP

Here's an easy way to have cooked bacon at the ready—a lot less expensive than buying it precooked. When you have time, cook a pound of bacon in the oven to the desired crispness. Drain and cool on paper towels, then wrap in plastic wrap and store in a tightly sealed container in the refrigerator. Whenever you need (or want) bacon, heat what you need in the microwave between 2 paper towels for 30 to 45 seconds. Let cool. It will be crisp and taste like fresh-cooked!

FOR INFORMATION ON SELECTING AND STORING ASPARAGUS, SEE PAGE 18; FOR INFORMATION ON LETTUCES, SEE PAGE 11.

Steamed Cauliflower

START TO FINISH: 20 MINUTES   MAKES: 4 SIDE-DISH SERVINGS

MANCHEGO—A HARD-TEXTURED AND SOMEWHAT SALTY SPANISH CHEESE—IS EASY TO FIND AT THE CHEESE COUNTER. ITS BLACK RIND IS PRESSED WITH THE IMPRINT OF AN INTRICATELY WOVEN BASKET.

2 small heads cauliflower and/or Romanesca cauliflower

2 to 3 ounces thinly sliced Serrano ham or other cooked ham

1 ounce thinly sliced Manchego cheese

¼ cup olive oil

2 tablespoons lemon juice

1 clove garlic, minced

½ teaspoon salt

¼ teaspoon sugar

¼ teaspoon dry mustard

¼ teaspoon freshly ground black pepper

2 tablespoons pine nuts, toasted

2 tablespoons capers, drained

1. Remove heavy leaves and tough stems from cauliflower; cut into wedges. Place a steamer basket in a large saucepan. Add water to just below the bottom of the basket. Bring water to boiling. Add cauliflower to steamer basket. Cover and reduce heat. Steam for 8 to 12 minutes or until crisp-tender. Divide cauliflower among serving plates. Arrange ham and cheese on cauliflower.

2. In a screw-top jar combine olive oil, lemon juice, garlic, salt, sugar, mustard, and pepper. Cover and shake well to combine; drizzle over cauliflower, ham, and cheese. Sprinkle with pine nuts and capers.

MICROWAVE DIRECTIONS: Place cauliflower in a microwave-safe 3-quart casserole. Add ½ cup water. Microwave, covered, on high for 7 to 9 minutes or until crisp-tender.

PER SERVING *207 cal., 18 g total fat (3 g sat. fat), 10 mg chol., 848 mg sodium, 7 g carbo., 4 g fiber, 9 g pro.*

KITCHEN TIP
Pale green Romanesca cauliflower is a cross between cauliflower and broccoli.

Steamed Red Chard

START TO FINISH: 45 MINUTES MAKES: 6 SIDE-DISH SERVINGS

A SIMPLE VINAIGRETTE COMPLEMENTS THE EARTHY FLAVOR OF THIS SIMPLE CHARD DISH.

3 pounds red Swiss chard, stems removed, and leaves cut crosswise into ½-inch strips

2 tablespoons olive oil

2 cups chopped onions (2 large)

¼ cup sherry vinegar or red wine vinegar

½ teaspoon salt

½ teaspoon freshly ground black pepper

1. Fill a 4-quart pot with water to a depth of 1 inch. Bring water to boiling. Place a steamer basket in the pot. Place one-third of the chard in the steamer basket. Cover and steam for 5 minutes or until chard is tender. Remove chard from steamer basket and place in a large colander placed over a large bowl to drain; set aside. Repeat with remaining chard in two batches.

2. Meanwhile, in the same pot heat oil over medium heat. Add onions; cook until tender. Add steamed chard, vinegar, salt, and pepper. Cook and stir until heated through.

PER SERVING *76 cal., 4 g total fat (1 g sat. fat), 0 mg chol., 463 mg sodium, 10 g carbo., 3 g fiber, 3 g pro.*

VINEGAR VENTURES

Substitute one variety for another to vary the taste of this—and other—vinegar-containing recipes.

- Cider vinegar lends a fruity apple element to foods and is particularly good paired with pork.
- The flavor of red wine vinegar is bold and assertive, perfect with strongly flavored greens and beef.
- Sherry vinegar is sweet and complex, which makes it an intriguing addition to most anything.
- Champagne vinegar, subtle and sublime, is gentle enough to use with mild-flavor foods.

FOR INFORMATION ON SELECTING AND STORING SWISS CHARD, SEE PAGE 23.

FOR INFORMATION ON SELECTING AND STORING GREEN BEANS, SEE PAGE 22.

Green Beans with Cilantro

START TO FINISH: 20 MINUTES   MAKES: 4 SIDE-DISH SERVINGS

A BUNCH OF FRESH CILANTRO WILL BE MORE THAN YOU NEED FOR THIS RECIPE. TO STORE THE REMAINING HERB, CLIP THE BOTTOM ½ INCH OF THE STEMS, PLACE STEMS IN A GLASS FILLED WITH 1 INCH OF WATER, COVER GLASS LOOSELY WITH A PLASTIC BAG, AND REFRIGERATE FOR UP TO 1 WEEK.

12 ounces fresh green beans

2 teaspoons olive oil

2 cloves garlic, minced

¼ teaspoon salt

¼ teaspoon black pepper

2 tablespoons snipped fresh cilantro

1. Wash beans; remove ends and strings. Place a steamer basket in large saucepan. Add water to just below the bottom of the basket. Bring water to boiling. Add beans to steamer basket. Cover and reduce heat. Steam for 8 to 10 minutes or until beans are crisp-tender. Remove steamer basket from saucepan; set aside.

2. In a large skillet heat olive oil over medium heat. Add garlic; cook for 15 seconds. Add beans, salt, and pepper. Cook for 3 minutes, stirring occasionally. Sprinkle with cilantro.

PER SERVING *50 cal., 2 g total fat (0 g sat. fat), 0 mg chol., 152 mg sodium, 7 g carbo., 3 g fiber, 2 g pro.*

SENSATIONAL CILANTRO
- Cilantro leaves are prone to harboring sand. Swish leaves well in cool water to remove grit.
- When purchasing fresh cilantro, sniff the bunch to make sure it is not flat-leaf parsley—the leaves of the two herbs are nearly identical.

Asparagus and Sweet Pepper Rolls

START TO FINISH: 45 MINUTES MAKES: 24 ROLLS (6 TO 8 SERVINGS)

TO SIMPLIFY PREPARATION AND CUT KITCHEN TIME, REPLACE HOMEMADE OLIVE PASTE WITH PURCHASED TAPENADE. MANY EXCELLENT OPTIONS ARE AVAILABLE IN SUPERMARKETS.

24 asparagus spears

6 ounces thinly sliced serrano ham or prosciutto

12 pitted kalamata olives, chopped

1 clove garlic, minced

1 teaspoon capers

1 teaspoon olive oil

¼ teaspoon lemon juice

24 basil leaves

¾ cup roasted sweet peppers, cut into 48 thin strips*

1. Snap off and discard woody bases from asparagus. Place a steamer basket in a large saucepan. Add water to just below the bottom of the basket. Bring water to boiling; add asparagus to steamer basket. Cover and reduce heat. Steam about 3 minutes or until crisp-tender. Drain and rinse under cold water until cool; drain on paper towels.

2. Cut ham into 24 strips, about 8×1½ inches each; set aside. For olive paste, using a mortar and pestle or fork, mash olives, garlic, capers, olive oil, and lemon juice into a chunky paste. Spread a heaping ¼ teaspoon olive paste on each ham strip. Lay one asparagus spear at one end of each slice of ham. Place a basil leaf and 2 strips of red pepper next to asparagus. Roll ham tightly around fillings, covering each except for tops; repeat with remaining ingredients. Serve immediately or cover and chill for up to 4 hours.

PER 4-ROLL SERVING *123 cal., 10 g total fat (0 g sat. fat), 4 mg chol., 846 mg sodium, 7 g carbo., 4 g fiber, 2 g pro.*

*TO ROAST PEPPERS
Preheat oven to 425°F. Halve a medium red sweet pepper and a medium yellow sweet pepper. Remove stems, membranes, and seeds. Place peppers, cut sides down, on a foil-lined baking sheet. Roast for 20 to 25 minutes or until skin is bubbly and browned. Wrap peppers in foil. Let stand for 20 to 30 minutes or until cool enough to handle. Pull the skin off gently and slowly, using a paring knife.

FOR INFORMATION ON SELECTING AND STORING ASPARAGUS, SEE PAGE 18; FOR INFORMATION ON SWEET PEPPERS, SEE PAGE 24.

Lemon Broccoli

START TO FINISH: 20 MINUTES MAKES: 6 SIDE-DISH SERVINGS

ENTRENCHED BROCCOLI SKEPTICS MAY BE PERSUADED TO TRY THIS SIMPLE DISH. THE PAIRING OF LEMON AND GARLIC IS A NATURAL WITH THE FRESH AND CRISP FLORETS.

6 cups broccoli florets

2 tablespoons olive oil

½ teaspoon finely shredded lemon peel

4 teaspoons lemon juice

1 clove garlic, minced

¼ teaspoon salt

⅛ teaspoon black pepper

1. Place a steamer basket in a large saucepan. Add water to just below the bottom of the basket. Bring water to boiling. Add broccoli to steamer basket. Cover and reduce heat. Steam for 8 to 10 minutes or until crisp-tender.
2. Meanwhile, combine oil, lemon peel, lemon juice, garlic, salt, and pepper. Drizzle over hot broccoli; toss to coat.
PER SERVING *66 cal., 5 g total fat (1 g sat. fat), 0 mg chol., 121 mg sodium, 5 g carbo., 3 g fiber, 3 g pro.*

PLEASING SQUEEZING

- One medium lemon yields about 3 tablespoons of juice.
- Room-temperature lemons will yield more juice.
- To extract just a few drops of juice from a lemon, pierce the lemon with a paring knife and squeeze the juice through the hole.
- Roll a room-temperature lemon firmly between your palms to make it release more juice.

FOR INFORMATION ON SELECTING AND STORING BROCCOLI, SEE PAGE 14.

Baked

PIZZA, BREADS, CAKES, PASTRIES & CASSEROLES

Whether harvested from garden, field, patch, bramble, or orchard, nearly every kind of produce eventually works its way to the oven. Tucked into this hot box, fruits rise to great heights in cakes or thicken under blankets of pastry, and vegetables embellish breads or bubble in gratins.

Herbed Leek Tart

PREP: 20 MINUTES BAKE: 25 MINUTES OVEN: 375°F MAKES: 24 SERVINGS

TO PREPARE LEEKS, START SLICING AT THE WHITE ROOT END, THEN CONTINUE UP THE STALK THROUGH THE PALE GREEN FLESH. STOP WHEN YOU REACH THE LEAVES. FOR INFORMATION ON CLEANING LEEKS, SEE PAGE 144.

9 medium leeks, thinly sliced (3 cups)

4 cloves garlic, minced

2 tablespoons olive oil

½ cup chopped red sweet pepper

2 tablespoons Dijon-style mustard

1 teaspoon dried herbes de Provence or dried basil, crushed

1½ cups Gruyère cheese or Swiss cheese (6 ounces)

1 15-ounce package rolled refrigerated unbaked piecrust (2 crusts)

2 tablespoons chopped almonds or walnuts

1. Preheat oven to 375°F. For filling, in a large skillet cook leeks and garlic in hot oil about 5 minutes or until tender. Remove from heat; stir in sweet pepper, mustard, and herbes de Provence. Cool slightly; stir in shredded cheese. Set filling aside.

2. Unroll piecrust according to package directions. On a lightly floured surface, roll one piecrust into a 12-inch circle. Transfer piecrust to a baking sheet. Spread half the filling into the center of the crust, leaving a 1½-inch border. Fold border up and over filling, pleating to build up a crust. Sprinkle 1 tablespoon of the nuts over the filling. Repeat with remaining piecrust, filling, and nuts.

3. Bake about 25 minutes or until crusts are golden. Cool for 10 minutes on baking sheets. Cut each tart into 12 wedges. Serve warm or at room temperature.

PER SERVING *133 cal., 9 g total fat (4 g sat. fat), 11 mg chol., 100 mg sodium, 11 g carbo., 0 g fiber, 3 g pro.*

FAST FLAVOR
In a tightly covered jar vigorously shake 2 teaspoons Dijon-style mustard, 2 tablespoons red wine vinegar, 3 tablespoons extra virgin olive oil, salt, and pepper. Pour over hot oven-roasted leeks.

FOR INFORMATION ON SELECTING AND STORING LEEKS, SEE PAGE 17.

FOR INFORMATION ON SELECTING AND STORING TOMATOES, SEE PAGE 21.

Three-Tomato Tart

PREP: 30 MINUTES BAKE: 35 MINUTES OVEN: 450°F/325°F MAKES: 10 TO 12 APPETIZER SERVINGS

A LOVELY APPETIZER, THIS TART IS ALSO A DELICIOUS MEAT-FREE MAIN DISH FOR LUNCH OR A LIGHT SUMMER SUPPER.

1 recipe Pastry for Single-Crust Pie

3 tablespoons grated Parmesan cheese

1 cup low-fat ricotta cheese

2 egg whites

1 tablespoon snipped fresh lemon thyme or thyme

2 cloves garlic, minced

2 large tomatoes, sliced

5 yellow or red cherry tomatoes, sliced

2 red cherry tomatoes, sliced

1 tablespoon olive oil

2 teaspoons snipped fresh lemon thyme or thyme

1. Preheat oven to 450°F. Prepare Pastry for Single-Crust Pie. On a lightly floured surface, roll pastry into a circle about 12 inches in diameter. Line a 10-inch tart pan with pastry. Press pastry into fluted sides of pan. Trim pastry even with rim of pan. Do not prick pastry. Line pastry shell with a double thickness of foil. Bake pastry for 5 minutes. Remove foil. Bake for 5 to 7 minutes more or until pastry is set and dry. Remove from oven. Reduce oven temperature to 325°F. Sprinkle tart shell with Parmesan cheese.

2. Meanwhile, in a small bowl stir together ricotta cheese, egg whites, 1 tablespoon thyme, and garlic; spread over pastry.

3. Overlap large tomato slices in a circle around edge. Arrange yellow cherry tomato slices in a circle within the tomato ring. Fill center with red cherry tomato slices. Stir together olive oil and 2 teaspoons thyme. Brush tomatoes with oil mixture.

4. Bake tart for 25 to 30 minutes or until heated through and nearly set. Serve warm or at room temperature. Refrigerate any leftover tart.

PER SERVING *179 cal., 11 g total fat (3 g sat. fat), 9 mg chol., 134 mg sodium, 14 g carbo., 6 g pro.*

PASTRY FOR SINGLE-CRUST PIE: In a large bowl stir together 1¼ cups all-purpose flour and ¼ teaspoon salt. Using a pastry blender, cut in ⅓ cup shortening until pieces are pea size. Sprinkle 1 tablespoon cold water over part of the mixture; gently toss with a fork. Push moistened dough to the side of the bowl. Repeat moistening dough, using 1 tablespoon cold water at a time, until all the dough is moistened (4 to 5 table-spoons cold water total). Form dough into a ball.

Baba Ghanoush

THIS LEMON-AND GARLIC-INFUSED EGGPLANT AND TAHINI DIP IS JUST ONE OF THE MANY LITTLE DISHES THAT MAKE UP THE MEZZE, OR APPETIZER TABLE, OF THE ARAB WORLD.

1 large eggplant (about 1½ pounds)

2 tablespoons lemon juice

2 tablespoons tahini (sesame seed paste)

1 tablespoon olive oil

2 cloves garlic, minced

1 teaspoon salt

2 tablespoons snipped fresh parsley

Pita bread rounds, toasted

1. Preheat oven to 400°F. Halve the eggplant lengthwise and place, cut sides down, on a baking sheet lined with foil. Prick skin all over with a fork. Bake about 25 minutes or until tender when pierced with a fork.

2. Peel eggplant; cut eggplant into chunks. Transfer eggplant to a food processor or blender; add the lemon juice, tahini, olive oil, garlic, and salt. Cover and process or blend until smooth.

3. Transfer dip to a bowl; stir in the parsley. Serve with toasted pita bread.

PER 1 TABLESPOON DIP *34 cal., 1 g total fat (0 g sat. fat), 0 mg chol., 113 mg sodium, 6 g carbo., 1 g fiber, 1 g pro.*

EGGPLANT MADE EASY

- Infuse eggplant with smoky flavor by charring it whole over a gas burner.
- To prevent eggplant from discoloring, brush the cut flesh with lemon juice.
- To easily brown eggplant, slice, coat with cooking spray, place on a baking sheet, and broil for about 2 minutes per side.

FOR INFORMATION ON SELECTING AND STORING EGGPLANT, SEE PAGE 23.

FOR INFORMATION ON SELECTING AND STORING CABBAGE, SEE PAGE 35.

Cabbage Strudel

PREP: 1 HOUR COOK: 15 MINUTES BAKE: 35 MINUTES COOL: 30 MINUTES
OVEN: 375°F MAKES: 12 SIDE-DISH SERVINGS

CABBAGE SELDOM MAKES IT TO THE AMERICAN TABLE UNLESS IT'S IN THE FORM OF COLESLAW. CRADLED IN CRISP PHYLLO, THE HUMBLE VEGETABLE BECOMES A BUTTERY DELIGHT.

8 tablespoons butter

1 cup chopped onion (1 large)

1 small head green cabbage (2 pounds), thinly sliced (8 cups)

1 cup shredded carrots (2 medium)

1 teaspoon salt

4 ounces feta cheese, crumbled

¾ cup plain dry bread crumbs

1 tablespoon snipped fresh dill

½ teaspoon caraway seeds

⅛ teaspoon black pepper

12 sheets frozen phyllo dough (14×9-inch rectangles), thawed

1. Preheat oven to 375°F. Grease a 15×10×1-inch baking pan; set aside.
2. In a large skillet melt 2 tablespoons of the butter over medium-high heat. Add onion; cook about 5 minutes or until tender. Add cabbage and carrots; sprinkle with salt. Cook about 10 minutes or until tender. Remove from heat; stir in feta cheese, ½ cup of the bread crumbs, the dill, caraway seeds, and pepper.
3. In a small saucepan melt the remaining 6 tablespoons butter. Unroll phyllo dough; cover with waxed paper and damp towel. Working quickly, place one sheet on work surface. Brush with some butter; top with 1 teaspoon bread crumbs. Repeat layers with 5 more sheets phyllo, melted butter, and bread crumbs. Spread half the cabbage filling over phyllo layers, leaving a 2-inch border on one of the long sides and both short sides. Fold both short sides over filling; roll up from long side. Place roll, seam side down, in prepared pan. Repeat with remaining ingredients to make a second roll.
4. Bake about 35 minutes or until golden. Transfer to a wire rack; cool for 30 minutes. To serve, use a serrated knife to cut into slices.
PER SERVING *205 cal., 11 g total fat (7 g sat. fat), 29 mg chol., 515 mg sodium, 22 g carbo., 3 g fiber, 5 g pro.*

FAST FLAVOR
Add a whole star anise to the cooking water with cabbage. The spice will infuse the cabbage with incredible sweetness.

White Pizza with Spring Vegetables

PREP: 30 MINUTES BAKE: 7 MINUTES PER PIZZA OVEN: 500°F MAKES: 8 MAIN-DISH SERVINGS

TO TRIM WOODY BOTTOMS FROM ASPARAGUS SPEARS, SIMPLY HOLD THE TIP IN ONE HAND AND THE BASE IN THE OTHER HAND, THEN BEND IT. THE STALK WILL SNAP TO SEPARATE THE WOODY BASE FROM THE TENDER STALK.

1 recipe Basic Pizza Dough

2 teaspoons finely shredded lemon peel

1 tablespoon snipped fresh dill or tarragon

¼ cup olive oil, plus additional for oiling baking pans

Dash salt

Dash black pepper

1 pound fresh asparagus spears, trimmed and sliced lengthwise*

1 cup sliced wild mushrooms, such as oyster or chanterelle

1 small sweet onion, thinly sliced

1 cup fresh shelled peas or frozen peas

1 cup crumbled feta or goat cheese

Olive oil

Salt and black pepper

1. Prepare Basic Pizza Dough. In a small bowl combine lemon peel, dill, ¼ cup olive oil, dash salt, and dash pepper; set aside.

2. Preheat oven to 500°F. Divide Basic Pizza Dough in half. On a lightly floured surface, roll each half to a circle. Transfer dough circles to round oiled pizza pans or two oiled baking sheets. Lightly brush dough with lemon-dill oil.

3. In a large bowl combine asparagus, mushrooms, onion, and peas. Sprinkle vegetables over crusts. Sprinkle with feta cheese. Lightly drizzle with additional olive oil. Sprinkle lightly with additional salt and pepper.

4. Bake crusts individually for 7 to 9 minutes or until crust is browned and vegetables are crisp-tender.

PER SERVING 357 cal., 16 g total fat (5 g sat. fat), 17 mg chol., 325 mg sodium, 42 g carbo., 4 g fiber, 10 g pro.

*TIP: To get very thin slices of asparagus, lay a stalk on a flat surface and slice with a vegetable peeler the length of the stalk.

BASIC PIZZA DOUGH: In a small bowl stir together 3 cups all-purpose flour and a dash salt; set aside. In a large mixing bowl stir together 1 cup warm water (105°F to 115°F) and 2 tablespoons olive oil; sprinkle 1 package active dry yeast over surface. Stir until yeast dissolves. With an electric mixer on low, beat about 2 cups of the flour mixture into yeast mixture until combined. Stir in as much of the remaining flour mixture as you can. On a lightly floured surface, knead in remaining flour until smooth. Shape into a ball. Cover and let rest for 10 minutes.

FOR INFORMATION ON SELECTING AND STORING ASPARAGUS, SEE PAGE 18; FOR INFORMATION ON GARDEN PEAS, SEE PAGE 12.

FOR INFORMATION ON SELECTING AND STORING GARLIC, SEE PAGE 39; FOR INFORMATION ON TOMATOES, SEE PAGE 21.

Roasted Garlic and Tomato Pizza

START TO FINISH: 25 MINUTES   OVEN: 450°F   MAKES: 6 TO 8 SIDE-DISH SERVINGS

DON'T LET THE 42 CLOVES OF GARLIC ALARM YOU. OVEN-ROASTING SOOTHES THE BULBS' ASSERTIVE FLAVOR, TRANSFORMING THE TASTE TO BE SOFT, SUBTLE, AND SUPERB.

3 bulbs garlic (about 42 cloves)

⅓ cup olive oil

1 12-inch Italian bread shell (such as Boboli brand) or prepared pizza crust

2 small tomatoes, sliced

⅓ cup pitted black olives

3 to 4 ounces mild goat cheese, crumbled, or shredded mozzarella cheese

2 tablespoons snipped fresh basil or other herbs

1. Peel garlic. In a medium saucepan heat olive oil over medium heat. Add garlic; cook and stir for 10 to 15 minutes or until garlic is golden. Use a slotted spoon to remove garlic, reserving oil. Cool garlic.

2. Preheat oven to 450°F. Place bread shell on a baking sheet. Brush with some of the garlic-flavor olive oil. Arrange sliced tomatoes and olives on bread shell; sprinkle with cheese. Top with garlic cloves; drizzle with additional garlic-flavor oil.

3. Bake about 10 minutes or until cheese begins to brown. Sprinkle with basil.

PER SERVING *403 cal., 22 g total fat (5 g sat. fat), 17 mg chol., 557 mg sodium, 42 g carbo., 1 g fiber, 14 g pro.*

FAST FLAVOR

To quickly roast a head of garlic, trim about ¼ inch from the top of the bulb—enough to expose the tips of the cloves. Pour ¼ inch of milk in a microwavable container and place the garlic, cut side down, in the milk. Cover container; microwave for about 6 minutes. Uncover, turn garlic upright, drizzle with 1 teaspoon of olive oil and finish in a 375° oven for about 20 minutes.

Stuffed Peppers

PREP: 40 MINUTES BAKE: 35 MINUTES OVEN: 350°F MAKES: 4 MAIN-DISH SERVINGS

TAKE LIBERTIES WITH THIS RECIPE. SUBSTITUTE COOKED BROWN RICE FOR THE WHITE RICE OR REPLACE CHEDDAR WITH ANOTHER CHEESE OF YOUR CHOICE.

4 medium sweet peppers (any color), tops cut off, seeded, and membranes removed

1 tablespoon olive oil

½ cup chopped onion (1 medium)

2 cloves garlic, minced

½ teaspoon ground cumin

8 ounces ground beef

1 8-ounce can tomato sauce

2 tablespoons ketchup

2 tablespoons Worcestershire sauce

½ teaspoon prepared horseradish

½ teaspoon salt (optional)

¼ teaspoon black pepper

1½ cups cooked white rice

1 cup shredded cheddar cheese (4 ounces)

2 tablespoons snipped fresh parsley

1. In a large pot cook sweet peppers, covered, in simmering water for 8 minutes. Drain; cool under running water. Drain peppers, cut sides down, on paper towels.

2. Preheat oven to 350°F. In a large skillet heat oil over medium heat. Add onion and garlic; cook about 5 minutes or until onion is tender. Stir in cumin; cook for 2 minutes. Add beef; cook about 5 minutes or until browned. Add tomato sauce, ketchup, Worcestershire sauce, horseradish, salt (if desired), and black pepper. Bring to boiling; reduce heat. Simmer, covered, for 5 minutes. Remove from heat. Stir in cooked rice and cheese. Spoon beef mixture into green pepper shells. Place the stuffed peppers in a 9×9×2-inch baking pan.

3. Bake for 35 to 40 minutes or until the filling is hot. Sprinkle with parsley.

PER SERVING *428 cal., 25 g total fat (11 g sat. fat), 70 mg chol., 687 mg sodium, 31 g carbo., 21 g pro.*

PECK OF PEPPERS

- To easily remove skins from freshly roasted peppers, rub off skins with a sheet of paper towel.
- To remove the white membranes from the insides of peppers, scrape them with a melon baller.

FOR INFORMATION ON SELECTING AND STORING SWEET PEPPERS, SEE PAGE 24.

Acorn Squash with Sausage and Corn Bread Stuffing

PREP: 50 MINUTES BAKE: 1 HOUR OVEN: 400°F/350°F MAKES: 8 MAIN-DISH SERVINGS

TO PREVENT SQUASH FROM TIPPING, CAREFULLY CUT A SMALL, FLAT PLATFORM ON THE BOTTOM OF EACH. PLACE SQUASH IN THE BAKING PAN AND TEST TO MAKE SURE EACH ONE IS STURDY BEFORE ADDING THE FILLING.

1 8.5-ounce package corn muffin mix

4 small acorn squash (12 to 16 ounces each), halved lengthwise and seeds removed

¼ teaspoon salt

¼ teaspoon black pepper

8 ounces bulk pork sausage

1 cup coarsely chopped onion (1 large)

1 cup sliced celery (2 stalks)

3 cloves garlic, minced

1 tablespoon snipped fresh sage or thyme

½ cup chicken broth

1 tablespoon butter, melted

1. Preheat oven to 400°F. Prepare and bake muffin mix according to package directions for an 8×8×2-inch baking pan. Cool corn bread in pan. Cut into ¾-inch cubes; set aside. Reduce oven temperature to 350°F.

2. Meanwhile, lightly grease a 15×10×1-inch baking pan. Sprinkle cavities of the squash with salt and pepper. Arrange squash halves, cut sides down, in prepared pan.

3. Bake squash halves, uncovered, for 30 to 40 minutes or until tender. Remove pan from oven. Using a wide metal spatula, carefully turn squash halves over.

4. Meanwhile, in an extra-large skillet cook sausage, onion, celery, and garlic until sausage is browned and vegetables are tender. Drain off fat. Stir in sage. Add corn bread cubes; toss gently to combine. Drizzle with broth and melted butter; toss gently to moisten. Spoon stuffing into squash cavities, mounding the stuffing.

5. Bake, uncovered, about 30 minutes or until top of stuffing is golden brown and mixture is heated through.

PER SERVING *304 cal., 14 g total fat (3 g sat. fat), 44 mg chol., 578 mg sodium, 38 g carbo., 3 g fiber, 9 g pro.*

MAKE-AHEAD DIRECTIONS

To make ahead, prepare as directed through Step 3. Place squash halves in airtight container(s) and refrigerate up to 24 hours. Place stuffing in another airtight container and refrigerate for up to 24 hours. To serve, let stuffing and squash stand at room temperature for 30 minutes. Preheat oven to 350°F. Place squash halves in a 15×10×1-inch baking pan and continue as directed in Step 5.

FOR INFORMATION ON SELECTING AND STORING ACORN SQUASH, SEE PAGE 40.

FOR INFORMATION ON SELECTING AND STORING SUGAR SNAP PEAS, SEE PAGE 12; FOR INFORMATION ON CARROTS, SEE PAGE 13.

Fish and Sugar Snap Peas en Papillote

PREP: 20 MINUTES BAKE: 12 MINUTES OVEN: 400°F MAKES: 6 MAIN-DISH SERVINGS

COOKING THE FISH AND VEGETABLES *EN PAPILLOTE* (IN AN ENVELOPE) ALLOWS THEM TO COOK IN WINE-ENHANCED JUICES FOR A WONDERFUL MELDING OF FLAVORS. WHEN THE PARCHMENT IS FIRST OPENED, THE AROMA IS AMAZING.

2 tablespoons butter, cut into 6 slices

6 8-ounce red snapper or white fish fillets

½ teaspoon sea salt

¼ teaspoon freshly ground black pepper

1 cup sugar snap peas, halved diagonally

12 baby carrots with tops, trimmed and quartered lengthwise, or 1 cup julienned carrots

6 slices lemon

¼ cup finely chopped shallots

12 sprigs fresh thyme or lemon thyme

6 tablespoons dry white wine

Lemon wedges (optional)

1. Position oven racks in the top third and center of the oven. Preheat oven to 400°F.

2. Cut six 18×12-inch pieces of parchment paper. Place sheets of parchment on a work surface with short ends toward you. Fold each sheet of parchment crosswise in half to crease, then unfold. Place 1 slice of butter on the lower half of each sheet of parchment. Place snapper fillets on the butter; sprinkle with salt and pepper. Top each fillet with sugar snap peas, carrots, lemon slice, shallots, and 2 thyme sprigs. Drizzle each with 1 tablespoon wine.

3. Fold each sheet of parchment over to enclose the fish and vegetables. To seal, turn up a corner of the cut edges of the paper and fold, then fold again, forming the second fold on top of the first fold. Continue folding to enclose all the way around the packet. When you reach the end, twist the last fold to seal. Repeat with remaining packets. Place the packets on 2 large baking sheets.

4. Bake both sheets at once about 12 minutes or until the paper is well browned and fish begins to flake when tested with a fork, switching the position of the baking sheets halfway through baking for even cooking. Transfer packets to plates and serve, allowing each guest to cut open the packet at the table. If desired, pass lemon wedges.

PER SERVING *301 cal., 7 g total fat (3 g sat. fat), 94 mg chol., 324 mg sodium, 7 g carbo., 2 g fiber, 48 g pro.*

KITCHEN TIP

Make shallot peeling a minor task! Just break the cloves apart and blanch them in boiling water for 1 minute. Drain, cool, and peel. Blanching softens the outer layer of skin, making it much easier to remove.

Caramelized Balsamic Onions

PREP: 20 MINUTES BAKE: 50 MINUTES OVEN: 425°F MAKES: 8 SIDE-DISH SERVINGS

AS THE ONION HALVES COOK, THE BALSAMIC MIXTURE BECOMES SYRUPY AND CARAMELIZES THE ONIONS, GIVING THEM A BRONZED CARAMEL COLOR AND A LUSCIOUS, RICH FLAVOR.

2 tablespoons butter, melted

1 tablespoon olive oil

⅓ cup balsamic vinegar

2 tablespoons dry white wine, chicken broth, or water

1 tablespoon granulated sugar

¼ teaspoon salt

⅛ teaspoon freshly ground black pepper

4 medium yellow onions

Salt and freshly ground black pepper

Fresh thyme leaves (optional)

1. Preheat oven to 425°F. In a 3-quart rectangular baking dish combine butter and olive oil. Whisk in vinegar, wine, sugar, ¼ teaspoon salt, and ⅛ teaspoon pepper. Set aside.

2. Peel off papery outer layers of onions, but do not cut off either end. Cut onions in half from stem through root end. Place onions in dish, cut sides up. Cover loosely with foil. Bake for 25 minutes.

3. Remove foil. Using tongs, carefully turn onions to cut sides down. Bake, uncovered, for 25 to 30 minutes more or until onions are tender and balsamic mixture is thickened and caramelized. Season to taste with additional salt and pepper. Sprinkle with fresh thyme, if desired. Serve cut sides up.

PER SERVING *81 cal., 5 g total fat (2 g sat. fat), 8 mg chol., 116 mg sodium, 9 g carbo., 1 g fiber, 1 g pro.*

MAKE-AHEAD DIRECTIONS: Prepare onions as directed. Cool, cover, and chill overnight. To reheat, preheat oven to 325°F. Bake, covered, about 40 minutes or until warm.

FAST FLAVOR
To give slow-to-caramelize onions a jump-start, sprinkle them with a bit of brown sugar.

FOR INFORMATION ON SELECTING AND STORING ONIONS, SEE PAGE 39.

FOR INFORMATION ON SELECTING AND STORING POTATOES, SEE PAGE 38.

Walnut-Sage Potatoes au Gratin

PREP: 30 MINUTES BAKE: 1 HOUR 10 MINUTES STAND: 10 MINUTES OVEN: 350°F
MAKES: 10 TO 12 SIDE-DISH SERVINGS

UPDATE TRADITIONAL SCALLOPED POTATOES WITH SNIPS OF FRESH SAGE, NUTTY GRUYÈRE CHEESE, AND A SPRINKLING OF CRUNCHY WALNUTS.

6 medium Yukon gold or Finnish yellow potatoes (2 pounds)

½ cup chopped onion (1 medium)

2 cloves garlic, minced

3 tablespoons walnut oil

3 tablespoons all-purpose flour

½ teaspoon salt

¼ teaspoon freshly ground black pepper

2½ cups milk

3 tablespoons snipped fresh sage

1 cup shredded Gruyère cheese (4 ounces)

⅓ cup broken walnut pieces

Fresh sage leaves (optional)

1. Preheat oven to 350°F. Peel potatoes, if desired, and thinly slice (should have 6 cups). Place slices in a colander. Rinse with cold water; set aside to drain.

2. For sauce, in a medium saucepan cook onion and garlic in walnut oil over medium heat until tender. Stir in flour, salt, and pepper. Add milk all at once. Cook and stir until thickened and bubbly. Remove from heat; stir in the snipped sage.

3. Grease a 2- to 2½-quart rectangular baking dish or 2-quart round glass casserole. Layer half the potatoes in casserole. Cover with half the sauce. Sprinkle with ½ cup of the cheese. Repeat layering with the potatoes and sauce. (Cover and chill remaining cheese until needed.)

4. Bake, covered, for 40 minutes. Uncover; bake about 25 minutes more or until potatoes are tender. Sprinkle the remaining ½ cup cheese and the walnuts over the top. Bake, uncovered, for 5 minutes more. Let stand for 10 minutes before serving. If desired, garnish with sage leaves.

PER SERVING *217 cal., 12 g total fat (3 g sat. fat), 17 mg chol., 187 mg sodium, 20 g carbo., 2 g fiber, 9 g pro.*

KITCHEN TIP
Avoid storing potatoes and onions in close proximity. In storage, each emits a gas that causes the other to spoil.

Mashed Root Vegetables with Parmesan

PREP: 25 MINUTES COOK: 20 MINUTES BAKE: 15 MINUTES
OVEN: 400°F MAKES: 12 SIDE-DISH SERVINGS

SERVE THIS RICH DISH IN PLACE OF PLAIN MASHED POTATOES AT YOUR NEXT HOLIDAY FEAST.

6 pounds assorted root vegetables such as carrots, parsnips, turnips, rutabagas, and/or red or yellow potatoes

6 cloves garlic, peeled

1 tablespoon kosher salt

½ cup milk, half-and-half, or light cream

2 tablespoons olive oil

2 tablespoons butter

½ to 1 teaspoon freshly ground black pepper

1½ cups shredded Parmesan cheese (6 ounces)

⅓ cup snipped fresh Italian parsley

1. Preheat oven to 400°F. Peel root vegetables and cut into 2- to 3-inch pieces. In a 4- to 6-quart Dutch oven combine the root vegetables, garlic, and 1½ teaspoons of the salt; add enough cold water to cover vegetables. Bring to boiling; reduce heat. Simmer, covered, about 20 minutes or until very tender. Meanwhile, in a small saucepan heat milk, olive oil, and butter until warm and butter is melted.

2. Drain vegetables in a colander. Return to pot. Mash with potato masher. Stir milk mixture, the remaining 1½ teaspoons salt, and the pepper into vegetables. Stir in ¾ cup of the cheese and the parsley. Transfer mashed vegetable mixture to a 3-quart au gratin dish; spread evenly. Sprinkle with the remaining ¾ cup cheese.

3. Bake, uncovered, about 15 minutes or until cheese is melted and mixture is heated through. If desired, preheat broiler; place broilersafe dish 4 to 5 inches from the heat and broil about 2 minutes or until top is browned.

PER SERVING *206 cal., 8 g total fat (3 g sat. fat), 13 mg chol., 727 mg sodium, 29 g carbo., 6 g fiber, 7 g pro.*

FOR INFORMATION ON SELECTING AND STORING ROOT VEGETABLES, SEE PAGE 37; FOR INFORMATION ON CARROTS, SEE PAGE 13; FOR INFORMATION ON POTATOES, SEE PAGE 38.

FOR INFORMATION ON SELECTING AND STORING BLUEBERRIES, SEE PAGE 29.

Fresh Blueberry Pie

PREP: 40 MINUTES **BAKE:** 13 MINUTES **CHILL:** 2 HOURS **OVEN:** 450°F **MAKES:** 8 SERVINGS

WHEN FRESH PLUMP BLUEBERRIES ROLL TO MARKET, BUY PLENTY—ENOUGH TO EAT OUT OF HAND, TO TUMBLE ON CEREAL, AND TO MAKE THIS PERFECT PIE.

1 recipe Lemon Pie Shell or 1 purchased 9-inch pie shell

½ cup sugar

3 tablespoons cornstarch

¼ teaspoon salt

⅓ cup water

2 tablespoons lemon juice

6 cups fresh blueberries

1 tablespoon butter

Vanilla ice cream (optional)

1. Prepare Lemon Pie Shell, if using; set aside.

2. In a large saucepan combine sugar, cornstarch, and salt. Add the water and lemon juice. Add 2 ½ cups of the blueberries; toss lightly to coat. Cook and stir over medium heat until bubbly. Cook and stir for 2 minutes more (mixture will be thick). Remove from heat and stir in butter; cool.

3. Add remaining 3 ½ cups blueberries to cooled filling, stirring gently. Turn into Lemon Pie Shell. Cover and chill at least 2 hours before serving. If desired, serve with vanilla ice cream.

LEMON PIE SHELL: In a medium bowl stir together 1 ¼ cups all-purpose flour and 3 tablespoons sugar. Using a pastry blender, cut in ⅓ cup cold butter until pieces are pea size. In a small bowl combine 1 beaten egg yolk, 1 tablespoon water, and 1 teaspoon finely shredded lemon peel. Gradually stir egg yolk mixture into flour mixture. (Dough will not be completely moistened.) Using your fingers, gently knead the dough just until a ball forms. If necessary, cover dough with plastic wrap and chill for 30 to 60 minutes or until dough is easy to handle. Preheat oven to 450°F. On a lightly floured surface, roll pastry from center to edges into a circle 12 inches in diameter. Line a 9-inch pie plate with pastry circle. Trim pastry to ½ inch beyond edge of pie plate. Fold under extra pastry. Crimp edge as desired. Generously prick bottom and side of pastry in pie plate with a fork. Prick all around where bottom and sides meet. Line pastry with a double thickness of foil. Bake for 8 minutes. Remove foil. Bake for 5 to 6 minutes more or until golden. Cool on a wire rack.

PER SERVING *300 cal., 10 g total fat (6 g sat. fat), 50 mg chol., 141 mg sodium, 51 g carbo., 3 g fiber, 3 g pro.*

FAST FLAVOR

Celebrate the blueberry season with this quick concoction: Heat 1 tablespoon sugar with ¼ cup rum until sugar is dissolved. Stir in 1 tablespoon finely grated lemon peel and 2 tablespoons lemon juice. Cool, then drizzle over fresh blueberries.

FOR INFORMATION ON SELECTING AND STORING RASPBERRIES, SEE PAGE 28.

Simple Raspberry Pie

PREP: 30 MINUTES BAKE: 1 HOUR OVEN: 350°F MAKES: 8 SERVINGS

"SIMPLE" IS SUCH A LOVELY WORD AND SO APPROPRIATE FOR FRESH RASPBERRIES, WHICH ARE AT THEIR FLAVORFUL BEST WHEN BARELY ADORNED.

5 cups fresh or frozen raspberries

1¼ cups sugar

⅓ cup all-purpose flour or 3 tablespoons cornstarch

1 recipe Pastry for Two-Crust Pie

1. Preheat oven to 375°F. For filling, in a large bowl combine berries, sugar, and flour. Gently toss berries until coated. (If using frozen fruit, let mixture stand for 45 minutes or until fruit is partially thawed but still icy.)

2. Prepare Pastry for Two-Crust Pie. On a lightly floured surface, roll pastry from center to edges into a circle 12 inches in diameter. Line a 9-inch pie plate with pastry circle. Stir filling. Transfer filling to pastry-lined pie plate. Trim bottom pastry to ½ inch beyond edge of pie plate. Roll remaining ball into a 12-inch-diameter circle. Cut slits in pastry circle; place on filling and seal. Crimp edge as desired.

3. To prevent overbrowning, cover edge of pie with foil. Place a foil-lined baking sheet on the rack below the pie in the oven. Bake for 30 minutes (50 minutes for frozen fruit). Remove foil. Bake for 30 to 45 minutes more or until filling is bubbly. Cool on a wire rack.

PER SERVING *484 cal., 19 g total fat (7 g sat. fat), 15 mg chol., 334 mg sodium, 74 g carbo., 6 g fiber, 6 g pro.*

PASTRY FOR TWO-CRUST PIE: In a large bowl stir together 2½ cups all-purpose flour and salt. Using a pastry blender, cut in ½ cup shortening and ¼ cup butter, cut up, until pieces are pea size. Sprinkle 1 tablespoon ice water over part of the flour; toss with a fork. Push moistened pastry to sides of bowl. Repeat moistening flour mixture, 1 tablespoon of ice water at time, until flour mixture is moistened (using a total ½ to ⅔ cup water). Gather flour mixture into a ball, kneading gently until it holds together. Divide pastry in half; form halves into balls.

KITCHEN TIP

Wash raspberries right before using them—not before. To wash, gently swish berries around in a bowl of cool water—do not run water over them. Drain berries on paper towels. Remove damaged berries, stems, and other debris.

Pumpkin Pie

PREP: 30 MINUTES **BAKE:** 50 MINUTES **COOL:** 1 HOUR **OVEN:** 375°F **MAKES:** 8 SERVINGS

GROW OR PURCHASE COOKING PUMPKINS—SUCH AS SUGAR, SWEET, OR PIE—TO MAKE PUMPKIN PIE FROM SCRATCH. CARVING PUMPKINS DON'T WORK IN BAKING BECAUSE THEY HAVE DULL FLAVOR AND WET, STRINGY TEXTURE.

1 recipe Pastry for Single-Crust Pie (page 164)

2 cups Pumpkin Puree (page 85) or canned pumpkin

²/₃ cup sugar

1½ teaspoons ground cinnamon

½ teaspoon ground nutmeg

¼ teaspoon ground ginger

3 eggs, lightly beaten

1 5-ounce can evaporated milk

½ cup half-and-half or light cream

Whipped cream (optional)

Ground cinnamon (optional)

1. Preheat oven to 375°F. Prepare Pastry for Single-Crust Pie. On a lightly floured surface, roll pastry from center to edges into a circle about 12 inches in diameter. Line a 9-inch pie plate with pastry. Trim pastry to ½ inch beyond edge of pie plate. Fold under extra pastry; crimp edge. Set aside.

2. For filling, in a large bowl stir together the 2 cups Pumpkin Puree, sugar, 1½ teaspoons cinnamon, nutmeg, and ginger. Using a whisk, beat in eggs, milk, and half-and-half until combined. Pour into pastry-lined pie plate. To prevent overbrowning, cover edge of pie with foil.

3. Bake for 25 minutes. Remove foil. Bake 25 to 35 minutes more or until a knife inserted near the center comes out clean. Cool on a wire rack. Cover and chill within 2 hours. If desired, top with whipped cream and sprinkle with additional cinnamon.

PER SERVING *358 cal., 17 g total fat (8 g sat. fat), 105 mg chol., 239 mg sodium, 45 g carbo., 1 g fiber, 8 g pro.*

FOR INFORMATION ON SELECTING AND STORING PUMPKINS, SEE PAGE 41.

FOR INFORMATION ON SELECTING AND STORING RHUBARB, SEE PAGE 19.

Rhubarb Hand Tarts

START TO FINISH: 2 HOURS 30 MINUTES OVEN: 375°F MAKES: 8 TARTS

FLAVOR MAGIC HAPPENS WHEN RHUBARB AND APPLES ARE COMBINED. THE SWEETNESS OF THE APPLES
MELLOWS THE RHUBARB, AND THE TARTNESS OF THE RHUBARB HELPS PERK UP THE APPLE FLAVOR.

1 cup sugar

2 tablespoons quick-cooking tapioca

1 teaspoon grated fresh ginger

Dash ground nutmeg

3 cups ½-inch slices fresh rhubarb or frozen
sliced rhubarb

1 cup sliced, peeled tart apples

2 cups all-purpose flour

½ teaspoon salt

½ cup shortening

7 to 9 tablespoons water

Milk

Coarse sugar

1. Line a large baking sheet with foil; grease foil and set aside.

2. For filling, in a large saucepan stir together sugar, tapioca, ginger, and nutmeg. Stir in rhubarb and apples until coated. Let stand about 15 minutes or until a syrup begins to form, stirring occasionally. Cook, covered, over medium heat about 15 minutes or just until fruit is softened, stirring occasionally. Remove from heat. Cool for 30 minutes.

3. Meanwhile, preheat oven to 375°F. In a large bowl combine flour and salt. Using a pastry blender, cut in shortening until pieces are pea size. Sprinkle 1 tablespoon of the water over part of the mixture; toss with a fork. Push moistened mixture to sides of bowl. Repeat, using 1 tablespoon of water at a time, until all the dough is moistened. Divide dough in half. On a lightly floured surface, roll out each portion of pastry to a 12-inch square. Cut each portion into four 6-inch squares.

4. Spoon about ¼ cup of the filling on half of each pastry square, leaving a 1-inch border around edge of pastry. Brush edges of square with water. Fold pastry over filling, forming a triangle. Gently press edges to seal. Lightly brush edges with water again. Fold edges up and over about ¼ inch. Press edges with tines of a fork to seal again.

5. Place tarts on prepared baking sheet. Prick tops 2 or 3 times with the tines of a fork for steam to escape. Pat down top to remove excess air around filling. Brush tops with milk and sprinkle with coarse sugar. Bake for 30 to 35 minutes or until golden brown. Cool on wire rack about 30 minutes; serve warm.

PER TART *344 cal., 13 g total fat (3 g sat. fat), 0 mg chol., 149 mg sodium, 54 g carbo., 2 g fiber, 3 g pro.*

FAST FLAVOR
Tart plus tart equals wonderful. Blanket Greek yogurt with this simple rhubarb jam: Chop 2 large stalks of rhubarb into ¼-inch pieces. Place in a microwave-safe bowl and sprinkle with 2 tablespoons sugar. Microwave at 50 percent power for 10 minutes. Cool and refrigerate.

Strawberry-Cornmeal Shortcakes

PREP: 30 MINUTES **BAKE:** 15 MINUTES **STAND:** 30 MINUTES **OVEN:** 425°F **MAKES:** 8 SHORTCAKES

CORNMEAL GIVES COLOR AND CRUNCH TO THESE TENDER BISCUITS TOPPED WITH LUSCIOUS ORANGE-KISSED BERRIES .

1¾ cups all-purpose flour

½ cup cornmeal

2 teaspoons baking powder

½ teaspoon salt

10 tablespoons butter, cut into small pieces

¾ to 1 cup whipping cream

2 tablespoons butter, melted

1 pound small strawberries, hulled (halve any large berries), or combination of berries

¼ cup orange marmalade

2 tablespoons finely chopped crystallized ginger

1 cup whipping cream

2 tablespoons sugar

1 teaspoon finely shredded orange peel

1. Preheat oven to 425°F. Line a baking sheet with parchment paper or foil (or lightly grease a baking sheet); set aside.

2. In a large bowl combine flour, cornmeal, baking powder, and salt. Using a pastry blender, cut in 10 tablespoons butter until mixture resembles coarse crumbs. Add ¾ cup whipping cream, stirring with a fork just until moistened. If necessary, stir in additional cream, 1 tablespoon at a time, to evenly moisten flour mixture.

3. Turn dough out onto a lightly floured surface. Knead dough by folding and gently pressing it for 4 to 6 strokes or just until dough holds together. Pat or lightly roll dough to ½-inch thickness. Cut dough with a floured 3-inch round biscuit cutter to cut out 8 shortcakes (dip cutter in flour between cuts to prevent sticking). Place shortcakes on prepared baking sheet. Brush tops with some of the 2 tablespoons melted butter. Bake for 15 to 18 minutes or until golden. Remove shortcakes from oven; brush with any remaining melted butter. Cool completely on a wire rack.

4. Meanwhile, in a medium bowl combine strawberries, orange marmalade, and ginger. Cover and let stand at room temperature for 30 to 60 minutes.

5. In a large chilled mixing bowl beat 1 cup whipping cream, sugar, and orange peel with an electric mixer on medium until soft peaks form. To serve, split cooled shortcakes in half. Spoon strawberry mixture on bottom halves. Top with whipped cream and biscuit tops.

PER SHORTCAKE *530 cal., 37 g total fat (23 g sat. fat), 118 mg chol., 355 mg sodium, 48 g carbo., 2 g fiber, 5 g pro.*

Zucchini Chocolate Cake

PREP: 20 MINUTES BAKE: 35 MINUTES OVEN: 350°F MAKES: 12 SERVINGS

GOT A GARDEN FULL OF ZUCCHINI? PUT SOME IN THIS CHOCOLATE CAKE—THE ZUCCHINI IS WHAT
MAKES IT SO MOIST AND TENDER.

2½ cups all-purpose flour

1⅓ cups sugar

⅓ cup unsweetened cocoa powder

1 **teas**poon baking soda

½ teaspoon baking powder

½ teaspoon ground cinnamon

¼ teaspoon salt

½ cup vegetable oil

½ cup milk

½ cup butter, softened

1 teaspoon vanilla

2 eggs

2 cups shredded zucchini (2 medium)

Sifted powdered sugar

1. Preheat oven to 350°F. Grease and flour a
13×9×2-inch baking pan; set aside.
2. In a large mixing bowl combine flour, sugar,
cocoa powder, baking soda, baking powder,
cinnamon, and salt. Add oil, milk, butter, and
vanilla. Beat with an electric mixer on low until
combined. Add eggs and zucchini; beat on
medium to high for 2 minutes. Spread batter
into prepared pan.
3. Bake about 35 minutes or until a toothpick
inserted in center comes out clean. Let cake
cool in the pan on a wire rack. Sprinkle with
powdered sugar.
PER SERVING *360 cal., 18 g total fat (6 g sat. fat),
56 mg chol., 242 mg sodium, 46 g carbo., 2 g fiber,
5 g pro.*
MAKE-AHEAD DIRECTIONS: Cool cake but do not
sprinkle with powdered sugar. Cover tightly and
let stand at room temperature for 24 hours or
freeze up to 1 week. Thaw at room temperature.
Sprinkle with powdered sugar before serving.

FAST FLAVOR
When garden zucchini is overly ambitious,
grate the giant vegetable torpedoes in a food
processor. Place in 1-cup bags and freeze. Use
grated zucchini all through the winter to add
body and flavor to soups and casseroles and
moistness to meat loaf.

FOR INFORMATION ON SELECTING AND STORING ZUCCHINI, SEE PAGE 22.

Butter Cake with Fresh Strawberries and Grand Marnier Glaze

PREP: 45 MINUTES BAKE: 1 HOUR 20 MINUTES COOL: 1 HOUR OVEN: 325°F MAKES: 12 TO 16 SERVINGS

EGGS ALONE GIVE LOFT TO THIS TENDER CAKE—NO LEAVENING IS NEEDED. BE SURE TO BEAT FOR A FULL MINUTE AFTER ADDING EACH EGG.

1 cup butter

6 eggs

2 cups whipping cream

3 cups sugar

3 cups cake flour

1 tablespoon vanilla

2 tablespoons finely shredded orange peel

2 teaspoons orange extract

1 recipe Grand Marnier Glaze

1 pint fresh strawberries, sliced

1. Preheat oven to 325°F. Let butter, eggs, and whipping cream stand at room temperature for 30 minutes. Grease and flour a 10-inch fluted tube pan; set aside.

2. In a large mixing bowl beat butter on medium for 30 seconds. Gradually add sugar, 2 tablespoons at a time, beating about 10 minutes or until light and fluffy. Beat for 2 minutes more. Add eggs, one at a time, beating for 1 minute after each addition. Alternately add flour and cream, beating on low after each addition just until combined. Beat in vanilla, orange peel, and orange extract. Pour batter into prepared pan; spread evenly.

3. Bake about 1 hour 20 minutes or until center springs back when lightly touched. Cool in pan on a wire rack for 15 minutes; remove from pan. Cool completely on wire rack.

4. Place cake on rack over waxed paper. Drizzle with Grand Marnier Glaze. Serve with strawberries.

GRAND MARNIER GLAZE: In a medium bowl stir together 2 cups powdered sugar and 1 tablespoon Grand Marnier, other orange liqueur, or orange juice. Whisk in enough milk (1 to 2 tablespoons) to make a glaze consistency.

PER SERVING *724 cal., 33 g total fat (20 g sat. fat), 201 mg chol., 161 mg sodium, 101 g carbo., 1 g fiber, 7 g pro.*

FAST FLAVOR
Take a tip from the Italians, who have devised perhaps the world's most wonderful way to enjoy fresh strawberries—simply halved and drizzled with a bit of high-quality balsamic vinegar.

FOR INFORMATION ON SELECTING AND STORING STRAWBERRIES, SEE PAGE 27.

Lemon and Cherry Pudding Cake

PREP: 25 MINUTES BAKE: 40 MINUTES COOL: 30 MINUTES OVEN: 350°F MAKES: 6 SERVINGS

ONE SCOOP OF THIS DELECTABLE DESSERT DELIVERS A CHUNK OF CHERRY-STUDDED CAKE IN A POOL OF SILKY-SMOOTH PUDDING SAUCE.

⅔ cup granulated sugar

¼ cup all-purpose flour

2 teaspoons finely shredded lemon peel

3 tablespoons lemon juice

2 tablespoons butter, melted

2 egg yolks

¾ cup milk

2 egg whites

2 cups fresh sweet cherries, pitted and coarsely chopped, or 1¾ cups frozen pitted sweet cherries, thawed, drained, and coarsely chopped

Powdered sugar

1. Preheat oven to 350°F. In a medium bowl combine granulated sugar and flour. Stir in lemon peel, lemon juice, and melted butter. In a small bowl combine egg yolks and milk. Add to flour mixture; stir just until combined.

2. In a medium mixing bowl beat egg whites until stiff peaks form (tips stand straight). Gently fold egg whites into lemon batter. Fold in cherries. Transfer batter to a 1½- to 2-quart baking dish. Place the dish in a large pan on an oven rack. Pour hot water into the large pan around the baking dish to a depth of 1 inch.

3. Bake for 40 to 45 minutes or until lightly browned and edges of cake spring back when lightly touched. Cool on a wire rack for 30 minutes. Serve warm sprinkled with powdered sugar or cover and chill for up to 24 hours.

PER SERVING *222 cal., 6 g total fat (3 g sat. fat), 83 mg chol., 61 mg sodium, 40 g carbo., 1 g fiber, 4 g pro.*

FAST FLAVOR

Marinate pitted cherries overnight in red wine vinegar. Bring to a simmer over medium high heat, and serve as a sauce with roast pork.

FOR INFORMATION ON SELECTING AND STORING SWEET CHERRIES, SEE PAGE 29.

FOR INFORMATION ON SELECTING AND STORING PEACHES, SEE PAGE 30.

Peach Crisp

PREP: 20 MINUTES BAKE: 30 MINUTES OVEN: 375°F MAKES: 6 SERVINGS

AUGUST IS PEAK PEACH SEASON. DON'T LET IT PASS WITHOUT MAKING THIS CLASSIC FAMILY TREAT.

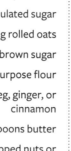

5 cups sliced, peeled fresh peaches*

2 to 4 tablespoons granulated sugar

¼ cup quick-cooking rolled oats

¼ cup packed brown sugar

2 tablespoons all-purpose flour

⅛ teaspoon ground nutmeg, ginger, or cinnamon

2 tablespoons butter

2 tablespoons finely chopped nuts or coconut

1. Preheat oven to 375°F. In a medium bowl combine peaches and granulated sugar. Divide peach mixture among six 6-ounce custard cups.** Place cups in a 15×10×1-inch baking pan.

2. For topping, in a small bowl combine oats, brown sugar, flour, and nutmeg. Using a pastry blender, cut in butter until mixture resembles coarse crumbs. Stir in nuts. Sprinkle topping over filling.

3. Bake for 30 to 35 minutes or until peaches are tender and topping is golden.

PER SERVING *187 cal., 6 g total fat (3 g sat. fat), 10 mg chol., 31 mg sodium, 32 g carbo., 3 g fiber, 3 g pro.*

*TIP: If fresh peaches are unavailable, substitute 5 cups frozen unsweetened sliced peaches for fresh peaches. Thaw peaches; do not drain. Combine the undrained peaches and granulated sugar. Continue as above.

**TIP: If desired, place peach mixture in a 2-quart square baking dish. Double the topping and sprinkle over the filling. Bake as above.

KITCHEN TIP

To make quick work of peeling peaches, cut a small X in the bottom of each fruit. Drop peaches in boiling water for 30 seconds; remove with a slotted spoon. Cool peaches in cold water. The peels will slip off with your fingers.

Rhubarb Surprise Crisp

PREP: 20 MINUTES BAKE: 30 MINUTES OVEN: 375°F MAKES: 6 SERVINGS

THE SURPRISE IN THIS DELICIOUS CRISP IS A TOUCH OF FRESH BASIL, WHICH IMPARTS ITS EXTRAORDINARY TASTE AND SCENT TO THE FRUIT MIXTURE.

⅔ cup granulated sugar

2 or 3 teaspoons cornstarch

¼ teaspoon ground cinnamon

2 cups sliced fresh rhubarb or frozen unsweetened sliced rhubarb, thawed

2 cups coarsely chopped strawberries

2 tablespoons snipped fresh basil

½ cup all-purpose flour

½ cup quick-cooking rolled oats

⅓ cup packed brown sugar

¼ teaspoon salt

3 tablespoons butter, melted

Fresh mint (optional)

1. Preheat oven to 375°F. In a medium bowl stir together granulated sugar, cornstarch, and cinnamon. (For fresh rhubarb, use 2 teaspoons cornstarch. For frozen, use 3 teaspoons cornstarch.) Stir in rhubarb, strawberries, and basil. Transfer fruit mixture to a 2-quart square baking dish; spread evenly. Set aside.

2. For topping, in another medium bowl stir together flour, oats, brown sugar, and salt. Stir in melted butter. Sprinkle topping evenly onto fruit.

3. Bake for 30 to 35 minutes or until fruit is tender and topping is golden brown. If desired, garnish with mint. Serve warm.

PER SERVING *276 cal., 7 g total fat (4 g sat. fat), 16 mg chol., 167 mg sodium, 52 g carbo., 3 g fiber, 3 g pro.*

FOR INFORMATION ON SELECTING AND STORING RHUBARB, SEE PAGE 19; FOR INFORMATION ON STRAWBERRIES, SEE PAGE 27.

Baked Pears with Maple-Orange Sauce

PREP: 10 MINUTES BAKE: 40 MINUTES COOK: 10 MINUTES OVEN: 425°F MAKES: 6 SERVINGS

SERVE ELEGANT BAKED PEARS TO COMPLETE A RICH DINNER IN A LIGHT, PALATE-CLEANSING WAY.

6 Bosc pears

3 tablespoons butter, melted

2 tablespoons sugar

¾ cup pure maple syrup

2 tablespoons Grand Marnier or other orange-flavor liqueur

½ cup heavy cream

1. Preheat oven to 425°F. Peel pears; cut in half lengthwise. Using melon baller or small spoon, scoop out seeds. Place pear halves, cut sides down, in a 15×10×1-inch baking pan. Brush pears with half the melted butter. Sprinkle with sugar. Brush again with the melted butter.

2. Bake pears for 15 minutes. Brush pears again with melted butter and with any juices that have collected in pan. Bake for 15 minutes more. Turn pears cut sides up. Baste again with butter and juices. Bake for 10 minutes.

3. Meanwhile, for sauce, in a small saucepan combine maple syrup and Grand Marnier. Bring to simmering over medium-low heat. Cook about 10 minutes or until reduced to ½ cup. Remove saucepan from heat. Stir in heavy cream.

4. To serve, arrange 2 pear halves on each plate. Pour some of the sauce on each serving.

PER SERVING *350 cal., 13 g total fat (8 g sat. fat), 43 mg chol., 53 mg sodium, 59 g carbo., 1 g pro.*

FAST FLAVOR
Brush cut sides of cored and peeled pear halves with butter. Grill over medium heat for about 5 minutes, basting with butter once or twice. Drizzle with pure maple syrup and fresh cream.

FOR INFORMATION ON SELECTING AND STORING PEARS, SEE PAGE 43.

FOR INFORMATION ON SELECTING AND STORING SCALLIONS, SEE PAGE 17.

Cornmeal Pie with Scallions and Feta

PREP: 10 MINUTES   BAKE: 45 MINUTES   STAND: 15 MINUTES
OVEN: 400°F   MAKES: 6 MAIN-DISH SERVINGS

FOR A MAIN COURSE, TEAM WITH A GREEN SALAD OR JUICY RIPE TOMATOES, SLICED AND SEASONED
WITH COARSELY GROUND BLACK PEPPER AND A DRIZZLE OF OLIVE OIL. OR CUT THE PIE INTO WEDGES
TO ACCOMPANY SAVORY SOUPS OR STEWS.

4 eggs, lightly beaten

1½ cups yellow cornmeal

12 ounces small-curd cottage cheese

1 cup chopped scallions (about 8)

¼ cup butter, melted

2 teaspoons snipped fresh thyme

¼ teaspoon salt

4 ounces feta cheese, crumbled

1. Preheat oven to 400°F. Grease a 9-inch pie plate; set aside.
2. In medium bowl stir together eggs, cornmeal, cottage cheese, scallions, melted butter, thyme, and salt. Pour into prepared pie plate; spreading evenly. Sprinkle feta cheese over the top.
3. Bake about 45 minutes or until golden brown and slightly puffed. Transfer to a wire rack; let stand for 15 minutes. Serve warm.
PER SERVING *364 cal., 19 g total fat (11 g sat. fat), 189 mg chol., 584 mg sodium, 31 g carbo., 3 g fiber, 17 g pro.*

Scallion Buttermilk Biscuits

PREP: 20 MINUTES   BAKE: 12 MINUTES   OVEN: 450°F   MAKES: 8 BISCUITS

SHAKE THE BUTTERMILK CONTAINER VIGOROUSLY BEFORE MEASURING. ITS THICKEST, MOST FLAVORFUL LIQUID SETTLES TO THE BOTTOM.

2 cups all-purpose flour

2 teaspoons baking powder

½ teaspoon baking soda

½ teaspoon salt

⅓ cup shortening

¾ cup buttermilk

⅓ cup chopped scallions

⅛ teaspoon cayenne pepper

1. Preheat oven to 450°F. In a large bowl combine flour, baking powder, baking soda, and salt. Using a pastry blender, cut in shortening until mixture resembles coarse crumbs. Make a well in the center of the flour mixture.

2. In a small bowl whisk together buttermilk, scallions, and cayenne pepper. Add buttermilk mixture all at once to flour mixture. Using a fork, stir just until mixture is moistened.

3. Turn dough out onto a lightly floured surface. Knead dough by folding and gently pressing it for four to six strokes or just until dough holds together. Pat or lightly roll dough into an 8×6-inch rectangle about ½ inch thick.

4. Cut dough into eight 3×2-inch rectangles. Place dough rectangles 1½ inches apart on an ungreased baking sheet.

5. Bake for 12 to 15 minutes or until biscuits are puffy and slightly browned on top. Transfer biscuits to wire rack and cool slightly. Serve warm.

PER BISCUIT *200 cal., 9 g total fat (2 g sat. fat), 1 mg chol., 345 mg sodium, 25 g carbo., 1 g fiber, 4 g pro.*

FAST FLAVOR

Scallions have many attributes. One of the best is that they are nearly waste-free, allowing you to use one or two and have no leftover onion to wrap and store. Whenever you need a small bit of onion, call on scallions.

FOR INFORMATION ON SELECTING AND STORING SCALLIONS, SEE PAGE 17.

Leek and Chive Bread

PREP: 15 MINUTES **RISE:** 1 HOUR 45 MINUTES **BAKE:** 15 MINUTES **OVEN:** 375°F
MAKES: 4 LOAVES (16 SERVINGS)

FRESH CHIVES, SCALLIONS, LEEKS, AND PARSLEY CELEBRATE SPRING.

4 to 4½ cups all-purpose flour

1 package active dry yeast

1 cup milk

3 tablespoons sugar

2 tablespoons butter

½ teaspoon salt

2 eggs, lightly beaten

1 cup shredded Asiago or Parmesan cheese
(4 ounces)

2 tablespoons snipped fresh chives

1 egg white, lightly beaten

1 tablespoon water

1 whole scallion

1 leek, thinly sliced (white part only)

Fresh chives

Italian parsley sprigs

1 tablespoon olive oil

1. In a large mixing bowl stir together 2 cups of the flour and the yeast; set aside.

2. In a medium saucepan heat and stir milk, sugar, butter, and salt just until warm (120°F to 130°F) and butter almost melts. Add milk mixture and 2 eggs to the flour mixture. Beat with mixer on low to medium for 30 seconds, scraping sides of bowl constantly. Beat on high for 3 minutes. Stir in cheese, 2 tablespoons chives, and as much of the remaining flour as you can.

3. Turn dough out onto a lightly floured surface. Knead in enough remaining flour to make a moderately stiff dough that is smooth and elastic (6 to 8 minutes total). Shape dough in a ball. Place in a lightly greased bowl; turn to grease dough. Cover; let rise in a warm place 1 hour or until double in size.

4. Punch dough down. Turn out onto a lightly floured surface; divide into 4 portions. Cover; let rest 10 minutes. Grease 2 baking sheets.

5. Shape dough by gently pulling each portion of dough into a 10×4½ rectangle. Place on prepared baking sheets. In a small bowl stir together egg white and water. Brush loaves with egg white mixture. On loaves press the green onion, leek, chives, or parsley. Gently brush herbs with olive oil to stay moist. Cover and let rise in a warm place until nearly double in size (about 45 minutes).

6. Preheat oven to 375°F. Bake 15 to 18 minutes or until golden. (If necessary, loosely cover with foil the last 5 minutes of baking to prevent overbrowning.) Remove from baking sheets; cool on wire racks.

PER SERVING *193 cal., 6 g total fat (3 g sat. fat), 39 mg chol., 174 mg sodium, 28 g carbo., 1 g fiber, 7 g pro.*

MAKE-AHEAD DIRECTIONS

Prepare the bread as directed; cool completely. Place bread in a freezer container or bag and freeze for up to 1 month. Before serving, let thaw at room temperature.

Scallion and Cheddar Popovers

PREP: 10 MINUTES BAKE: 30 MINUTES OVEN: 450°F/350°F MAKES: 8 POPOVERS

STEAMING POPOVERS WILL MAKE THE SIMPLEST DINNERS SPECIAL. SERVE THEM WARM SO BUTTER MELTS INTO THE HOLLOW CAVITIES.

Nonstick cooking spray

1 cup all-purpose flour

½ teaspoon salt

2 eggs

1 cup milk

1 cup shredded sharp cheddar cheese (4 ounces)

3 scallions, chopped

1. Preheat oven to 450°F. Coat 8 cups of a popover pan or eight 2½-inch muffin cups with nonstick cooking spray. Fill any empty cups with ½ inch of water to prevent pan from burning.

2. In a medium bowl whisk together flour and salt. In a second bowl whisk together eggs and milk. Add egg mixture to flour mixture; stir just until mixed. Stir in cheese and scallions. Fill prepared cups about three-fourths full (about ⅓ cup batter in each).

3. Bake for 15 minutes. Reduce oven temperature to 350°F; bake for 10 to 15 minutes more or until browned and puffed. Do not open oven door until end of baking time or popovers will collapse.

4. Remove popovers from oven and immediately remove from pan. Pierce sides once with a knife to release steam. Serve warm. If necessary, reheat popovers at 350°F for 5 minutes to crisp outside edges.

PER POPOVER *149 cal., 7 g total fat (4 g sat. fat), 70 mg chol., 264 mg sodium, 14 g carbo., 1 g fiber, 8 g pro.*

KITCHEN TIP

To clean and trim scallions, cut off the top of the green stem and a little bit off the root end. Pull off any slimy leaves at the root end and rinse in cold water. Dry thoroughly before using.

FOR INFORMATION ON SELECTING AND STORING SCALLIONS, SEE PAGE 17.

Roasted

MEAT, VEGETABLE & FRUIT ENTRÉES & SIDES

Within the cozy confines of a toasty oven, fruits and vegetables—often side by side with meats—benefit from high, dry heat to tenderize juicy roots, tubers, florets, stalks, and fruits with rich, caramelized flavor.

Proscuitto-Wrapped Roasted Asparagus

PREP: 20 MINUTES   ROAST: 17 MINUTES   OVEN: 425F°   MAKES: 4 TO 6 APPETIZER SERVINGS

ROASTING HEIGHTENS THE SWEET, SLIGHTLY NUTTY FLAVOR OF ASPARAGUS. DRESS IT UP IN PROSCIUTTO AND YOU HAVE AN APPETIZER THAT'S ELEGANT AND IMPRESSIVE YET SIMPLE TO PREPARE.

1½ pounds medium to large asparagus (about 24 spears)

1 tablespoon olive oil

⅛ teaspoon salt

⅛ teaspoon freshly ground black pepper

3 tablespoons balsamic vinegar

3 ounces thinly sliced prosciutto, cut into ½- to 1-inch wide strips

1. Preheat oven to 425°F. Snap off and discard woody bases from asparagus; rinse. If desired, scrape off scales. Place asparagus in a 15×10×1-inch baking pan. Drizzle with oil and sprinkle with salt and pepper; toss to coat.

2. Roast for 8 minutes, stirring once. Sprinkle vinegar over asparagus; roast for 4 to 5 minutes more or until crisp-tender, stirring once. Cool in pan on a wire rack until cool enough to handle.

3. Wrap 1 or 2 strips of prosciutto around each set of 2 of the roasted asparagus spears. Place bundles on the baking pan. Roast for 5 to 6 minutes more or until prosciutto is lightly browned and starting to look crisp. Arrange on serving platter.

PER SERVING *100 cal., 6 g total fat (2 g sat. fat), 27 mg chol., 715 mg sodium, 3 g carbo., 1 g fiber, 11 g pro.*

FAST FLAVOR
When you have leftover fat from cooking bacon, save a tablespoon or two to sauté asparagus spears.

FOR INFORMATION ON SELECTING AND STORING ASPARAGUS, SEE PAGE 18.

Beef Rib Roast with Port-Glazed Potatoes and Pearl Onions

PREP: 25 MINUTES ROAST: 1 HOUR 55 MINUTES STAND: 15 MINUTES OVEN: 325°F
MAKES: 12 TO 16 MAIN-DISH SERVINGS

PORT WINE AND HONEY COMBINE TO MAKE A GLORIOUSLY STICKY AND SWEET GLAZE THAT MEETS ITS PERFECT MATCH IN CREAMY, PIQUANT BLUE CHEESE.

1 4- to 6-pound beef rib roast

6 cloves garlic, quartered

2 teaspoons kosher salt

1 teaspoon coarsely ground black pepper

2 pounds tiny Yukon gold, fingerling, or new potatoes, halved

10 ounces pearl onions, peeled

1 cup port

1 tablespoon honey

2 ounces blue cheese, crumbled

1 teaspoon snipped fresh thyme

1. Preheat oven to 325°F. Using a paring knife, cut small evenly spaced slits into the meat. Insert garlic quarters into slits in meat. Sprinkle meat with salt and pepper.

2. Place meat, fat side up, in a 15×10×1-inch baking pan. Insert an oven-going meat thermometer into center of roast; thermometer should not touch bone. Roast, uncovered, for 1¾ to 2¼ hours or until meat thermometer registers 135°F for medium rare or for 2¼ to 2¾ hours or until 150°F for medium, adding potatoes and onions to the roasting pan the last hour of roasting time. Remove meat from pan. Drain and discard pan juices. Cover meat with foil and let stand for 15 minutes before carving. Meat temperature after standing should be 145°F for medium rare or 160°F for medium.

3. Meanwhile, for glaze, in a small saucepan bring port and honey to boiling. Reduce heat and simmer, uncovered, about 15 minutes or until reduced to ⅓ cup.

4. Drizzle potatoes and onions in pan with port glaze and return to oven for 10 to 15 minutes or until glazed, stirring occasionally. Sprinkle with blue cheese and thyme. Serve potatoes and onions with beef.

PER SERVING *443 cal., 25 g total fat (11 g sat. fat), 73 mg chol., 477 mg sodium, 20 g carbo., 2 g fiber, 26 g pro.*

KITCHEN TIP
For tearless peeling, cut off the tip of the onion opposite the root end with a paring knife. Cook in boiling water 2 minutes. Drain. Let stand until cool enough to handle. Squeeze the onion gently at root end. The onion will slip right out of its skin! Slice off remaining roots.

FOR INFORMATION ON SELECTING AND STORING POTATOES, SEE PAGE 38; FOR INFORMATION ON ONIONS, SEE PAGE 39.

Roasted Pork with Fennel and Mushrooms

PREP: 30 MINUTES CHILL: 1 HOUR ROAST: 1 HOUR STAND: 15 MINUTES OVEN: 400°F
MAKES: 7 TO 8 MAIN-DISH SERVINGS

FENNEL IS QUICKLY TAKING ITS PLACE AS COOKS LEARN TO LOVE ITS HINT-OF-LICORICE TASTE. ROASTING IT
MELLOWS THE FLAVOR AND GIVES IT AN ALMOST BUTTERY TEXTURE SIMILAR TO ROASTED ONIONS.

1 teaspoon coriander seeds

1 teaspoon fennel seeds

1 teaspoon cumin seeds

1½ teaspoons kosher salt

2 cloves garlic, cut up

5 tablespoons olive oil

1 3- to 3½-pound pork loin center rib roast

4 or 5 bulbs fennel, trimmed (reserve tops),
cored, and cut into 6 wedges each

8 ounces assorted fresh mushrooms, such as
stemmed shiitake, cremini, stemmed oyster, or
button, sliced

1 cup dry white wine

1 tablespoon chopped fennel tops

½ teaspoon freshly ground black pepper

1. Preheat oven to 400°F. In a spice grinder combine coriander seeds, fennel seeds, cumin seeds, and ½ teaspoon of the salt. Process until finely ground. Add garlic; process until mixture is a thick paste. Transfer spice mixture to a small bowl; stir in 2 tablespoons of the olive oil. Trim fat from the roast. Rub spice mixture onto pork roast. Cover loosely and chill for 1 hour.

2. In a large roasting pan toss together fennel wedges, mushrooms, wine, the remaining 3 tablespoons olive oil, and ½ teaspoon salt. Place the pork roast, bone side down, on top of the vegetable mixture in pan. Insert an oven-going meat thermometer into center of roast.

3. Roast, uncovered, for 1 to 1¼ hours or until meat thermometer registers 150°F. Transfer roast to a cutting board; cover with foil and let stand for 15 minutes. The temperature of the meat after standing should be 160°F.

4. Meanwhile, in a small bowl combine fennel tops, pepper, and the remaining ½ teaspoon salt. Sprinkle over roast. To serve, slice the roast between the bones and serve with vegetables. Spoon cooking juices from pan over pork and vegetables.

PER SERVING *441 cal., 19 g total fat (4 g sat. fat), 109 mg chol., 466 mg sodium, 16 g carbo., 5 g fiber, 45 g pro.*

FAST FLAVOR
The anise flavor of fennel is delicious with citrus. Try tossing thin slivers of fennel bulb with segments of oranges or grapefruit, snipped fresh basil, a drizzle of extra virgin olive oil, and a little bit of salt and pepper for a fresh salad that will brighten a winter or fall meal.

FOR INFORMATION ON SELECTING AND STORING FENNEL, SEE PAGE 36.

FOR INFORMATION ON SELECTING AND STORING SWEET CORN, SEE PAGE 25.

Pork Chops with Roasted Corn Salsa

PREP: 30 MINUTES MARINATE: 3 HOURS ROAST: 35 MINUTES OVEN: 375°F
MAKES: 8 MAIN-DISH SERVINGS

WHEN REMOVING PEEL FROM THE ORANGE, SHRED ONLY THE BRIGHT ORANGE SURFACE. THE PITHY
WHITE MEMBRANE BENEATH THE PEEL MAY ADD BITTERNESS TO THESE CITRUSY CHOPS.

8 boneless pork loin chops,
cut 1¼ inches thick

½ cup olive oil

1 tablespoon finely shredded orange peel

½ cup orange juice

2 tablespoons lime juice

1 small dried hot pepper, broken

6 cloves garlic, crushed and peeled

2 teaspoons salt

1 recipe Roasted Corn Salsa

1. Trim fat from chops; place chops in a large resealable plastic bag. For marinade, in a small bowl combine olive oil, orange peel, orange juice, lime juice, dried pepper, garlic, and salt. Pour marinade over chops in bag; seal bag. Turn to coat chops. Marinate in the refrigerator for 3 to 6 hours.

2. Preheat oven to 375°F. Drain chops. Place chops on rack in a shallow roasting pan. Roast for 35 to 45 minutes or until chops are 160°F and juices run clear. Serve chops with Roasted Corn Salsa.

PER SERVING *363 cal., 23 g total fat (5 g sat. fat), 52 mg chol., 989 mg sodium, 20 g carbo., 22 g pro.*

ROASTED CORN SALSA: Preheat oven to 425°F. Place 1 small onion, halved; 1 whole fresh serrano or other hot chile pepper (see tip, page 51); and 2 unpeeled cloves garlic on a square of heavy foil. Drizzle with 1 tablespoon olive oil. Bring up opposite sides of foil; seal with a double fold. Fold remaining edges to enclose, leaving room for steam to build. Roast packet for 20 minutes. Meanwhile, cut kernels from 6 ears of fresh sweet corn (3 cups). Spread corn in a shallow roasting pan. Add corn to oven. Roast packet and corn for 15 to 20 minutes more or until vegetables are tender and corn starts to brown. Carefully open packet; cool. Peel garlic; chop onion and chile pepper. In a medium bowl combine the corn; onion; garlic; chile pepper; any oil remaining in packet; 1 cup chopped, seeded tomatoes (2 medium); 2 tablespoons lime juice; and 1½ teaspoons salt. Transfer 1 cup of corn mixture to a blender. Cover and blend until coarsely chopped; return to salsa.

KITCHEN TIP

To butter corn on the cob, thickly butter a slice of sandwich bread. Hold the bread in one hand and roll the hot ear of corn over the buttered bread, coating the corn evenly with butter.

Plum and Rosemary Pork Roast

PREP: 35 MINUTES   ROAST: 40 MINUTES   STAND: 15 MINUTES   OVEN: 300°F   MAKES: 6 MAIN-DISH SERVINGS

SWEET FORTIFIED PORT WINES ARE AVAILABLE IN FOUR CATEGORIES—VINTAGE PORT, TAWNY PORT, RUBY PORT, AND WHITE PORT. FOR COOKING, CHOOSE TAWNY OR RUBY PORT; RESERVE VINTAGE AND WHITE PORTS FOR SIPPING.

1 2-pound boneless pork top loin roast (single loin)

Kosher salt

Freshly ground black pepper

1 tablespoon olive oil

½ cup chopped onion (1 medium)

½ cup chopped carrot (1 medium)

2 tablespoons snipped fresh rosemary

2 cloves garlic, minced

1½ cups port wine

¼ cup reduced-sodium chicken broth

6 fresh plums, pitted and quartered

Fresh rosemary sprigs (optional)

1. Preheat oven to 300°F. Sprinkle meat with kosher salt and pepper. In a 4- to 5-quart oven-going Dutch oven heat oil over medium heat. Add meat; cook for 5 to 8 minutes or until brown, turning to brown evenly on all sides. Remove meat from Dutch oven; set aside.

2. Add onion and carrot to Dutch oven. Cook about 5 minutes or until onion is golden, stirring frequently. Stir in 2 tablespoons snipped rosemary and garlic; cook and stir for 1 minute more. Add port wine and broth. Return meat to the Dutch oven. Heat just until boiling.

3. Roast, covered, for 20 minutes. Add plums to Dutch oven. Roast, covered, for 20 to 25 minutes more or until internal temperature of meat registers 150°F on an instant-read thermometer.

4. Transfer meat to a cutting board; cover with foil and let stand for 15 minutes. Meat temperature after standing should be 160°F.

5. Meanwhile, using a slotted spoon, transfer plums to a serving platter. For sauce, place Dutch oven over medium-high heat on the rangetop. Reduce heat; boil gently, uncovered, about 10 minutes or until sauce is reduced to about ¾ cup.

6. To serve, thinly slice meat. Arrange meat slices on platter with plums. Serve with sauce. If desired, garnish with fresh rosemary sprigs.

PER SERVING *367 cal., 10 g total fat (3 g sat. fat), 83 mg chol., 249 mg sodium, 19 g carbo., 2 g fiber, 34 g pro.*

FAST FLAVOR

Create a plum dessert in minutes by combining sliced plums with vanilla yogurt and crushed amaretti cookies.

FOR INFORMATION ON SELECTING AND STORING PLUMS, SEE PAGE 31.

Roast Pork Loin with Red Cabbage, Apples, and Onions

PREP: 25 MINUTES   ROAST: 1 HOUR 20 MINUTES   STAND: 15 MINUTES   OVEN: 450°F/400°F
MAKES: 6 MAIN-DISH SERVINGS

THIS CRUMB-CRUSTED PORK LOIN, ACCOMPANIED BY CABBAGE, APPLES, AND ONIONS, IS THE QUINTESSENTIAL AUTUMN MEAL.

2½ pounds red and yellow onions, cut into ½-inch wedges

½ of a head red cabbage, cut into wedges

10 garlic cloves

3 tablespoons olive oil

Salt

5 slices white bread, torn into pieces

2 tablespoons coarsely chopped fresh sage

Black pepper

1 3-pound pork center loin roast

¼ cup Dijon-style mustard

2 pounds apples (Granny Smith, Rome, or Empire), halved, cored, and halves cut into thirds

1 tablespoon cider vinegar

Fresh sage leaves (optional)

1. In a large roasting pan toss together onion wedges, cabbage, 6 of the garlic cloves, and 2 tablespoons of the olive oil; sprinkle with salt.

2. Peel and coarsely chop the remaining 4 cloves garlic. In a food processor or blender combine chopped garlic, the bread, and chopped sage. Cover and process or blend until crumbs form. Season with salt and pepper. Set crumb mixture aside.

3. Preheat oven to 450°F. Sprinkle pork with salt and pepper. In a large skillet heat the remaining 1 tablespoon olive oil over medium-high heat. Add pork to skillet; cook about 5 minutes or until brown on all sides. Place pork, fat side up, in the center of roasting pan on onion mixture; spread mustard on top of pork. Sprinkle bread crumb mixture on mustard, pressing to adhere. Insert an oven-going meat thermometer into center of roast.

4. Roast for 20 minutes. Reduce oven temperature to 400°F. Add apples to pan; roast for 1 to 1¼ hours more or until thermometer registers 155°F, covering loosely with foil if crumbs begin to brown too quickly.

5. Remove pork from pan. Cover with foil; let stand for 15 minutes before carving. (Meat temperature after standing should be 160°F.)

6. Meanwhile, drizzle vegetables with vinegar. Season with salt and pepper, and, if desired, additional vinegar. Cut pork into ½-inch slices. Serve pork slices on onion mixture. If desired, garnish with fresh sage leaves.

PER SERVING *775 cal., 38 g total fat (11 g sat. fat), 153 mg chol., 533 mg sodium, 57 g carbo., 9 g fiber, 53 g pro.*

KITCHEN TIP

Apple corers have not kept up with the ever-growing size of American apples, so leave the tool in the drawer. Instead, place the apple on a cutting board and slice quarters away from the core with a sharp knife.

FOR INFORMATION ON SELECTING AND STORING CABBAGE, SEE PAGE 35; FOR INFORMATION ON APPLES, SEE PAGE 42; FOR INFORMATION ON ONIONS, SEE PAGE 39.

Herb-Crusted Rack of Lamb with Roasted Radishes and Orange Vinaigrette

PREP: 25 MINUTES   ROAST: 45 MINUTES   STAND: 15 MINUTES   OVEN: 325°F   MAKES: 6 MAIN-DISH SERVINGS

SOMETHING QUITE UNEXPECTED HAPPENS TO RADISHES WHEN THEY ARE ROASTED—THEY BECOME SWEET, SUCCULENT, AND MELLOW. THEY ARE A FINE ACCOMPANIMENT TO ROASTED MEATS.

2 1- to 1½-pound lamb rib roasts (6 to 8 ribs each)

½ teaspoon salt

3 tablespoons Dijon-style mustard

2 tablespoons snipped fresh Italian parsley

1 tablespoon snipped fresh oregano

2 teaspoons snipped fresh thyme

2 cloves garlic, minced

½ teaspoon cracked black pepper

1½ pounds radishes, washed, trimmed, and halved

3 tablespoons olive oil

1 tablespoon sherry vinegar or white wine vinegar

½ teaspoon finely shredded orange peel

1 tablespoon orange juice

1 teaspoon honey

1. Preheat oven to 325°F. Trim fat from meat. Sprinkle meat with salt. Brush meat with mustard. In a small bowl combine parsley, oregano, thyme, garlic, and pepper. Sprinkle onto meat and press to adhere.

2. Place meat on a rack in a shallow roasting pan, arranging roasts to stand upright. Insert an oven-going meat thermometer into one of the roasts; thermometer should not touch the bone. Drizzle radishes with 1 tablespoon of the olive oil and place around roasts in roasting pan. Roast, uncovered, for 45 to 60 minutes or until meat thermometer registers 135°F for medium rare. Cover with foil; let stand for 15 minutes. Temperature of meat after standing should be 145°F. (For medium, roast for 1 to 1½ hours or until thermometer registers 150°F. Cover; let stand for 15 minutes. Temperature of meat after standing should be 160°F.) To carve, slice between ribs.

3. In a small screw-top jar combine the remaining 2 tablespoons olive oil, sherry vinegar, orange peel, orange juice, and honey. Cover and shake well to combine. Season with salt and pepper. Drizzle vinaigrette over roasted radishes and serve with lamb.

PER SERVING *451 cal., 40 g total fat (15 g sat. fat), 79 mg chol., 470 mg sodium, 5 g carbo., 2 g fiber, 17 g pro.*

KITCHEN TIP

Radish bulbs keep much longer in cold storage than their green tops, which can become slimy and unappealing in a matter of days. If you're not going to use a bunch of radishes right away, cut off the tops and discard them. Scrub the radish bulbs under cold running water, pat dry, and store them in a sealed container in the crisper drawer of the refrigerator.

FOR INFORMATION ON SELECTING AND STORING RADISHES, SEE PAGE 16.

FOR INFORMATION ON SELECTING AND STORING APPLES, SEE PAGE 42.

Apple-Glazed Roast Chicken

PREP: 30 MINUTES   ROAST: 2 HOURS 15 MINUTES   OVEN: 325°F   MAKES: 6 MAIN-DISH SERVINGS

FOR THE JUICIEST, EASY-TO-CARVE CHICKEN, LET THE BIRD STAND, TENTED WITH FOIL, FOR 10 MINUTES AFTER TAKING IT OUT OF THE OVEN.

1 cup apple cider vinegar

1 cup apple jelly

1 teaspoon apple pie spice

1 5-pound whole roasting chicken

Salt

1 6-ounce package long grain and wild rice mix

2¼ cups water

1 tablespoon butter

6 small baking apples, cored (with stems intact, if desired)

½ teaspoon freshly ground black pepper

3 scallions, thinly sliced

Sage leaves (optional)

1. For glaze, in a 1½- to 2-quart saucepan stir together vinegar and jelly. Heat and stir over medium heat until boiling. Boil glaze gently, uncovered, about 20 minutes or until syrupy and reduced to about 1 cup, stirring frequently. Remove from heat. Stir in apple pie spice. Divide glaze in half and set aside. (Glaze will thicken as it stands; stir before brushing over chicken and apples.)

2. Preheat oven to 325°F. Skewer neck skin to back; tie legs to tail. Twist wing tips under back. Place chicken, breast side up, on a rack in a shallow roasting pan. Sprinkle with salt. (If desired, insert meat thermometer into center of inside thigh muscle; thermometer should not touch bone.) Roast, uncovered, for 1¼ hours. Cut string.

3. Meanwhile, in a 1-quart casserole combine rice and seasoning mix, water, and butter; cover. Add apples to roasting pan around chicken. Stir one portion of the glaze; brush some on chicken and apples. Sprinkle with pepper. Roast chicken and rice for 1 to 1¼ hours more or until drumsticks move easily in sockets and chicken is no longer pink (180°F), brushing with remaining glaze portion twice. Stir scallions into rice. Place chicken and apples on a serving platter; cover with foil.

4. For sauce, skim fat from pan juices in the roasting pan and discard. Pour remaining glaze portion into the juices in roasting pan. Place roasting pan on burner over medium heat. Cook and stir, scraping up browned bits in bottom of pan. If desired, strain sauce. Season to taste with salt and freshly ground pepper. Serve chicken, apples, and rice mixture with sauce. If desired, garnish with fresh sage.

PER SERVING *885 cal., 25 g total fat (8 g sat. fat), 331 mg chol., 1,041 mg sodium, 81 g carbo., 5 g fiber, 87 g pro.*

Roasted Chicken with 20 Cloves of Garlic

PREP: 15 MINUTES   ROAST: 1 HOUR 10 MINUTES   OVEN: 375°F/450°F   MAKES: 6 MAIN-DISH SERVINGS

THIS DISH WILL SURPRISE YOU WITH ITS SWEET, EXCEPTIONALLY SOFT, AND SUBTLE FLAVOR—NOT AT ALL WHAT ONE WOULD EXPECT FROM 20 CLOVES OF GARLIC. THE FLAVOR OF THIS "STINKING ROSE" MELLOWS SIGNIFICANTLY WHEN IT'S ROASTED.

1 3½- to 4-pound chicken

1 small onion, peeled and cut in half

1 small lemon, cut in half

2 teaspoons olive oil

1½ teaspoons snipped fresh rosemary

1 teaspoon snipped fresh thyme

1 teaspoon black pepper

20 cloves garlic, unpeeled (from 2 whole heads)

1 14-ounce can chicken broth

¾ cup dry white wine

2 tablespoons snipped fresh parsley

½ teaspoon salt

1. Preheat oven to 375°F. Rinse chicken body cavity; pat dry with paper towels. Place onion and lemon in cavity of chicken. Skewer neck skin to back. Tie legs to tail. Twist wing tips under back. In a small bowl stir together olive oil, rosemary, thyme, and pepper. Brush oil mixture over chicken.

2. Place chicken, breast side up, in an oven-going Dutch oven. (If desired, insert meat thermometer into center of inside thigh muscle; thermometer should not touch bone.) Sprinkle garlic around chicken. Add broth and white wine. Bring to boiling over high heat.

3. Transfer Dutch oven to oven. Roast, covered, for 25 minutes. Increase oven temperature to 450°F. Uncover; bake about 45 minutes more or until drumsticks move easily in sockets and chicken is no longer pink (180°F). Transfer chicken and garlic to platter. Cover with foil; let stand for 10 minutes.

4. Meanwhile, skim as much fat as possible from cooking liquid. Squeeze out 6 cloves cooked garlic into a small bowl. Mash to a paste; stir in a few tablespoons of the cooking liquid. Whisk garlic mixture into cooking liquid in Dutch oven. Stir in parsley and salt. Serve broth and the remaining garlic cloves with chicken. To eat garlic, gently press with a fork to squeeze pulp from skin.

PER SERVING *344 cal., 20 g total fat (5 g sat. fat), 112 mg chol., 574 mg sodium, 4 g carbo., 0 g fiber, 35 g pro.*

FOR INFORMATION ON SELECTING AND STORING GARLIC, SEE PAGE 39.

Quinoa with Roasted Beets and Chive Vinaigrette

PREP: 20 MINUTES ROAST: 40 MINUTES STAND: 15 MINUTES COOK: 15 MINUTES OVEN: 400°F

MAKES: 6 SIDE-DISH SERVINGS

QUINOA [KEEN-WAH] IS A TINY GRAIN THAT PACKS A HUGE PROTEIN PUNCH. OF ALL THE GRAINS, IT CONTAINS THE HIGHEST LEVEL OF PROTEIN AND ALL THE ESSENTIAL AMINO ACIDS. IT IS MILD AND TASTES MUCH LIKE COUSCOUS.

1½ pounds baby beets

4 cloves garlic, peeled

4 tablespoons olive oil

¼ teaspoon salt

¼ teaspoon black pepper

1½ cups quinoa, rinsed and drained

3 cups water

¼ teaspoon salt

3 tablespoons white balsamic or white wine vinegar

1 tablespoon snipped fresh chives

1 teaspoon Dijon-style mustard

¾ cup crumbled ricotta salata or feta cheese

⅓ cup chopped walnuts, toasted

1 medium shallot, thinly sliced

Snipped fresh chives

1. Preheat oven to 400°F. Cut tops off beets and trim root ends. Halve or quarter beets. Place beets and garlic in a 15×10×1-inch baking pan. Drizzle with 1 tablespoon of the olive oil and sprinkle with salt and pepper; toss to coat. Cover with foil.

2. Roast for 40 to 45 minutes or until tender. Let stand, covered, for 15 minutes. To remove skins, wrap beets, one at a time, in a paper towel and gently rub to remove skins. (If skins are very tender, you do not need to remove them). Mash garlic and set aside.

3. Meanwhile, in a medium saucepan combine quinoa, the water, and salt. Bring to boiling; reduce heat. Simmer, covered, about 15 minutes or until liquid is absorbed.

4. For vinaigrette, in a screw-top jar combine the remaining 3 tablespoons olive oil, the balsamic vinegar, 1 tablespoon chives, and the mustard. Season with salt and pepper.

5. In a medium bowl combine the quinoa, the vinaigrette, cheese, walnuts, and shallot. Toss to combine.

6. Divide quinoa mixture among serving plates. Top with roasted beets. Sprinkle with additional snipped chives. Serve warm or at room temperature.

PER SERVING *364 cal., 19 g total fat (2 g sat. fat), 13 mg chol., 521 mg sodium, 38 g carbo., 6 g fiber, 11 g pro.*

FOR INFORMATION ON SELECTING AND STORING BEETS, SEE PAGE 34.

FOR INFORMATION ON SELECTING AND STORING CARROTS, SEE PAGE 13.

Roasted Carrots with Cumin

PREP: 15 MINUTES   ROAST: 45 MINUTES   OVEN: 400°F   MAKES: 6 SIDE-DISH SERVINGS

A TOUCH OF AROMATIC, NUTTY-FLAVOR CUMIN SEEDS ADDS A SPICY FLAVOR TO THE SWEET CARROTS IN THIS AUTUMNAL SIDE DISH.

2 pounds baby carrots with tops

⅓ cup olive oil

1½ teaspoons cumin seeds, crushed

1 teaspoon kosher salt

3 cloves garlic, minced

3 sprigs fresh thyme

Fresh thyme leaves

Plain yogurt (optional)

1. Preheat oven to 400°F. Snip tops from carrots. Scrub carrots and, if deisred, peel. Slice any large carrots in half lengthwise.

2. In a large bowl combine carrots, oil, cumin seeds, kosher salt, garlic, and thyme sprigs; toss to mix. Transfer carrot mixture to a shallow roasting pan.

3. Roast, uncovered, for 35 to 45 minutes or until tender, stirring occasionally. Discard thyme sprigs. Sprinkle carrots with fresh thyme leaves. If desired, serve with yogurt.

PER SERVING *164 cal., 12 g total fat (2 g sat. fat), 0 mg chol., 441 mg sodium, 13 g carbo., 5 g fiber, 1 g pro.*

KITCHEN TIP

Young carrots—harvested from backyard gardens or farmers' markets—seldom need peeling. A good scrub with a stiff brush is all they need.

FOR INFORMATION ON SELECTING AND STORING BEETS, SEE PAGE 34.

Oven-Roasted Beets

PREP: 5 MINUTES ROAST: 1 HOUR OVEN: 425°F MAKES: 4 SIDE-DISH SERVINGS

BEETS STAIN LIKE THE DICKENS. BE SURE TO WEAR AN APRON AND AVOID DRIPPING BEET JUICE ON POROUS OR LIGHT-COLOR COUNTERTOPS.

6 medium-size beets

½ cup coarsely chopped walnuts, toasted

1 tablespoon balsamic vinegar

2 teaspoons olive oil

¼ teaspoon salt

¼ teaspoon black pepper

1. Preheat oven to 425°F. Cut tops off beets and trim ends. Wrap each beet individually in aluminum foil. Roast beets for 1 hour or until fork-tender.

2. Remove beets from oven; let stand until cool enough to handle. Remove foil. Using paring knife, slip skins off beets. Cut beets into quarters or eighths, depending on size of beets.

3. In a large bowl combine beets, walnuts, vinegar, oil, salt, and pepper; toss to mix. Serve slightly warm or at room temperature.

PER SERVING *149 cal., 11 g total fat (0 g sat. fat), 0 mg chol., 191 mg sodium, 10 g carbo., 5 g pro.*

Oven-Roasted Broccoli

PREP: 5 MINUTES ROAST: 20 MINUTES OVEN: 450°F MAKES: 4 TO 6 SIDE-DISH SERVINGS

ALTHOUGH BROCCOLI IS USUALLY QUICKLY STEAMED TO RETAIN ITS VERDANT HUE, ROASTING CONCENTRATES ITS SWEETNESS—AND THE SHORT ROASTING TIME ALLOWS THE FLORETS TO REMAIN QUITE GREEN.

2 tablespoons olive oil

4 cups broccoli florets

1 cup thinly sliced leeks

½ teaspoon salt

¼ teaspoon black pepper

1. Preheat oven to 450°F. Add olive oil to a shallow baking pan. Heat in oven for 1 minute. Stir broccoli into hot oil; cover with foil. Roast, covered, for 15 minutes.

2. Stir leeks, salt, and pepper into baking pan. Roast, covered, for 5 to 7 minutes more or until broccoli is crisp-tender.

PER SERVING *98 cal., 7 g total fat (1 g sat. fat), 0 mg chol., 319 mg sodium, 8 g carbo., 3 g fiber, 3 g pro.*

FOR INFORMATION ON SELECTING AND STORING BROCCOLI, SEE PAGE 14.

Oven-Roasted Fries

PREP: 15 MINUTES ROAST: 20 MINUTES OVEN: 450°F MAKES: 4 SIDE-DISH SERVINGS

THESE CHUNKY POTATO WEDGES WITH A TOUCH OF OLIVE OIL ARE PERFECT WITH STEAK OR BURGERS, AND THE CRISP STRIPS CONTAIN A MINIMAL AMOUNT OF FAT.

2 teaspoons olive oil

4 large baking potatoes (2½ pounds)

1 teaspoon salt

¼ teaspoon freshly ground black pepper

1. Preheat oven to 450°F. Line a baking sheet with foil; brush with 1 teaspoon of the oil. Scrub potatoes. Cut potatoes lengthwise into ½-inch wedges. Transfer to a large bowl. Add remaining 1 teaspoon oil, salt, and pepper; toss. Spread potatoes in a single layer on prepared baking sheet.

2. Roast for 20 to 25 minutes or until golden and crisp. Serve immediately.

PER SERVING *230 cal., 3 g total fat (1 g sat. fat), 0 mg chol., 705 mg sodium, 47 g carbo., 6 g pro.*

KITCHEN TIP

To test unidentified potatoes for starch content, slice the raw potato with a sharp knife. If the knife is coated with a creamy white substance that clings to the knife, it is a starchy potato. If not, it is a wax potato.

FOR INFORMATION ON SELECTING AND STORING POTATOES, SEE PAGE 38.

Spicy Roasted Cauliflower

PREP: 15 MINUTES ROAST: 30 MINUTES OVEN: 450°F MAKES: 4 TO 6 SIDE-DISH SERVINGS

ROASTED CAULIFLOWER IS A POPULAR STREET FOOD IN INDIA. AS THE FLORETS CARAMELIZE, THEY LOSE THEIR CABBAGELIKE CHARACTER AND BECOME TOASTY AND SWEET.

⅓ cup olive oil

1 teaspoon kosher salt

¼ to ½ teaspoon crushed red pepper

1 medium head cauliflower (2¾ to 3 pounds), cut into florets

1. Preheat oven to 450°F. In a large bowl combine olive oil, salt, and crushed red pepper. Add cauliflower florets and toss to coat. Place cauliflower in a shallow baking pan. Roast for 30 to 40 minutes or until browned, stirring once.

PER SERVING *125 cal., 12 g total fat (2 g sat. fat), 0 mg chol., 346 mg sodium, 4 g carbo., 2 g fiber, 2 g pro.*

FAST FLAVOR

Roast cauliflower florets, then toss the hot florets with bottled blue cheese vinaigrette. These tender vegetable bites are delectable alongside broiled steak.

FOR INFORMATION ON SELECTING AND STORING CAULIFLOWER, SEE PAGE 14.

FOR INFORMATION ON SELECTING AND STORING TOMATOES, SEE PAGE 21.

Oven-Roasted Tomatoes

PREP: 10 MINUTES ROAST: 14 MINUTES OVEN: 400°F MAKES: 8 SIDE-DISH SERVINGS

SERVE THIS DISH WITH SOME CRUSTY BREAD TO SOAK UP THE BALSAMIC- AND BASIL-INFUSED LIQUID.

Roma and/or pear tomatoes (about 7 cups)

2 tablespoons olive oil

2 tablespoons balsamic vinegar*

2 cloves garlic, minced

1 teaspoon kosher salt

½ teaspoon freshly ground black pepper

2 tablespoons snipped fresh basil

Fresh basil leaves (optional)

Crusty bread slices (optional)

1. Preheat oven to 400°F. Line a 13×9×2-inch baking pan with foil. If desired, remove and discard stems from tomatoes. Wash tomatoes; pat tomatoes dry with paper towels. Arrange tomatoes in a single layer in the prepared pan. In a small bowl whisk together olive oil, vinegar, garlic, salt, and pepper. Pour over tomatoes and toss to coat.

2. Roast, uncovered, for 14 to 18 minutes or just until the tomatoes are soft and skins begin to split, gently stirring once.

3. Transfer the tomatoes to a shallow serving bowl. Drizzle the vinegar mixture from the pan over the tomatoes. Sprinkle with snipped basil. Serve warm or at room temperature. If desired, garnish with fresh basil sprigs and serve with bread to dip in the vinegar mixture.

PER SERVING *61 cal., 4 g total fat (1 g sat. fat), 0 mg chol., 249 mg sodium, 7 g carbo., 2 g fiber, 1 g pro.*

*TIP: For a richer flavor, in a small saucepan heat ⅓ cup balsamic vinegar over medium heat until boiling. Boil gently, uncovered, for 6 to 8 minutes or until reduced to 2 tablespoons, watching carefully toward the end of cooking time because vinegar reduces quickly.

FAST FLAVOR

Consider making a double batch of these tangy roasted tomatoes—and instead of serving them whole, puree the roasted tomatoes in a food processor to make a simple sauce for fresh pasta.

FOR INFORMATION ON STORING AND SELECTING TURNIPS, SEE PAGE 37.

Roasted Baby Turnips with Garlic

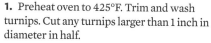

PREP: 20 MINUTES   ROAST: 45 MINUTES   OVEN: 425°F   MAKES: 8 SIDE-DISH SERVINGS

BABY TURNIPS HAVE A DELICATE, SLIGHTLY SWEET FLAVOR THAT BECOMES EVEN SWEETER AND MORE DELECTABLE WHEN ROASTED.

2 pounds baby turnips, ¾ to 1½ inches in diameter

3 tablespoons olive oil

¼ teaspoon salt

¼ teapoon freshly ground black pepper

20 large garlic cloves, peeled

1. Preheat oven to 425°F. Trim and wash turnips. Cut any turnips larger than 1 inch in diameter in half.

2. Place turnips in a 13×9×2-inch baking pan or shallow roasting pan. Drizzle with olive oil and sprinkle with salt and pepper. Toss to coat.

3. Roast, uncovered, for 15 minutes. Remove from oven; stir in garlic. Roast for 15 minutes; stir again. Roast for 10 to 15 minutes more or until golden brown and tender. Season with additional salt and pepper.

PER SERVING *82 cal., 5 g total fat (1 g sat. fat), 0 mg chol., 136 mg sodium, 8 g carbo., 2 g fiber, 1 g pro.*

GARLICKY GOODNESS

- To remove garlic odor from a cutting board, scrub the board with a paste of baking soda and water.
- To remove garlic odor from hands, under running water rub a stainless-steel spoon across your fingers and palm.
- To mash garlic into a paste, cover the cloves with a double sheet of kitchen parchment and mash with a meat pounder.
- To keep garlic from sticking to your knife when mincing, sprinkle the garlic with a bit of kosher salt. The salt will absorb the liquid in the garlic, making it less sticky.

Roasted Turnip Gratin

PREP: 15 MINUTES BAKE: 40 MINUTES OVEN: 425°F/375°F MAKES: 10 TO 12 SIDE-DISH SERVINGS

USE PURE MAPLE SYRUP IN THIS RECIPE. IT MAY BE PRICEY, BUT IT IS MUCH MORE FLAVORFUL THAN ARTIFICIAL PANCAKE SYRUP, MADE MOSTLY WITH CORN SYRUP. THE FLAVOR OF PURE MAPLE SYRUP IS WORTH EVERY PENNY.

1½ pounds turnips, peeled and cut into 1-inch chunks

1 small sweet onion, cut into 1-inch chunks

1 tablespoon olive oil

3 cups cooked long grain rice

1 medium cooking apple, peeled, cored, and chopped

4 ounces Gruyère cheese, shredded (1 cup)

¾ cup half-and-half

1 tablespoon pure maple syrup

½ teaspoon snipped fresh thyme

½ teaspoon salt

¼ teaspoon ground black pepper

1 cup coarse soft bread crumbs

2 tablespoons butter, melted

1. Preheat oven to 425°F. Place turnips and onion in a 15×10×1-inch baking pan. Drizzle with olive oil and toss to coat. Roast, uncovered, 20 to 25 minutes or until tender and edges begin to brown, stirring once. Reduce oven temperature to 375°F.

2. In a large bowl combine roasted turnips and onion, rice, apple, cheese, half-and-half, maple syrup, thyme, salt, and pepper.

3. Spread mixture in a 2-quart oval or rectangular baking dish. In a small bowl combine bread crumbs and melted butter. Sprinkle over the top.

4. Bake, uncovered, 20 to 25 minutes or until topping is browned and mixture is heated through.

PER SERVING *206 cal., 10 g total fat (5 g sat. fat), 25 mg chol., 247 mg sodium, 24 g carbo., 2 g fiber, 6 g pro.*

MAKE-AHEAD DIRECTIONS
Spread vegetable-rice mixture in the baking dish and cool slightly. Top with buttered bread crumbs, cover, and chill for up to 24 hours. Uncover and bake in a 400°F oven for 30 minutes or until heated through.

FOR INFORMATION ON SELECTING AND STORING TURNIPS, SEE PAGE 37.

Braised

HEARTY MEAT DISHES & STURDY VEGETABLE SIDES

Great meals result from great ingredients and slow cooking. In covered casseroles or stew pots, just a small amount of liquid slowly teases out flavorful juices of meats and vegetables as they meld into an aromatic and rustic melange of comfort and richness.

Beef Short Ribs with Smashed Horseradish Parsnips

PREP: 25 MINUTES BAKE: 2 HOURS OVEN: 350°F MAKES: 4 MAIN-DISH SERVINGS

HORSERADISH KICKS BACK AT SOME OF THE NATURAL SWEETNESS OF PARSNIPS, MAKING THE SMASHED ROOTS TASTE SMOOTH AND SAVORY. THE BITE OF THE MASH CONTRASTS WITH SUCCULENT RIBS.

3 pounds bone-in beef short ribs

½ teaspoon salt

¼ teaspoon black pepper

1 tablespoon olive oil

1 14-ounce can lower-sodium beef broth

½ cup water

1½ pounds parsnips, peeled and cut into 1½-inch chunks

½ cup chopped onion (1 medium)

8 cloves garlic, peeled

1 teaspoon snipped fresh rosemary

¼ cup half-and-half or light cream

2 tablespoons butter

1 tablespoon prepared horseradish

Snipped fresh rosemary (optional)

1. Preheat oven to 350°F. Trim fat from ribs. Sprinkle ribs with salt and pepper. In a Dutch oven heat oil over medium-high heat. Add ribs; cook until browned on all sides. Remove ribs from Dutch oven; set aside. Drain fat from Dutch oven.

2. Add broth and the water to Dutch oven, stirring to scrape up any browned bits from the bottom of the pan. Bring to boiling. Return beef ribs to Dutch oven. Add parsnips, onion, garlic, and 1 teaspoon rosemary to Dutch oven. Return to boiling. Cover Dutch oven and place in oven. Bake about 2 hours or until ribs are very tender.

3. Transfer ribs to a serving platter. With a slotted spoon transfer parsnips and garlic to a medium bowl. Using a potato masher, coarsely mash parsnips. Stir in half-and-half, butter, and horseradish. Season with salt and pepper.

4. Skim fat from cooking liquid; serve with ribs and parsnips. If desired, sprinkle with additional snipped fresh rosemary.

PER SERVING *761 cal., 63 g total fat (28 g sat. fat), 135 mg chol., 435 mg sodium, 21 g carbo., 5 g fiber, 26 g pro.*

FAST FLAVOR

To enrich plain mashed potatoes with sweet parsnips, add 1 part peeled and sliced parsnips to 3 parts potatoes. Cook and mash just as you would potatoes.

FOR INFORMATION ON SELECTING AND STORING PARSNIPS, SEE PAGE 37.

Beef and Sweet Potato Pot Roast

PREP: 30 MINUTES COOK: 2 HOURS MAKES: 8 MAIN-DISH SERVINGS

SWEET POTATOES MAKE A COLORFUL, HEALTHFUL ADDITION TO THIS SLOW-SIMMERED POT ROAST.

1 3- to 3½-pound boneless beef chuck
pot roast

Salt and black pepper

2 tablespoons vegetable oil

1 14-ounce can beef broth

1 tablespoon Worcestershire sauce

3 medium sweet potatoes, peeled and sliced
½ inch thick

12 ounces fresh green beans

1 large onion, cut into wedges

¼ teaspoon ground cinnamon

½ cup apple juice

2 tablespoons cornstarch

¼ teaspoon salt

1. Trim fat from meat. Sprinkle with salt and pepper. In a 4- to 6-quart Dutch oven heat oil over medium heat; add roast and brown on all sides. Drain off fat. Pour broth and Worcestershire sauce over roast. Bring to boiling; reduce heat. Simmer, covered, for 1¾ hours.

2. Add sweet potatoes, whole green beans, onion wedges, and cinnamon to Dutch oven. Return to boiling; reduce heat. Simmer, covered, for 15 to 20 minutes more or until meat and vegetables are tender. Transfer meat and vegetables to a serving platter, reserving juices in Dutch oven.

3. Stir together apple juice and cornstarch. Stir into juices. Cook and stir over medium heat until thickened and bubbly. Cook and stir for 2 minutes more. Stir in ¼ teaspoon salt. Serve over roast and vegetables.

PER SERVING 456 cal., 25 g total fat (9 g sat. fat), 109 mg chol., 441 mg sodium, 21 g carbo., 3 g fiber, 34 g pro.

KITCHEN TIP

There is often confusion about the difference between a sweet potato and a yam. Although they are similar, true yams are not widely available. Their flesh can range from off-white and yellow to purple or pink. Widely available sweet potatoes have the deep orange flesh you see here.

FOR INFORMATION ON SELECTING AND STORING SWEET POTATOES, SEE PAGE 38.

Braised Pork and Butternut Squash

PREP: 20 MINUTES COOK: 50 MINUTES MAKES: 4 MAIN-DISH SERVINGS

HUMBLE PORK SHOULDER IS ONE OF THE MOST INEXPENSIVE CUTS OF PORK. BUT ITS TERRIFIC TENDERNESS AND EXCEPTIONALLY RICH FLAVOR SURPASS MOST EXPENSIVE CUTS.

1 pound boneless pork shoulder, cut into 1½-inch pieces

1 teaspoon salt

¼ teaspoon black pepper

1 tablespoon olive oil

1 medium fresh poblano or Anaheim chile pepper, seeded and chopped (see tip, page 51)

½ cup chopped onion (1 medium)

2 cloves garlic, minced

2 tablespoons tequila or cider vinegar

1 14-ounce can chicken broth

1 teaspoon ground cumin

1½ pounds butternut squash, peeled and cut into 1-inch pieces

Small fresh sage leaves

1. Trim fat from meat. Sprinkle with ½ teaspoon of the salt and and the pepper. In a large skillet heat olive oil over medium-high heat. Add pork; cook until brown. Remove pork from skillet. Drain all but 1 tablespoon fat from skillet.

2. Add chile pepper, onion, and garlic to skillet. Cook and stir about 5 minutes or until tender. Remove skillet from heat. Carefully add tequila to skillet. Return to heat; cook, stirring to scrape up any browned bits from the bottom of the skillet. Add broth to skillet. Bring to boiling. Stir in the pork, cumin, and the remaining ½ teaspoon salt. Return to boiling; reduce heat. Simmer, covered, for 20 minutes. Add squash. Simmer, covered, for 30 to 40 minutes or until pork and squash are tender. Sprinkle with sage before serving.

PER SERVING *342 cal., 18 g total fat (6 g sat. fat), 61 mg chol., 1,044 mg sodium, 23 g carbo., 4 g fiber, 18 g pro.*

KITCHEN TIP

Make butternut squash a bit easier to peel—simply prick the squash in several places with a fork, then microwave on high for 1 minute. The peel will come off easily with a vegetable peeler.

FOR INFORMATION ON SELECTING AND STORING BUTTERNUT SQUASH, SEE PAGE 40.

FOR INFORMATION ON SELECTING AND STORING CABBAGE, SEE PAGE 35.

Roast Pork Tenderloin with Braised Cabbage

PREP: 20 MINUTES   COOK: 18 MINUTES   ROAST: 25 MINUTES   STAND: 10 MINUTES   OVEN: 450°F
MAKES: 6 MAIN-DISH SERVINGS

THE TENDERLOIN IS THE MOIST, TENDER MEAT NEXT TO THE LOIN. PORK TENDERLOIN USUALLY COMES TWO PER PACKAGE. ALTHOUGH HIGHER IN PRICE PER POUND THAN LOIN ROAST, TENDERLOIN IS AN EXCELLENT VALUE BECAUSE IT PRODUCES NO WASTE.

4 cloves garlic, minced

1¼ teaspoons salt

¾ teaspoon freshly ground black pepper

2½ teaspoons snipped fresh thyme

2 12-ounce pork tenderloins

1 cup chopped onion (1 large)

1 small head green cabbage (2 pounds), cored and sliced thin

1 cup thinly sliced Golden Delicious apple (1 medium)

¾ cup chicken broth

1 cup apple cider

1. For pork, preheat oven to 450°F. In a small bowl mash garlic with 1 teaspoon of the salt, ½ teaspoon of the pepper, and 1½ teaspoons of the thyme. Rub the garlic mixture over pork. Place onion in bottom of a roasting pan; place pork tenderloins on top of onions. Roast, uncovered, about 25 minutes or until meat thermometer registers 155°F.

2. Meanwhile, for braised cabbage, in a large skillet combine cabbage, apple, broth, the remaining ¼ teaspoon salt, and the remaining ¼ teaspoon pepper. Cover and cook over medium-high heat about 10 minutes or until cabbage is crisp-tender. Stir in the remaining 1 teaspoon thyme. Cook, uncovered, for 3 to 4 minutes or until most of the liquid is evaporated. Cover and keep warm.

3. Remove pork from roasting pan. Cover; let stand for 10 minutes. Temperature of the meat after standing should be 160°F. Pour apple cider into roasting pan. Place pan over burners on stovetop. Bring to boiling, stirring to scrape up onions and browned bits in bottom of pan. Serve pork with braised cabbage and pan juices.

PER SERVING *204 cal., 4 g total fat (1 g sat. fat), 72 mg chol., 685 mg sodium, 13 g carbo., 4 g fiber, 25 g pro.*

KITCHEN TIP
To core cabbage, first cut the head through the stem end into four wedges. Lay each wedge on its side and cut out its core.

Apple-Glazed Chicken with Braised Spinach and Leeks

PREP: 20 MINUTES BROIL: 12 MINUTES MAKES: 4 MAIN-DISH SERVINGS

LEMON-SCENTED APPLE JELLY SERVES AS A BASTE FOR THE CHICKEN DURING BROILING AND AS A DRESSING FOR THE WARM SPINACH SALAD. YOU'LL NEED A DUTCH OVEN OR LARGE KETTLE TO HOLD THE FRESH SPINACH WHILE IT COOKS.

½ cup apple jelly

2 tablespoons reduced-sodium soy sauce

1 tablespoon snipped fresh thyme

1 teaspoon finely shredded lemon peel

1 teaspoon grated fresh ginger

4 skinless, boneless chicken breast halves

Nonstick cooking spray

1⅓ cups coarsely chopped, peeled apples (2 medium)

1 medium leek, trimmed, cleaned thoroughly, and sliced (white part only), or ⅓ cup chopped onion

2 cloves garlic, minced

10 ounces fresh spinach, stems removed (about 10 cups)

Salt and black pepper

1. For glaze, in a small saucepan heat apple jelly, soy sauce, thyme, lemon peel, and ginger just until jelly is melted. Remove from heat. Reserve ¼ cup glaze.

2. Preheat broiler. Place chicken on the unheated rack of a broiler pan. Broil chicken 4 to 5 inches from the heat for 12 to 15 minutes or until chicken is tender and no longer pink (170°F), turning once and brushing with remaining glaze halfway through broiling.

3. Meanwhile, lightly coat a 4-quart pot with cooking spray. Heat over medium heat. Add apples, leek, and garlic; cook for 3 minutes, stirring occasionally. Add the reserved ¼ cup glaze; heat to boiling. Add spinach; toss just until wilted. Season with salt and pepper.

4. To serve, slice each chicken breast half crosswise into 6 to 8 pieces. Divide spinach mixture among 4 dinner plates. Top with sliced chicken.

PER SERVING *304 cal., 2 g total fat (1 g sat. fat), 66 mg chol., 420 mg sodium, 43 g carbo., 4 g fiber, 30 g pro.*

FOR INFORMATION ON SELECTING AND STORING SPINACH, SEE PAGE 13; FOR INFORMATION ON LEEKS, SEE PAGE 17.

Jerk Braised Chicken Thighs with Sweet Potatoes

PREP: 25 MINUTES   COOK: 35 MINUTES   MAKES: 4 MAIN-DISH SERVINGS

JERK SEASONING—A BODACIOUS BLEND OF CHILE PEPPERS, HERBS, AND SWEET SPICES—INFUSES CHICKEN THIGHS AND SWEET POTATOES WITH AN INTRIGUING, SWEET-HOT KICK.

8 chicken thighs with bone, skinned

½ teaspoon salt

¼ teaspoon black pepper

1 tablespoon olive oil

1 medium onion, halved and thinly sliced

1 tablespoon grated fresh ginger

2 cloves garlic, minced

1 cup chicken broth

2 teaspoons Jamaican jerk seasoning

2 small sweet potatoes, peeled, halved lengthwise, and sliced ½ inch thick (about 1 pound)

Snipped fresh cilantro

1. Sprinkle chicken thighs with salt and pepper. In an extra-large skillet heat oil over medium-high heat. Add chicken; cook until browned on both sides. Remove chicken from skillet. Drain fat; reserving 1 tablespoon.

2. In the same skillet cook onion, ginger, and garlic in the 1 tablespoon fat. Cook and stir about 4 minutes or until tender. Add broth, stirring to scrape up any browned bits from the bottom of the skillet. Bring to boiling.

3. Return chicken to skillet. Sprinkle chicken with jerk seasoning. Return to boiling; reduce heat. Simmer, covered, for 20 minutes. Add sweet potatoes to skillet. Cover and simmer about 15 minutes more or until chicken is done (180°F) and sweet potatoes are tender. Sprinkle with cilantro.

PER SERVING *283 cal., 9 g total fat (2 g sat. fat), 115 mg chol., 846 mg sodium, 20 g carbo., 3 g fiber, 29 g pro.*

FAST FLAVOR
To boost the flavor of ordinary roasted sweet potatoes before baking, toss 1 pound of peeled raw sweet potato wedges in a mixture of 1 tablespoon sesame oil, 1 tablespoon bottled chile-garlic sauce, and 1 tablespoon soy sauce.

FOR INFORMATION ON SELECTING AND STORING SWEET POTATOES, SEE PAGE 38.

FOR INFORMATION ON SELECTING AND STORING SPINACH, SEE PAGE 13.

Braised Beans and Greens

PREP: 20 MINUTES STAND: 1 HOUR COOK: 1 HOUR 15 MINUTES MAKES: 16 SIDE-DISH SERVINGS

YOU'LL RELISH THE COMBINATION OF TENDER COOKED BEANS AND FRESH SPINACH IN THIS WHOLESOME JALAPEÑO-SPIKED DISH. USE THE CHILE SEEDS IF YOU LIKE MORE HEAT.

1 pound dry cranberry beans, dry Christmas (calico) lima beans, or dry pinto beans

1 onion, cut into thin wedges

⅓ cup snipped fresh thyme

3 cloves garlic, thinly sliced

1 bay leaf

4 cups fresh spinach

¾ cup olive oil

3 fresh red or green jalapeño chile peppers, seeded and chopped (see tip, page 51)

1 teaspoon salt

¼ teaspoon black pepper

1. Rinse dry beans. In a large pot combine beans and 8 cups water. Bring to boiling; reduce heat. Simmer for 2 minutes. Remove from heat. Cover and let stand for 1 hour. (Or place beans in water in pot. Cover and let soak in a cool place overnight.) Drain and rinse beans.

2. Return beans to pot. Stir in 8 cups fresh water, the onion, ¼ cup of the thyme, garlic, and bay leaf. Bring to boiling; reduce heat. Simmer, covered, for 1¼ to 1½ hours or until tender for cranberry and pinto beans, or 45 to 60 minutes for Christmas lima beans or until tender. Stir in spinach; drain.

3. Transfer bean-spinach mixture to a large serving bowl. Cool slightly. Discard bay leaf. Stir in olive oil, chile peppers, the remaining thyme, the salt, and black pepper. Serve at room temperature. (Or cover and chill up to 6 hours.) Season to taste with additional salt and black pepper.

PER SERVING *192 cal., 11 g total fat (2 g sat. fat), 0 mg chol., 154 mg sodium, 19 g carbo., 7 g fiber, 7 g pro.*

KITCHEN TIP

To clean garden-fresh spinach, rinse the leaves in a basin of cool water. Sand and dirt will settle in the bottom of the basin. Several changes of water may be necessary. Immerse leaves in warm water on the final rinse—warmth will relax the spinach's crinkles and release any remaining sand.

Sweet Potato Stew

PREP: 15 MINUTES   COOK: 45 MINUTES   MAKES: 8 MAIN-DISH SERVINGS

THE FANTASTIC FLAVORS OF THIS MIDDLE EASTERN-INSPIRED STEW IMPROVE WHEN THE DISH IS
REFRIGERATED OVERNIGHT AND REHEATED.

2 tablespoons vegetable oil

1 cup chopped onion (1 cup)

1 red sweet pepper, cut into 1-inch pieces

1 green sweet pepper, cut into 1-inch pieces

1 yellow sweet pepper, cut into 1-inch pieces

2 jalapeño chile peppers, finely chopped (see tip, page 51)

2 cloves garlic, minced

2 14-ounce cans diced tomatoes, undrained

2 cups water

2 tablespoons packed brown sugar

1½ teaspoons ground cumin

¾ teaspoon ground cinnamon

1 teaspoon salt

2 pounds sweet potatoes, peeled and cut into 1-inch pieces

1 15-ounce can garbanzo beans (chickpeas), rinsed and drained

1 10-ounce package couscous

2 tablespoons snipped fresh cilantro

1. In a large saucepan heat oil over medium-high heat. Add onion, sweet peppers, chile peppers, and garlic; cook about 5 minutes or until tender.

2. Add undrained tomatoes, the water, brown sugar, cumin, cinnamon, and salt; stir to dissolve sugar. Add sweet potatoes and garbanzo beans. Bring to boiling; reduce heat. Simmer, covered, about 40 minutes or until potatoes are tender, stirring occasionally.

3. Stir uncooked couscous into stew; cook for 5 minutes more. Sprinkle with cilantro.

PER SERVING *419 cal., 5 g total fat (0 g sat. fat), 0 mg chol., 614 mg sodium, 82 g carbo., 9 g fiber, 11 g pro.*

FOR INFORMATION ON SELECTING AND STORING SWEET POTATOES, SEE PAGE 38; FOR INFORMATION ON SWEET PEPPERS, SEE PAGE 24.

Braised Red Cabbage with Apple Cider and Pears

PREP: 15 MINUTES   COOK: 30 MINUTES   STAND: 10 MINUTES   MAKES: 6 SIDE-DISH SERVINGS

FEW ACCOMPANIMENTS ARE AS PERFECT WITH ROAST PORK AS BRAISED RED CABBAGE, ESPECIALLY WHEN SWEETENED WITH PEAR, AS IT IS IN THIS QUICK RECIPE.

½ cup cider vinegar

½ cup apple cider

¼ cup sugar

1 medium head red cabbage, shredded (8 cups)

1 teaspoon pickling spice

2 tablespoons butter

1 medium pear, peeled, cored, and thinly sliced

1 small onion, thinly sliced

Salt and black pepper

1. In a large bowl combine vinegar, apple cider, and sugar. Stir to dissolve sugar. Add cabbage and toss to combine. Let stand for 10 minutes. Make a spice bag by placing pickling spice in the center of a double-thick, 6-inch square of 100%-cotton cheesecloth. Bring edges of the cheesecloth together and tie closed with clean kitchen string.

2. In an extra-large skillet melt butter over medium heat. Add pear and onion; cook until tender. Add cabbage mixture and spice bag. Bring to boiling; reduce heat. Simmer, covered, for 30 minutes, stirring occasionally. Discard spice bag. Season with salt and pepper.

PER SERVING *129 cal., 4 g total fat (2 g sat. fat), 10 mg chol., 539 mg sodium, 21 g carbo., 3 g fiber, 2 g pro.*

FAST FLAVOR

For a quick vegetable side featuring red cabbage, sauté thinly sliced red cabbage with slivers of red onion and a little bit of fresh thyme.

FOR INFORMATION ON SELECTING AND STORING CABBAGE, SEE PAGE 35.

FOR INFORMATION ON SELECTING AND STORING SWISS CHARD, SEE PAGE 23.

Braised Swiss Chard

START TO FINISH: 20 MINUTES MAKES: 4 SIDE-DISH SERVINGS

WHEN YOU BUY CHARD, YOU MAY FIND THREE VARIETIES. THE VARIETY THAT RESEMBLES RHUBARB, WITH DEEP RED STALKS, HAS THE STRONGEST FLAVOR. LIGHT PINK—OR RUBY CHARD—AND MULTICOLOR RAINBOW CHARD ARE MUCH MILDER IN TASTE.

1 pound Swiss chard

2 tablespoons olive oil

3 cloves garlic, minced

¼ teaspoon salt

¼ teaspoon black pepper

2 tablespoons grated Parmesan cheese

1. Cut tough stems from chard; discard. If desired, cut tender stems into thin slices. Coarsely chop leaves.
2. In an extra-large skillet heat olive oil over medium heat. Add the chard and garlic. (If necessary, add half the chard at the beginning; add remaining after chard begins to wilt.) Cook for 4 to 6 minutes or just until leaves are wilted, stirring occasionally. Stir in salt and pepper. Transfer to a serving dish. Sprinkle with Parmesan cheese.
PER SERVING *94 cal., 8 g total fat (1 g sat. fat), 2 mg chol., 406 mg sodium, 5 g carbo., 2 g fiber, 3 g pro.*

Cabbage with Fennel Seeds

PREP: 20 MINUTES COOK: 14 MINUTES MAKES: 4 SIDE-DISH SERVINGS

CRINKLY LEAVED VERZA DI VERONA, SAVOY, AND NAPA CABBAGES ARE ELITE MEMBERS OF THE CABBAGE CLAN, OFFERING SWEET, DELICATE FLAVORS AND QUICK COOKING TIMES.

1 tablespoon olive oil

1 large onion, sliced and separated into rings

6 cups thinly sliced Verza di Verona, savoy, or napa cabbage

1 teaspoon fennel seeds

2 tablespoons chicken broth or water

Salt and black pepper

1. In a 4-quart pot heat olive oil over medium heat. Add onion; cook about 10 minutes or until tender, stirring occasionally.
2. Add cabbage and fennel seeds to pan; cook and stir for 2 minutes. Add broth. Cook and stir for 1 minute more. Season with salt and pepper. Serve immediately.
PER SERVING *73 cal., 4 g total fat (1 g sat. fat), 0 mg chol., 196 mg sodium, 10 g carbo., 3 g fiber, 2 g pro.*

FOR INFORMATION ON SELECTING AND STORING CABBAGE, SEE PAGE 35.

FOR INFORMATION ON SELECTING AND STORING CAULIFLOWER, SEE PAGE 14.

Curried Cauliflower

PREP: 15 MINUTES COOK: 45 MINUTES MAKES: 6 SIDE-DISH SERVINGS

WHEN PURCHASING COCONUT MILK, READ THE LABEL CAREFULLY. IT'S EASILY CONFUSED WITH CREAM OF COCONUT—THE INGREDIENT USED IN EXOTIC COCKTAILS.

2 tablespoons vegetable oil

1 cup chopped onion (1 large)

1 teaspoon curry powder

½ teaspoon ground turmeric

½ teaspoon ground cardamom

Dash ground cloves

Dash cayenne pepper

4 cups cauliflower florets (about 1 pound)

1 14-ounce can unsweetened coconut milk

1 teaspoon salt

2 tablespoons snipped fresh cilantro

1. In a large skillet heat oil over medium heat. Add onion for 8 to 10 minutes or until tender.

2. Stir in curry powder, turmeric, cardamom, cloves, and cayenne pepper; cook for 1 minute.

3. Add cauliflower, coconut milk, and salt. Cook, uncovered, about 30 minutes or until very tender, stirring occasionally. Stir in cilantro. If desired, season with additional salt.

PER SERVING *237 cal., 18 g total fat (1 g sat. fat), 0 mg chol., 313 mg sodium, 15 g carbo., 3 g fiber, 4 g pro.*

KITCHEN TIP

Commercial curry powders vary greatly, so try several until you find a product that suits your taste. To boost the flavor of a purchased curry powder blend, add ¼ teaspoon ground cumin and ¼ teaspoon ground coriander to each tablespoon of commercial curry powder.

Braised Brussels Sprouts with Bacon and Crumb Topper

PREP: 20 MINUTES BAKE: 5 MINUTES COOK: 13 MINUTES OVEN: 425°F MAKES: 6 SIDE-DISH SERVINGS

BACON, OF COURSE, MAKES EVERYTHING BETTER—INCLUDING BRUSSELS SPROUTS. GIVE THIS YUMMY DISH A TRY AND YOU'LL SEE.

½ cup coarse soft bread crumbs

1 tablespoon butter, melted

3 slices bacon

1 tablespoon snipped fresh Italian parsley

1½ pounds Brussels sprouts, trimmed and halved

1 medium shallot, thinly sliced

½ teaspoon salt

¼ teaspoon black pepper

3 tablespoons dry sherry

½ cup chicken broth

1. Preheat oven to 425°F. In a small bowl combine bread crumbs and butter; toss to coat. Spread crumbs in a shallow baking pan. Bake, uncovered, about 5 minutes or until golden brown; set aside.

2. In a large skillet cook bacon over medium heat until crisp. Remove from skillet and drain on paper towels. When cool enough to handle, crumble bacon. In a small bowl combine bacon, bread crumb mixture, and parsley; set aside. Drain off fat, reserving 1 tablespoon.

3. In the same skillet cook Brussels sprouts, shallot, salt, and pepper in the 1 tablespoon fat over medium heat about 5 minutes or until vegetables are lightly browned, stirring occasionally. Remove from heat. Carefully add sherry to skillet. Return skillet to heat. Cook about 3 minutes or until nearly all the sherry has evaporated, stirring occasionally. Add broth to skillet. Bring to boiling; reduce heat. Simmer, covered, for 5 to 7 minutes or until Brussels sprouts are tender. Sprinkle with crumb mixture.

PER SERVING *126 cal., 6 g total fat (3 g sat. fat), 12 mg chol., 435 mg sodium, 12 g carbo., 4 g fiber, 5 g pro.*

FAST FLAVOR
When steaming or boiling Brussels sprouts, add a generous pinch of caraway seeds to the sprouts. The seeds infuse the sprouts with nutty, aniselike flavor, and the seeds' sweet, warm aroma will mask the strong cooking odor.

FOR INFORMATION ON SELECTING AND STORING BRUSSELS SPROUTS, SEE PAGE 35.

Kohlrabi Braised In Apple Cider

PREP: 15 MINUTES   COOK: 25 MINUTES   MAKES: 8 SIDE-DISH SERVINGS

KOHLRABI—PERHAPS THE ODDEST-LOOKING VEGETABLE IN THE GARDEN—HAS A SASSY-SWEET FLAVOR THAT TASTES LIKE A BLEND OF CELERY ROOT AND BROCCOLI. SAVE ITS LEAVES FOR SALAD OR STIR-FRY.

1 tablespoon butter

1 small sweet onion, cut into thin wedges

1¼ pounds baby kohlrabi, cut into wedges, or kohlrabi (about 3), peeled and cut into bite-size strips

1 cup apple cider or apple juice

1 tablespoon lemon juice

½ teaspoon salt

¼ teaspoon black pepper

¼ teaspoon freshly grated nutmeg

Fresh Italian parsley (optional)

1. In a large skillet melt butter over medium heat. Add onion; cook about 5 minutes or until tender. Add kohlrabi, cider, lemon juice, salt, pepper, and nutmeg. Bring to boiling; reduce heat. Simmer, covered, for 20 to 25 minutes or until kohlrabi is tender. If desired, sprinkle with parsley.

PER SERVING *38 cal., 2 g total fat (1 g sat. fat), 4 mg chol., 163 mg sodium, 3 g carbo., 1 g fiber, 1 g pro.*

FAST FLAVOR

Cut peeled kohlrabi into large matchstick pieces. Sauté in butter over medium heat until crisp-tender. Add a little cream, salt, and pepper and continue cooking until cream has thickened slightly and kohlrabi is tender. Serve with roasted meats and chicken.

FOR INFORMATION ON SELECTING AND STORING KOHLRABI, SEE PAGE 36.

Grilled

On a grill, fruits and vegetables get along well with fire and smoke. Spicy chiles, greens, luscious stone fruits, and plump tomatoes sizzle with flavor.

Grilled Ribeye Steaks with Smoked Tomatoes

PREP: 20 MINUTES GRILL: 16 MINUTES STAND: 1 HOUR 5 MINUTES MAKES: 4 MAIN-DISH SERVINGS

SMOKED TOMATOES ARE LAYERED WITH RICH FLAVOR THAT COMPLEMENTS GRILLED MEAT. THROW VINE-RIPENED TOMATOES ON THE GRILL WHEN THEY ARE INEXPENSIVE AND PLENTIFUL. AT SEASON'S END, TRY SMOKING GREEN TOMATOES TOO.

2 cups hickory or oak chips

2 teaspoons paprika

1 teaspoon kosher salt

½ teaspoon ground sage

¼ teaspoon garlic powder

¼ teaspoon dry mustard

¼ teaspoon black pepper

4 boneless beef ribeye steaks, cut 1 inch thick (2½ to 3 pounds)

6 to 8 small heirloom, Campari, or roma tomatoes, halved

8 to 12 scallions, trimmed

1. Soak wood chips in enough water to cover for at least 1 hour before grilling.

2. In a small bowl combine paprika, salt, sage, garlic powder, dry mustard, and pepper; set aside ½ teaspoon of the spice mixture. Sprinkle the remaining spice mixture over steaks; rub the mixture over both sides of the steaks.

3. Drain wood chips. For a charcoal grill, arrange medium-hot coals around a drip pan. Sprinkle wood chips over coals. Place steaks on grill rack over drip pan. Cover and grill for 16 to 20 minutes for medium rare (145°F) or 20 to 24 minutes for medium (160°F), turning once halfway through grilling. Sprinkle tomatoes with reserved spice mixture. Place tomatoes, cut sides up, on grill rack over the drip pan and scallions on grill rack over coals for the last 8 to 10 minutes of grilling time, turning onions once. (For a gas grill, preheat grill. Reduce heat to medium. Add wood chips to grill according to manufacturer's directions. Adjust for indirect cooking. Place steaks on grill rack over burner that is turned off. Cover; grill as directed.) Let steaks stand for 5 minutes before serving. Serve steaks with tomatoes and scallions.

PER SERVING *782 cal., 61 g total fat (25 g sat. fat), 185 mg chol., 646 mg sodium, 8 g carbo., 3 g fiber, 50 g pro.*

FAST FLAVOR

Lay a thick slice of ripe tomato on a piece of hearty country bread. Top with a little salt and pepper and a slice of mozzarella or other mild, meltable cheese. Broil until the cheese is lightly browned and bubbly. Enjoy immediately!

FOR INFORMATION ON SELECTING AND STORING TOMATOES, SEE PAGE 21.

Bison Steaks with Grilled Balsamic-Honey Peaches

PREP: 20 MINUTES   GRILL: 15 MINUTES   MAKES: 4 MAIN-DISH SERVINGS

BISON IS A NATURALLY FLAVORFUL, LEAN, AND TENDER MEAT AND CAN BE PREPARED MUCH THE SAME AS BEEF. BECAUSE IT IS LOW IN FAT, HOWEVER, IT IS IMPORTANT NOT TO OVERCOOK IT—MEDIUM DONENESS IS PERFECT.

3 cups sliced peaches (3 medium)

2 tablespoons honey

2 tablespoons balsamic vinegar

1 tablespoon packed brown sugar

2 teaspoons finely chopped crystalized ginger

4 10-ounce boneless bison top loin steaks, cut 1 inch thick

1 tablespoon cracked black pepper

¾ teaspoon salt or kosher salt

1. Fold a 36×18-inch piece of heavy foil in half to make an 18-inch square. Place peach slices in the center of foil. In a small bowl combine honey, vinegar, brown sugar, and ginger; drizzle over peaches. Bring up two opposite edges of foil; seal with a double fold. Fold in the remaining ends to completely enclose peaches, leaving space for steam to build.

2. Trim fat from steaks. Sprinkle steaks with pepper and salt; rub in with your fingers.

3. For a charcoal grill, grill steaks and peaches in foil packet on the rack of an uncovered grill directly over medium coals until steaks reach desired doneness and peaches are tender, turning once halfway through grilling. For steaks, allow 14 to 18 minutes for medium rare (145°F) or 18 to 22 minutes for medium (160°F). For peaches, allow 15 to 20 minutes. (For a gas grill, preheat grill. Reduce heat to medium. Place steaks and peaches in foil packet on grill rack over heat. Cover and grill as above.) Serve steaks with grilled peach slices.

PER SERVING *437 cal., 7 g total fat (3 g sat. fat), 201 mg chol., 588 mg sodium, 29 g carbo., 2 g fiber, 62 g pro.*

A PEACHY MARGARITA

Enjoy this margarita during the peak of peach season: Rub a lime wedge around each of four 8-ounce margarita glasses. Dip rims of glasses in margarita salt. In a blender combine 1 ripe peach, pitted and cut into chunks; ½ cup tequila; ½ cup fresh lime juice; ⅓ cup triple sec; 3 tablespoons fresh lemon juice; 2 tablespoons sugar; 1 tablespoon grenadine syrup; and 2½ cups ice cubes. Cover and blend until smooth. Pour into prepared glasses.

Spring Herbs and Prosciutto Grilled Chicken

PREP: 20 MINUTES **GRILL:** 1 HOUR 45 MINUTES **STAND:** 10 MINUTES **MAKES:** 6 MAIN-DISH SERVINGS

FOR A SIMPLE SIDE DISH, TOSS ASSORTED VEGETABLES (SUCH AS FENNEL WEDGES, SWEET PEPPERS, AND WHOLE MUSHROOMS) WITH OLIVE OIL. GRILL THE VEGETABLES—IN A GRILL BASKET OR ON SKEWERS—ALONGSIDE THE CHICKEN JUST UNTIL TENDER.

1 lemon

½ cup snipped fresh chervil or tarragon

¼ cup snipped fresh chives

1 shallot, finely chopped, or 3 tablespoons finely chopped onion

2 tablespoons butter, softened

1 teaspoon freshly ground black pepper

3 ounces prosciutto, finely chopped (about ½ cup)

1 5- to 5½-pound whole chicken

½ teaspoon kosher salt or coarse sea salt

1 tablespoon butter, melted

1. Finely shred peel from the lemon; halve the lemon. Set peel and lemon aside.

2. In a small bowl stir together chervil, chives, shallot, lemon peel, 2 tablespoons softened butter, and ½ teaspoon of the pepper. Stir in prosciutto; set aside.

3. Rinse chicken cavity with cold running water. Pat dry with paper towels and place on work surface. Using your fingers, gently separate skin from meat along breasts and legs to create pockets (being careful not to tear the skin). Using a spoon or your fingers, insert butter mixture between the skin and meat. Rub surface of chicken to evenly disperse butter mixture. Sprinkle cavity with salt and the remaining ½ teaspoon black pepper. Add lemon halves to cavity. Tie the drumsticks securely to the tail; tuck wings under breasts. Brush entire chicken with 1 tablespoon melted butter. Cover and chill chicken until ready to grill.

4. For a charcoal grill, arrange preheated coals around a drip pan. Test for medium heat above the pan. Place chicken, breast side up, on grill rack over drip pan. Cover; grill for 1¾ to 2 hours or until drumsticks move easily in sockets and chicken is no longer pink (180°F), cutting string between legs after 1½ hours. (For a gas grill, preheat grill. Reduce heat to medium. Adjust for indirect cooking. Place chicken on a rack in a roasting pan. Grill as above.)

5. Remove chicken from grill. Cover with foil; let stand for 10 minutes before carving.

PER SERVING *628 cal., 44 g total fat (15 g sat. fat), 217 mg chol., 732 mg sodium, 3 g carbo., 1 g fiber, 52 g pro.*

MAKE-AHEAD DIRECTIONS
Prepare chicken through Step 3. Cover and chill up to 24 hours. Continue as above.

FOR INFORMATION ON SELECTING AND STORING FRESH HERBS, SEE PAGE 26.

Peppered Beef Flank Steak with Grilled Corn Relish

PREP: 25 MINUTES   GRILL: 17 MINUTES   STAND: 5 MINUTES   MAKES: 4 MAIN-DISH SERVINGS

PEPPERCORN MELANGE IS A BLEND OF BLACK, WHITE, PINK, AND GREEN PEPPERCORNS. THE BLACK VARIETY, THE STRONGEST, IS MELLOWED BY THE MILDER INFLUENCES OF PINK, WHITE, AND GREEN PEPPER BERRIES.

1 1¼- to 1½-pound beef flank steak

1 tablespoon peppercorn melange, coarsely ground

1 teaspoon kosher salt

4 ears fresh sweet corn, husks removed

1 small red onion, cut into ½-inch slices

1 medium poblano pepper, seeded and halved (see tip, page 51)

1 cup grape or cherry tomatoes, quartered

3 tablespoons olive oil

3 tablespoons lime juice

1 tablespoon snipped fresh cilantro or Italian parsley

1 teaspoon smoked paprika or paprika

½ teaspoon salt

¼ teaspoon black pepper

1. Trim fat from steak. Score both sides of steak in a diamond pattern. Sprinkle steak with peppercorn melange and kosher salt and rub in with your fingertips.

2. For a charcoal grill, grill steak on the rack of an uncovered grill directly over medium coals for 17 to 21 minutes for medium doneness (160°F), turning once halfway through grilling. Grill corn, onion, and poblano pepper about 10 minutes or until tender and lightly charred. (For a gas grill, preheat grill. Reduce heat to medium. Place steak, corn, onion, and poblano pepper on grill rack over heat. Cover and grill as directed.) Let steak stand for 5 minutes. Thinly slice steak diagonally across the grain.

3. For relish, cut corn from cobs. Chop onion and poblano pepper. In a medium bowl combine corn, onion, poblano pepper, tomatoes, olive oil, lime juice, cilantro, paprika, salt, and black pepper. Serve with steak.

PER SERVING *419 cal., 22 g total fat (6 g sat. fat), 50 mg chol., 868 mg sodium, 24 g carbo., 4 g fiber, 34 g pro.*

FAST FLAVOR
Although it could be argued that corn on the cob requires no embellishment but butter and salt, try amping up the flavor of grilled or boiled corn on the cob with herbed butter or just a light smear of basil mayonnaise.

FOR INFORMATION ON SELECTING AND STORING SWEET CORN, SEE PAGE 25; FOR INFORMATION ON TOMATOES, SEE PAGE 21; FOR INFORMATION ON CHILES, SEE PAGE 24.

Grilled Lamb Chops with Blueberry-Rosemary Barbecue Sauce

PREP: 40 MINUTES GRILL: 12 MINUTES MAKES: 4 MAIN-DISH SERVINGS

THE ZINGY TASTE OF FRESH BLUEBERRY BARBECUE SAUCE ACCENTUATES LAMB'S DELICATE BUT ULTRARICH MEAT. IF BLUEBERRIES ARE ABUNDANT, CONSIDER MAKING A DOUBLE BATCH OF SAUCE—IT IS WONDERFUL SPOONED OVER GRILLED CHICKEN AS WELL.

1 tablespoon olive oil

½ cup chopped onion (1 medium)

2 cloves garlic, minced

1 pint fresh blueberries

¼ cup ketchup

3 tablespoons red wine vinegar

2 tablespoons honey

1 tablespoon Dijon-style mustard

1½ teaspoons snipped fresh rosemary

1 teaspoon bottled hot pepper sauce

¼ teaspoon salt

8 lamb loin chops, cut 1 inch thick

½ teaspoon salt

¼ teaspoon black pepper

1. For barbecue sauce, in a small saucepan heat olive oil over medium heat. Add onion and garlic; cook and stir for 10 minutes or until tender. Stir in blueberries, ketchup, vinegar, honey, mustard, rosemary, hot pepper sauce, and salt. Bring to boiling; reduce heat. Simmer, uncovered, about 10 minutes or until desired consistency.

2. Sprinkle lamb chops with salt and pepper. For a charcoal grill, grill chops on the rack of an uncovered grill directly over medium coals until desired doneness, turning once halfway through grilling. Allow 12 to 14 minutes for medium rare (145°F) and 15 to 17 minutes for medium (160°F). (For a gas grill, preheat grill. Reduce heat to medium. Place chops on grill rack over heat. Cover and grill as directed.) Serve with barbecue sauce.

PER SERVING *488 cal., 28 g total fat (12 g sat. fat), 112 mg chol., 801 mg sodium, 26 g carbo., 2 g fiber, 32 g pro.*

FAST FLAVOR

Blueberries pair beautifully with the flavor of ginger. Toss a cup into a batch of gingerbread to give it a healthful boost.

FOR INFORMATION ON SELECTING AND STORIES BLUEBERRIES, SEE PAGE 29.

FOR INFORMATION ON SELECTING AND STORING LETTUCES, SEE PAGE 11.

Grilled Shrimp and Romaine

PREP: 15 MINUTES   GRILL: 7 MINUTES   MAKES: 4 MAIN-DISH SERVINGS

IF YOU OWN A GRILL WOK, PREHEAT IT ON THE GRILL AND TOSS IN THE SHRIMP INSTEAD OF THREADING THEM ON SKEWERS. GRILL, STIRRING OFTEN, FOR 5 TO 8 MINUTES OR UNTIL SHRIMP ARE OPAQUE.

¼ cup olive oil

½ teaspoon kosher salt

1 pound fresh or frozen large shrimp, peeled and deveined

2 hearts of romaine lettuce, halved lengthwise

¼ cup finely shredded Parmesan cheese (1 ounce)

2 lemons

Olive oil

Kosher salt and freshly ground black pepper

1. In a small bowl whisk together ¼ cup olive oil and ½ teaspoon kosher salt. Set aside. On four 10-inch metal skewers, thread shrimp, leaving a ¼-inch space between each shrimp. Brush oil mixture over shrimp and cut sides of lettuce. Transfer skewers and lettuce to a baking sheet or tray.

2. For a charcoal grill, place shrimp on the grill rack directly over medium coals. Grill, uncovered, for 5 to 8 minutes or until shrimp are opaque, turning once halfway through grilling. Grill lettuce, cut sides down, for 2 to 4 minutes or until grill marks appear and lettuce is slightly wilted. (For a gas grill, preheat grill. Reduce heat to medium. Place shrimp on grill rack over heat. Cover and grill shrimp and lettuce as above.)

3. Place lettuce in serving bowl. Remove shrimp from skewers and add to bowl with lettuce; sprinkle with Parmesan cheese. Squeeze the juice of 1 of the lemons over the shrimp and lettuce; drizzle with additional olive oil. Sprinkle with additional salt and freshly ground black pepper. Cut the remaining lemon into wedges and serve with the salad.

PER SERVING 267 cal., 20 g total fat (3 g sat. fat), 133 mg chol., 514 mg sodium, 2 g carbo., 0 g fiber, 19 g pro.

LOVELY LETTUCE

- Lettuce should be torn by hand. Cutting it with a knife can cause it to turn brown. If you must cut lettuce, be sure to use a stainless-steel knife blade.
- The darker outer leaves of lettuce contain more vitamins and nutrients than the pale inner leaves.
- When it is cooked, lettuce is most often grilled, but it can also be sautéed, steamed, or lightly braised.

Grilled California-Style Pizza

PREP: 30 MINUTES RISE: 45 MINUTES GRILL: 10 MINUTES STAND: 15 MINUTES MAKES: 4 SIDE-DISH SERVINGS

GRILLING PIZZA GIVES IT THE SMOKY FLAVOR AND DELIGHTFULLY CHARRED CRUST OF A TRADITIONAL WOOD-FIRED PIZZA OVEN. THIS ONE—STUDDED WITH MEDITERRANEAN TOPPINGS—MAKES A WONDERFUL APPETIZER OR MEAT-FREE MAIN DISH. (PICTURED ON THE COVER.)

1 purchased frozen pizza crust or 1 Homemade Grilled Pizza Crust

2 tablespoons olive oil

1 clove garlic, minced

¼ teaspoon crushed red pepper

1½ cups chopped yellow or red heirloom tomatoes (2 medium)

¾ cup red sweet pepper strips

½ of a small onion, cut into thin slivers

2 ounces semisoft goat cheese or feta cheese, crumbled or cut up

8 to 12 pitted kalamata olives, halved or quartered lengthwise

5 ounces fresh mozzarella cheese, cut into small cubes

Fresh oregano leaves or snipped fresh basil

1. Thaw purchased crust or prepare Homemade Grilled Pizza Crust. In a small bowl combine olive oil, garlic, and crushed red pepper. Brush over the top of the pizza crust.

2. For a charcoal grill, carefully slide pizza crust, oiled side down, onto the lightly greased rack of a grill directly over medium coals. Cover and grill about 6 minutes or until light brown and firm. Transfer crust, grilled side up, to the back of a baking sheet. (For a gas grill, preheat grill. Reduce heat to low. Place dough on greased grill rack over heat. Cover and grill as directed.)

3. Top grilled side of crust with tomato, sweet pepper, onion, goat cheese, and olives. Sprinkle with mozzarella. Slide onto grill rack. Cover; grill for 4 to 6 minutes or until cheese melts. Sprinkle with fresh oregano or basil.

PER SERVING *698 cal., 31 g total fat (10 g sat. fat), 36 mg chol., 1,150 mg sodium, 82 g carbo., 6 g fiber, 21 g pro.*

HOMEMADE GRILLED PIZZA CRUST: In a small bowl sprinkle 1 package active dry yeast and ¼ teaspoon sugar over 1 cup warm water (105°F to 115°F). Let stand about 5 minutes or until yeast is bubbly. Stir in 2 tablespoons olive oil. In a food processor combine 3 cups all-purpose flour, 1 teaspoon sugar, and 1 teaspoon salt. Cover and pulse until combined. With food processor running, pour yeast mixture in a steady stream through feed tube. Process for 1 minute. Place dough in a lightly greased bowl, turning once to grease surface. Cover; let rise in a warm place until double in size (45 to 60 minutes). Punch dough down. Turn out dough onto a lightly floured surface. Cover; let rest for 15 minutes. Pat or roll dough portion into a 14-inch circle.

KITCHEN TIP

To make pizza using a pizza stone, prepare crust as directed in Step 1. Preheat pizza stone according to manufacturer's directions. Top as directed in Step 3. Slide crust from baking sheet onto preheated pizza stone on grill. Cover and grill as directed.

FOR INFORMATION ON SELECTING AND STORING TOMATOES, SEE PAGE 21; FOR INFORMATION ON SWEET PEPPERS, SEE PAGE 24.

FOR INFORMATION ON SELECTING AND STORING CHILES, SEE PAGE 24; FOR INFORMATION ON TOMATOES, SEE PAGE 21.

Grilled Stuffed Green Chiles

PREP: 20 MINUTES GRILL: 13 MINUTES STAND: 20 MINUTES CHILL: 1 HOUR MAKES: 4 APPETIZERS

THESE DELICIOUS STUFFED CHILES ARE SERVED WITH A FRESH TOMATO SALSA. IN A PINCH, PURCHASED SALSA IS A PERFECTLY ACCEPTABLE SUBSTITUTE.

4 large fresh Anaheim chile peppers (see tip, page 51)

3 ounces soft goat cheese (chèvre) or cream cheese, softened

1 cup shredded Colby cheese or Colby and Monterey Jack cheese

Dash cayenne pepper

Vegetable oil

1 recipe Fresh Tomato Salsa

1. Rinse peppers; pat dry. Carefully cut a lengthwise slit down one side of each pepper. Using a small, sharp knife, gently scrape out as many seeds and as much membrane as possible without tearing the pepper. Leave stems attached.

2. For a charcoal grill, place peppers on the rack of an uncovered grill directly over hot coals. Grill for 10 to 12 minutes or until skin turns dark and blisters, turning often during grilling. (For a gas grill, preheat grill. Place peppers on the grill rack over heat. Cover and grill as directed.)

3. Wrap peppers in foil; let stand for 20 minutes. When cool enough to handle, hold peppers under cold running water, carefully peeling away blackened skin. Be careful not to tear peppers.

4. In a small bowl stir together goat cheese, Colby cheese, and cayenne pepper. Spoon 2 to 3 tablespoons of the cheese mixture into each of the whole peppers. Do not overstuff. Pinch edges together with cheese to nearly seal.

5. Lightly brush stuffed peppers with oil. If desired, place peppers in a grill basket. For a charcoal grill, place peppers on the grill rack directly over medium-hot coals (or place grill basket on rack directly over medium-hot coals). Grill for 3 to 4 minutes or just until cheese melts. Do not turn. (For a gas grill, reduce heat to medium-high. Place peppers on the grill rack over heat. Cover and grill as directed.) Serve warm with Fresh Tomato Salsa.

FRESH TOMATO SALSA: In a medium bowl combine 2 cups coarsely chopped tomatoes (2 large); ¼ cup finely chopped sweet onion; 1 to 2 small fresh serrano or jalapeño chile peppers, seeded and finely chopped (see tip, page 51); 1 teaspoon sugar; and ½ teaspoon salt. Cover and chill for 1 to 24 hours.

PER APPETIZER *278 cal., 21 g total fat (10 g sat. fat), 36 mg chol., 550 mg sodium, 12 g carbo., 2 g fiber, 13 g pro.*

MAKE-AHEAD DIRECTIONS
Prepare as above through Step 3. Cover and chill for up to 24 hours. Continue as above in Steps 4 and 5.

Grilled Eggplant Stacks with Basil Chiffonade

PREP: 25 MINUTES GRILL: 8 MINUTES COOL: 1 HOUR MAKES: 5 TO 6 SIDE-DISH SERVINGS

EGGPLANT IS LIKE A SPONGE WHEN IT COMES TO SOAKING UP THE MARVELOUS FLAVORS OF FOODS WITH WHICH IT IS PAIRED. PURPLE EGGPLANT WILL MAKE THE PRETTIEST DISH, BUT WHITE OR GOLDEN EGGPLANT WILL WORK AS WELL.

1 large eggplant, cut crosswise into ½-inch slices (10 to 12 slices)

5 tablespoons Basil-Infused Olive Oil*

½ teaspoon salt

½ teaspoon black pepper

1 19-ounce can cannellini (white kidney) beans, rinsed and drained

4 ounces feta cheese, crumbled

½ teaspoon finely shredded lemon peel

2 tablespoons lemon juice

1 clove garlic, minced

½ cup bottled roasted red sweet peppers, cut into bite-size strips

¼ cup fresh basil leaves

1. Brush eggplant slices with 2 tablespoons of the Basil-Infused Olive Oil. Sprinkle with salt and pepper.

2. For a charcoal grill, grill eggplant slices on the rack of an uncovered grill directly over medium-high coals for 8 to 10 minutes or until very tender and lightly charred, turning frequently. (For a gas grill, preheat grill. Reduce heat to medium-high. Place eggplant slices on grill rack directly over heat. Cover and grill as directed.)

3. In a food processor or blender combine cannellini beans, feta cheese, lemon peel, lemon juice, 2 tablespoons of the Basil-Infused Olive Oil, and the garlic. Cover and process or blend just until combined but still chunky. Season with additional salt and black pepper.

4. Arrange eggplant slices on serving plates. Top with bean mixture and roasted pepper strips. Drizzle with the remaining 1 tablespoon Basil-Infused Olive Oil. For basil chiffonade, roll up basil leaves and cut across the roll; sprinkle over eggplant stacks.

PER SERVING *302 cal., 19 g total fat (5 g sat. fat), 20 mg chol., 771 mg sodium, 27 g carbo., 10 g fiber, 11 g pro.*

*NOTE: If you like, substitute purchased basil-infused olive oil for the homemade.

BASIL-INFUSED OLIVE OIL

In a blender combine ½ cup extra virgin olive oil and ½ cup packed fresh basil leaves. Cover and blend until finely chopped. Transfer oil to a small saucepan. Cook over medium heat just until bubbles appear around edges. Remove from heat. Cool to room temperature. Strain mixture and store in a covered container in the refrigerator up to 3 days.

FOR INFORMATION ON SELECTING AND STORING EGGPLANT, SEE PAGE 23.

FOR INFORMATION ON SELECTING AND STORING SWEET POTATOES, SEE PAGE 38.

Chipotle Sweet Potatoes

PREP: 20 MINUTES   GRILL: 6 MINUTES   MAKES: 4 OR 5 SIDE-DISH SERVINGS

DRIED CHIPOTLES, SIMILAR TO THE CANNED VARIETY, ARE SUPER-SMOKY TASTING AND WICKEDLY HOT. THE SMOKE AND HEAT PUT AN INCENDIARY SPIN ON SWEET POTATOES.

4 medium sweet potatoes (about 1½ pounds)

2 to 3 dried chipotle peppers, seeded (see tip, page 51)

1 tablespoon olive oil

1½ teaspoons paprika

½ teaspoon chili powder

¼ teaspoon salt

1 to 2 tablespoons water

1. Scrub sweet potatoes; pat dry with paper towels. Cut sweet potatoes in half lengthwise; cut each half into 4 wedges.

2. In a covered large saucepan cook sweet potatoes in a small amount of boiling water for 5 to 7 minutes or until almost tender. Drain; cool.

3. Meanwhile, place chipotle peppers in a blender, food processor, or coffee mill. Cover and blend, process, or grind until peppers are ground. In a small bowl stir together the ground chipotle peppers, olive oil, paprika, chili powder, and salt. Stir in enough of the water to make the mixture brushing consistency. Brush the chipotle mixture over potatoes.

4. For a charcoal grill, place potatoes on the rack of an uncovered grill directly over medium coals. Grill about 6 minutes or until edges begin to brown and potatoes are tender, turning occasionally. (For a gas grill, preheat grill. Reduce heat to medium. Place sweet potatoes on grill rack over heat. Cover and grill as directed.)

PER SERVING *154 cal., 4 g total fat (1 g sat. fat), 0 mg chol., 221 mg sodium, 28 g carbo., 4 g fiber, 3 g pro.*

MAKE-AHEAD DIRECTIONS
Prepare sweet potatoes through Step 2. Cover and chill for up to 24 hours. Continue as directed.

FOR INFORMATION ON GROWING AND SELECTING SUMMER SQUASH, SEE PAGE 22; FOR INFORMATION ON TOMATOES, SEE PAGE 21; FOR INFORMATION ON FRESH HERBS, SEE PAGE 26.

Grilled Summer Squash Caprese

PREP: 20 MINUTES GRILL: 6 MINUTES MAKES: 12 SIDE-DISH SERVINGS

THIS GRILLED SQUASH RECIPE TAKES ITS INSPIRATION FROM CAPRESE SALAD—A TRADITIONAL ITALIAN DISH MADE WITH TOMATOES, BASIL, AND MOZZARELLA CHEESE.

3 pounds yellow summer squash (5 medium), cut lengthwise into ¼-inch slices

5 tablespoons olive oil

1 teaspoon salt

½ teaspoon freshly ground pepper

1 pint grape or cherry tomatoes, halved

½ cup fresh small basil leaves

1. Brush squash with 3 tablespoons of the olive oil; sprinkle with salt and pepper.

2. For a charcoal grill, grill squash, cut sides up, on the rack of an uncovered grill directly over medium coals about 6 minutes or until crisp-tender, turning once. (For a gas grill, preheat grill. Reduce heat to medium. Place squash on grill rack over heat. Cover and grill as directed.)

3. On a platter arrange squash, tomatoes, and basil. Drizzle with remaining olive oil .

PER SERVING *80 cal., 6 g total fat (1 g sat. fat), 0 mg chol., 200 mg sodium, 6 g carbo., 2 g fiber, 1 g pro.*

Fire-Roasted Acorn Squash

PREP: 10 MINUTES GRILL: 45 MINUTES MAKES: 4 SERVINGS

FALLING LEAVES AND CHILLY EVENINGS SET THE STAGE FOR WINTER SQUASH. RATHER THAN THE USUAL BROWN SUGAR AND BUTTER TREATMENT, BASTE RINGS OF SQUASH WITH TARRAGON BUTTER, THEN GRILL THEM. THEY'RE DELICIOUS WITH GRILLED PORK AND A DRY WHITE WINE.

1 tablespoon olive oil

½ teaspoon salt

¼ teaspoon black pepper

2 small acorn squash, cut crosswise into 1-inch rings and seeded

2 tablespoons butter, melted

2 teaspoons snipped fresh tarragon

1. In a small bowl combine olive oil, salt, and pepper; brush over squash rings. In another small bowl stir together melted butter and tarragon; set aside.

2. For a charcoal grill, arrange medium-hot coals around a drip pan. Test for medium heat above the pan. Place squash rings on grill rack over drip pan. Cover and grill about 45 minutes or until squash is tender, turning squash occasionally and brushing with butter mixture after 30 minutes of grilling. (For a gas grill, preheat grill. Reduce heat to medium. Adjust for indirect cooking. Place squash rings on grill rack over burner that is turned off. Grill as above.)

PER SERVING *156 cal., 9 g total fat (4 g sat. fat), 15 mg chol., 332 mg sodium, 20 g carbo., 4 g fiber, 2 g pro.*

FOR INFORMATION ON SELECTING AND STORING ACORN SQUASH, SEE PAGE 40.

Herbed Grilled Potatoes

PREP: 25 MINUTES GRILL: 16 MINUTES MAKES: 8 APPETIZER OR 4 SIDE-DISH SERVINGS

POTATOES IN HUES OF GOLD, RED, AND PURPLE MAKE THIS EASY APPETIZER OR SIDE DISH EXTRA SPECIAL. CHOOSE POTATOES OF EVEN SIZE TO BE SURE THE POTATOES BECOME UNIFORMLY TENDER.

2 pounds small red, yellow, and/or purple potatoes, halved

2 tablespoons olive oil

½ teaspoon salt

½ teaspoon freshly ground black pepper

1 to 2 tablespoons chopped fresh parsley, basil, and/or rosemary

1. In a covered large saucepan cook potatoes in enough boiling salted water to cover for 6 to 8 minutes or just until potatoes are tender. Drain.

2. In a large bowl gently toss potatoes with 1 tablespoon of the oil, the salt, and pepper. Transfer potatoes to a grill pan.

3. For a charcoal grill, place grill pan on the grill rack directly over medium coals. Grill for 16 to 18 minutes or until potatoes are tender and brown, stirring occasionally. (For a gas grill, preheat grill. Reduce heat to medium. Place grill pan on rack over heat. Cover and grill as directed.)

4. To serve, transfer potatoes to a serving bowl. Toss with the remaining 1 tablespoon olive oil and desired fresh herb. Serve warm.

PER APPETIZER SERVING *150 cal., 9 g total fat (2 g sat. fat), 5 mg chol., 226 mg sodium, 16 g carbo., 1 g fiber, 2 g pro.*

FAST FLAVOR

Mustard-roasted potatoes are a fast and flavorful side dish to all kinds of roasted and grilled meats. In a large bowl whisk together 5 tablespoons of Dijon-style mustard and 3 tablespoons of olive oil. Whisk in a bit of salt and black pepper to taste—and any fresh chopped herbs you might have on hand. Add 2 pounds of potatoes cut into 1½-inch pieces to the bowl. Toss until thoroughly coated. Spread in a single layer on a baking sheet and roast in a 400°F oven for 35 to 40 minutes.

FOR INFORMATION ON SELECTING AND STORING POTATOES, SEE PAGE 38.

Barley with Grilled Summer Squash and Herb Vinaigrette

PREP: 15 MINUTES COOK: 10 MINUTES GRILL: 10 MINUTES MAKES: 6 SIDE-DISH SERVINGS

THIS HEALTHFUL DISH WILL KEEP ANY SCHEDULE YOU WANT IT TO KEEP. THE MIX IS EXCELLENT HOT, WONDERFUL AT ROOM TEMPERATURE, AND EXCEEDINGLY GOOD SERVED COLD. IT WILL BE READY AT WHENEVER YOU ARE.

2 cups water

½ teaspoon salt

1¼ cups quick-cooking pearl barley

1 medium zucchini, quartered lengthwise

1 medium yellow summer squash, quartered lengthwise

1 small red onion, cut into 1-inch slices

3 tablespoons olive oil

¼ teaspoon black pepper

2 tablespoons white wine vinegar

1 teaspoon honey

1 teaspoon country Dijon-style mustard

½ teaspoon snipped fresh thyme

½ teaspoon snipped fresh oregano

½ teaspoon snipped fresh parsley

⅓ cup coarsely shredded Asiago or Romano cheese

1. In a small saucepan bring the water and ¼ teaspoon of the salt to boiling. Slowly add barley and return to boiling; reduce heat. Simmer, covered, for 10 to 12 minutes or until barley is tender. Drain, if necessary.
2. Brush zucchini, summer squash, and onion with 1 tablespoon of the olive oil. Sprinkle with the remaining ¼ teaspoon salt and the pepper.
3. For a charcoal grill, grill onion slices on the rack of an uncovered grill directly over medium coals for 5 minutes. Add zucchini and summer squash. Grill about 5 minutes more or until vegetables are tender and lightly charred, turning once. (For a gas grill, preheat grill. Reduce heat to medium. Place vegetables on grill rack directly over heat. Cover and grill as above.) Coarsely chop vegetables; set aside.
4. For vinaigrette, in a small screw-top jar combine remaining 2 tablespoons olive oil, white wine vinegar, honey, mustard, thyme, oregano, and parsley. Cover and shake well. Season with additional salt and pepper.
5. In a large bowl combine cooked barley, grilled vegetables, the vinaigrette, and the cheese.

PER SERVNG *380 cal., 14 g total fat (4 g sat. fat), 11 mg chol., 441 mg sodium, 55 g carbo., 11 g fiber, 10 g pro.*

SUMMER SQUASH SAVVY
- Place thin slices of zucchini or summer squash on a sandwich for a bit of crunch.
- Summer squash are excellent for stuffing. Cut in half horizontally and use a spoon to scrape out the seeds and create a channel for your favorite stuffing. Bake in a 400°F oven for 20 to 30 minutes or until crisp-tender.

FOR INFORMATION ON SELECTING AND STORING SUMMER SQUASH, SEE PAGE 22; FOR INFORMATION ON FRESH HERBS, SEE PAGE 26.

Grilled Peaches with Honey and Queso Fresco

PREP: 15 MINUTES   GRILL: 6 MINUTES   MAKES: 6 SERVINGS

QUESO FRESCO—OR "FRESH CHEESE"—IS A BRIGHT WHITE, MILD BUT TANGY CRUMBLING CHEESE FROM MEXICO. THE CHEESE IS OFTEN AVAILABLE IN SUPERMARKETS, BUT IF YOU ARE UNABLE TO FIND IT, STOP BY A LATIN MARKET AND TAKE YOUR PICK FROM MANY BRANDS.

½ cup honey

1 tablespoon white wine vinegar

½ teaspoon ground ancho chile pepper

1 teaspoon snipped fresh sage

6 ripe peaches

4 ounces queso fresco, coarsely crumbled (1 cup)

Fresh sage sprigs (optional)

1. In a small saucepan combine honey, vinegar, ancho chile pepper, and snipped sage. Heat and stir over medium heat just until mixture comes to boiling. Remove from heat; cool slightly.

2. Cut peaches in half lengthwise; remove pits. Brush cut sides of peaches with the honey mixture.

3. For a charcoal grill, grill peach halves, cut sides down, on the rack of an uncovered grill directly over medium coals for 6 to 8 minutes or until lightly browned and warmed through, turning once halfway through grilling. (For a gas grill, preheat grill. Reduce heat to medium. Place peach halves on grill rack over heat. Cover and grill as above.)

4. Place 2 peach halves on each of 6 dessert plates. Evenly drizzle the remaining honey mixture on top of peaches; sprinkle with queso fresco. If desired, garnish with sage sprigs. Serve warm.

PER SERVING *181 cal., 1 g total fat (0 g sat. fat), 0 mg chol., 4 mg sodium, 39 g carbo., 2 g fiber, 6 g pro.*

PEACH PERFECTION

- Nectarines, apricots, and plums may be substituted for peaches in equal measure in most recipes.
- The skin of peaches darkens with exposure to air, so they should be cooked or eaten immediately once cut. To slow darkening, dip slices in an acidic juice such lemon or pineapple—at full strength or diluted in water.
- Peaches and nectarines are nearly genetically identical, except peaches have fuzzy skin—nectarines do not.

Grilled Pears with Gianduja and Hazelnuts

PREP: 20 MINUTES GRILL: 10 MINUTES MAKES: 8 SERVINGS

GIANDUJA (*ZHAN-DOO-YAH*) IS A CREAMY HAZELNUT-FLAVOR CHOCOLATE FROM NORTHERN ITALY AND SWITZERLAND. THE POPULAR SPREAD MADE FROM GIANDUJA STARS IN THIS ELEGANT DESSERT. ALSO SERVE THE SPREAD WITH PURCHASED HAZELNUT OR LEMON SHORTBREAD COOKIES.

4 teaspoons butter, melted

1 tablespoon lemon juice

¼ teaspoon vanilla

4 medium pears, halved lengthwise and cored

2 tablespoons sugar

Vegetable oil

½ cup chocolate-hazelnut spread

2 tablespoons hazelnut liqueur (optional)

¼ cup chopped toasted hazelnuts

1. In a small bowl combine butter, lemon juice, and vanilla. Brush butter mixture over pear halves. Sprinkle with sugar. If desired, brush a grill pan with oil; place pear halves on grill pan.

2. For a charcoal grill, place pear halves in grill pan on the rack of an uncovered grill directly over medium heat. Grill for 10 to 15 minutes or until pears are lightly golden and tender, turning occasionally. (For a gas grill, preheat grill. Reduce heat to medium. Place pear halves in grill pan on grill rack. Cover and grill as directed). Remove from grill and place on 8 serving plates.

3. Meanwhile, in a small saucepan heat chocolate-hazelnut spread just until warm. If desired, drizzle liqueur over warm pears. Drizzle warm hazelnut spread over pears; sprinkle with nuts.

PER SERVING *181 cal., 9 g total fat (1 g sat. fat), 6 mg chol., 34 mg sodium, 26 g carbo., 3 g fiber, 2 g pro.*

FAST FLAVOR

Here's a perfect autumnal appetizer: Serve slices of perfectly ripe pears on a platter with hearty whole wheat crackers, a wedge of blue cheese, and pistachios or walnuts.

FOR INFORMATION ON SELECTING AND STORING PEARS, SEE PAGE 43.

Chilled

ICE CREAM & OTHER COOL FRUIT DESSERTS

Seasons are short and perfection is fleeting—especially for gifts from the garden. Prolong the pleasure of fresh berries, robust red cherries, luscious peaches, and juicy watermelon by placing them in a sweet state of suspended animation.

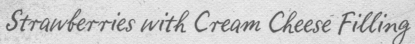

Strawberries with Cream Cheese Filling

START TO FINISH: 30 MINUTES MAKES: 32 FILLED STRAWBERRIES

WHEN JUICY-SWEET STRAWBERRIES FLOOD THE MARKET, TURN THEM INTO BEAUTIFUL TREATS LIKE THIS ONE, A PERFECT DESSERT FOR A CASUAL OUTDOOR MEAL.

1 8-ounce package cream cheese, softened

1 3-ounce package cream cheese, softened

½ cup powdered sugar

¼ teaspoon almond extract

2 tablespoons grated semisweet chocolate (about ½ ounce)

32 large strawberries

Chocolate curls or chocolate shavings (optional)

1. For filling, in a large mixing bowl beat cream cheese, powdered sugar, and almond extract with an electric mixer on medium until smooth. Stir in 2 tablespoons grated chocolate. Set aside.

2. Cut a thin slice from the stem end of a berry. With the berry upright on the flattened end, cut into 4 wedges, cutting to, but not through the stem end. Repeat for all berries. Gently pull apart wedges and pipe filling into center of strawberries, being careful not to pull strawberry wedges completely apart. Serve immediately or cover and chill up to 6 hours. If desired, garnish berries with chocolate curls before serving.

PER STRAWBERRY *48 cal., 4 g total fat (2 g sat. fat), 11 mg chol., 32 mg sodium, 4 g carbo., 0 g fiber, 1 g pro.*

KITCHEN TIP

To pipe the filling, spoon it into a piping bag fitted with a large round tip (or small resealable plastic bag, seal bag, and snip off a small corner of the plastic bag. Squeeze filling into strawberries.

Strawberry Ice Cream

PREP: 30 MINUTES FREEZE: ACCORDING TO MANUFACTURER'S DIRECTIONS
MAKES: 3 QUARTS (12 SERVINGS)

HOMEMADE ICE CREAM IS AN EXQUISITE TREAT THAT NEEDS NO EMBELLISHMENT—ESPECIALLY WHEN IT STARTS WITH FABULOUSLY FLAVORFUL RIPE STRAWBERRIES.

5 cups hulled fresh strawberries

3 cups whipping cream

1½ cups milk

1 12-ounce can evaporated milk

4 eggs* or pasteurized eggs or 1 cup refrigerated or frozen egg product, thawed

1½ cups sugar

1½ to 2 teaspoons vanilla

1. In a very large bowl mash strawberries with a potato masher. Stir in whipping cream, milk, evaporated milk, eggs, sugar, and vanilla. Freeze strawberry mixture in a 4- to 5-quart ice cream freezer according to the manufacturer's directions. If desired, ripen 4 hours.**

PER ½-CUP SERVING *402 cal., 27 g total fat (16 g sat. fat), 163 mg chol., 89 mg sodium, 36 g carbo., 1 g fiber, 7 g pro.*

*NOTE: Using raw eggs poses a higher risk of food-borne illness, especially in people who have weakened immune systems, children, and elderly people.

KITCHEN TIP**

Ripening ice cream: For a traditional ice cream freezer, after churning remove lid and dasher. Cover top with foil. Plug the lid hole with a cloth; replace lid on can and fill the outer freezer bucket with ice and rock salt (enough to cover top of the freezer can) in a ratio of 4 cups ice to 1 cup salt. Let stand at room temperature about 4 hours. For an ice cream freezer with an insulated freezer bowl, transfer the ice cream to a freezer container, cover, and store in the freezer for at least 4 hours.

FOR INFORMATION ON SELECTING AND STORING STRAWBERRIES, SEE PAGE 27.

FOR INFORMATION ON SELECTING AND STORING PEACHES, SEE PAGE 30.

Fresh Peach Ice Cream

PREP: 30 MINUTES **CHILL:** 4 TO 24 HOURS **RIPEN:** 4 HOURS **MAKES:** 1½ QUARTS (12 SERVINGS)

USE YOUR BLENDER OR FOOD PROCESSOR TO PREPARE ENOUGH PEACH PUREE FOR THE ICE CREAM AND THE CHOCOLATE-PEACH SAUCE. IF YOU HAVE LEFTOVER PEACH ICE CREAM, DROP SCOOPS INTO GLASSES OF COLD GINGER ALE OR LEMON-LIME SODA FOR A FANTASTIC FLOAT.

1½ pounds ripe peaches, peeled and pitted (5 medium)

3 cups half-and-half or light cream

1¼ cups sugar

6 egg yolks, lightly beaten

1 teaspoon vanilla

1 recipe Chocolate-Peach Sauce

1. Cut peaches into chunks and place in a food processor or blender. Cover and process or blend until smooth. Measure 2 cups of the peach puree for the ice cream; cover and chill. Measure and set aside 2 tablespoons of the peach puree for the Chocolate-Peach Sauce (if using). Cover and chill any remaining puree for another use.

2. In a large saucepan combine half-and-half and sugar. Cook and stir over medium heat until sugar is dissolved. Gradually stir about half the hot mixture into the egg yolks. Add yolk mixture to cream mixture in saucepan. Cook and stir about 5 minutes more or until mixture is slightly thickened and coats the back of a metal spoon. Remove from heat. Transfer to a large bowl; cover and cool for 30 minutes. Stir in vanilla.

3. Cover and chill for 4 to 24 hours. Stir in the 2 cups chilled peach puree. Freeze mixture in a 4- or 5-quart ice cream freezer according to the manufacturer's directions. Ripen at least 4 hours (see tip, page 279). If desired, serve ice cream with Chocolate-Peach Sauce.

PER ½-CUP SERVING *299 cal., 15 g total fat (9 g sat. fat), 134 mg chol., 38 mg sodium, 38 g carbo., 2 g fiber, 5 g pro.*

CHOCOLATE-PEACH SAUCE: In a small saucepan bring 1 cup half-and-half or light cream just to boiling. Remove from heat. Stir in 5 ounces finely chopped semisweet chocolate. Stir until the chocolate is completely melted (if necessary, whisk until mixture is smooth). Stir in 2 tablespoons reserved peach puree (from Fresh Peach Ice Cream recipe) and 2 tablespoons peach liqueur. Let cool slightly. Makes about 1½ cups sauce.

FAST FLAVOR

Drizzle this peachy treat with pureed raspberries to create a version of Peach Melba.

FOR INFORMATION ON SELECTING AND STORING BLUEBERRIES, SEE PAGE 29.

Lemon Blueberry Semifreddo

PREP: 10 MINUTES FREEZE: 4 HOURS STAND: 15 MINUTES MAKES: 10 SERVINGS

SEMIFREDDO IS ONE OF ITALY'S MOST WELL-KNOWN DESSERTS, ONE THAT APPEARS IN ALL SORTS OF CREATIVE FLAVOR COMBINATIONS ALL ACROSS THE COUNTRY.

1 pint lemon ice cream

Nonstick cooking spray

1 cup whipping cream

1 tablespoon honey

2 drops yellow food coloring (optional)

1 cup fresh blueberries

14 lemon or shortbread cookies, coarsely crushed

1. To soften ice cream, let stand at room temperature for 10 minutes. Meanwhile, lightly coat a 9×5×3-inch loaf pan with nonstick cooking spray. Line pan with plastic wrap; set aside.

2. In a large chilled mixing bowl beat whipping cream and honey with an electric mixer on medium until soft peaks form. Beat in ice cream. Beat ice cream mixture into whipped cream. If desired, beat in food coloring. Fold in berries and ⅔ cup of the crushed cookies.

3. Transfer ice cream mixture to pan. Tap pan gently on counter to release air bubbles. Sprinkle with remaining crushed cookies; gently press crumbs to adhere. Cover with plastic wrap. Freeze for at least 4 hours or until firm. Use plastic wrap to lift loaf from pan; invert on serving platter. Let stand for 15 minutes before slicing.

PER SERVING *283 cal., 16 g total fat (9 g sat. fat), 58 mg chol., 66 mg sodium, 23 g carbo., 0 g fiber, 3 g pro.*

FAST FLAVOR

This is one recipe that changes deliciously with your whims—and seasonal availability of ingredients. When the creative mood strikes, consider these adaptations and replace the lemon ice cream, blueberries, and cookies with:

● Key lime ice cream, blackberries, and graham crackers
● Chocolate ice cream, raspberries, and dark chocolate wafers
● Dulce de leche ice cream, cherries, and almond shortbread

Watermelon Cooler

PREP: 30 MINUTES CHILL: 2 HOURS FREEZE: 1 TO 2 HOURS MAKES: 10 SERVINGS

THIS REFRESHER IS LIKE DRINKING WATERMELON IN A GLASS!

5 cups seeded, cubed watermelon (about 3½ pounds)

⅓ cup raspberry or cherry syrup

Watermelon Ice Cubes or ice cubes

1 1-liter bottle carbonated water, chilled

Raspberry or cherry syrup (optional)

1. In a food processor or blender combine watermelon and ⅓ cup raspberry syrup. Cover and process or blend until smooth. Press mixture through a fine-mesh sieve into a medium bowl; discard pulp. Cover and refrigerate for 2 to 24 hours.

2. To serve, add Watermelon Ice Cubes to ten 12-ounce glasses. Pour enough watermelon mixture into glasses to fill half full. Add enough carbonated water to fill glasses. If desired, sweeten individual servings with additional syrup; stir to dissolve syrup.

PER SERVING *44 cal., 0 g total fat, 0 mg chol., 22 mg sodium, 11 g carbo., 0 g fiber, 0 g pro.*

WATERMELON ICE CUBES: Cut 1-inch cubes from watermelon flesh. Place the melon cubes in a single layer in a 15×10×1-inch baking pan. Freeze for 1 to 2 hours or until firm. If storing longer than 4 hours, transfer cubes to a resealable plastic freezer bag or freezer container and freeze until ready to use.

FOR INFORMATION ON SELECTING AND STORING WATERMELON, SEE PAGE 33.

FOR INFORMATION ON SELECTING AND STORING STRAWBERRIES, SEE PAGE 27.

Strawberry Zabaglione Loaf

PREP: 30 MINUTES COOK: 15 MINUTES FREEZE: 12 HOURS MAKES: 12 SERVINGS

ZABAGLIONE—PRONOUNCED *ZAH-BAHL-YOH-NAY*—USUALLY REQUIRES LAST-MINUTE PREPARATION, BUT THIS FROZEN VARIATION WILL ALLOW YOU TO TAKE YOUR TIME. PREPARE IT UP TO 4 DAYS BEFORE SERVING.

Nonstick cooking spray

4 cups chopped fresh strawberries

1 cup sugar

½ teaspoon finely shredded orange peel

4 egg yolks

2 eggs

¾ cup champagne or white grape juice

1 cup whipping cream

1 teaspoon vanilla

Halved fresh strawberries (optional)

Sweetened whipped cream* (optional)

Ground cinnamon (optional)

1. Lightly coat a 9×5×3-inch loaf pan with nonstick cooking spray. Line pan with plastic wrap; set aside.

2. In a food processor or blender process or blend 4 cups chopped strawberries until smooth. Transfer strawberry puree to a small bowl; stir in ¼ cup of the sugar; set aside.

3. In a double boiler set over simmering water combine egg yolks, whole eggs, and the remaining ¾ cup sugar. Stir in champagne. Cook and stir until mixture thickens and reaches 160°F on an instant-read thermometer, about 15 minutes.

4. Remove double boiler insert from the saucepan and place in a bowl of ice water. Whisk strawberry mixture about 5 minutes or until cool. Stir strawberry mixture into egg mixure.

5. In a medium chilled mixing bowl beat whipping cream and vanilla with an electric mixer until soft peaks form. Fold whipped cream into strawberry mixture. Spoon into prepared pan. Cover and freeze for 12 to 24 hours.

6. To serve, briefly dip the loaf pan into warm water. Invert onto a serving plate. Remove plastic wrap. Cut into slices. If desired, serve with halved strawberries, sweetened whipped cream, and cinnamon.

PER SERVING *232 cal., 14 g total fat (8 g sat. fat), 146 mg chol., 26 mg sodium, 24 g carbo., 1 g fiber, 3 g pro.*

KITCHEN TIP*
To make sweetened whipped cream, in a chilled mixing bowl combine 1 cup whipping cream, 2 tablespoons sugar, and ½ teaspoon vanilla. Beat with an electric mixer on medium until soft peaks form.

Royal Ann Cherry Compotes in Honeyed Syrup

PREP: 20 MINUTES COOK: 15 MINUTES CHILL: 4 TO 24 HOURS MAKES: 4 TO 6 SERVINGS

ROYAL ANN CHERRIES—PLUMP AND HEART SHAPE WITH GOLDEN ORANGE GLOW—ARE TRULY THE QUEEN OF CHERRIES, WITH FIRM FLESH THAT BURSTS WITH JUICE.

1 cup water

½ cup honey

1 3-inch piece stick cinnamon

3 cups fresh Royal Ann sweet cherries, pitted, or 2½ cups frozen pitted sweet cherries, thawed

1 tablespoon cherry brandy (optional)

1 cup cubed honeydew melon

2 fresh kiwifruits, peeled and sliced

Edible flowers (optional)

Small shortbread cookies (optional)

1. For syrup, in a medium saucepan stir together water, honey, and cinnamon. Bring to boiling; reduce heat. Boil gently, uncovered, about 15 minutes or until syrupy. Remove from heat; cool slightly. Transfer to a medium bowl. Cover and refrigerate 4 to 24 hours to chill thoroughly.

2. Discard cinnamon stick. Stir cherries and, if desired, brandy into syrup. Stir in honeydew and kiwifruit slices. If desired, garnish with flowers and serve with cookies.

PER SERVING *240 cal., 0 g total fat, 0 mg chol., 13 mg sodium, 63 g carbo., 4 g fiber, 2 g pro.*

GARDEN TIP

Chances are that you have edible flowers growing in your own yard. Bachelor's buttons, carnations, lavender, lilac, pansies, snapdragons, and violets are especially wonderful with sweets. Just be sure they have not been treated with any chemicals if you plan to eat them!

FOR INFORMATION ON SELECTING AND STORING SWEET CHERRIES, SEE PAGE 29; FOR INFORMATION ON HONEYDEW MELON, SEE PAGE 32.

Coffee-Chocolate-Cherry Icebox Pie

PREP: 35 MINUTES FREEZE: 4 HOURS 30 MINUTES STAND: 10 MINUTES MAKES: 8 SERVINGS

CONSIDER MAKING TWO OF THESE SCRUMPTIOUS ICEBOX PIES. THEY KEEP BEAUTIFULLY TIGHTLY WRAPPED AND FROZEN AND WILL BE READY TO GRAB FOR AN IMPROMPTU GRILL-OUT IN YOUR BACKYARD.

1 pint coffee-flavor frozen yogurt or ice cream

1 9-inch chocolate cookie crumb or chocolate-flavor crumb pie shell

⅓ cup light chocolate-flavor syrup or hot fudge sauce

1 pint vanilla frozen yogurt or ice cream

1 cup fresh sweet cherries, pitted and chopped, or ½ cup chopped frozen pitted sweet cherries

¼ cup chopped, toasted almonds

1 recipe Chocolate-Dipped Cherries; 1 cup fresh sweet cherries with stems, pitted; or 1 cup frozen pitted sweet cherries, thawed

1. In a large bowl use a large spoon to stir coffee yogurt until softened. Spoon into pie shell, spreading evenly. Drizzle with chocolate syrup. Cover and freeze for 30 minutes.

2. In a large bowl use a large spoon to stir vanilla yogurt until softened. Stir in chopped cherries and almonds until combined. Spoon mixture over frozen coffee layer in pie shell; spread evenly. Cover and freeze for 4 hours or until firm.

3. Remove pie from freezer 10 to 20 minutes before serving. Top with Chocolate-Dipped Cherries.

PER SERVING *398 cal., 15 g total fat (7 g sat. fat), 38 mg chol., 202 mg sodium, 59 g carbo., 2 g fiber, 9 g pro.*

CHOCOLATE-DIPPED CHERRIES: Pit 1 cup (about 16) fresh sweet cherries, leaving stems intact. Pat dry; set aside. In a small saucepan melt 2 ounces chopped bittersweet chocolate and 2 ounces chopped chocolate-flavor candy coating. Holding cherries by stems, dip into chocolate mixture to coat. Place on waxed pepper until set.

MAKE-AHEAD DIRECTIONS
Wrap pie tightly in freezer wrap and freeze for up to 2 months.

FOR INFORMATION ON SELECTING AND STORING SWEET CHERRIES, SEE PAGE 29.

FOR INFORMATION ON SELECTING AND STORING PEACHES, SEE PAGE 30; FOR INFORMATION ON FRESH HERBS, SEE PAGE 26.

Peaches in Basil-Peach Sauce

PREP: 10 MINUTES   **COOK:** 12 MINUTES   **MAKES:** 4 SERVINGS

BASIL IN A DESSERT? ABSOLUTELY. THE VERDANT GREEN HERB APPLIES ITSELF TO SWEET AND SAVORY COOKING—AND SEEMS TO TASTE BEST WITH FRUITS AND VEGETABLES THAT FLOURISH AT THE SAME TIME IT DOES, LIKE PEACHES.

8 medium peaches or nectarines

1 cup sweet white wine

⅓ cup torn fresh basil

1 to 2 tablespoons sugar (optional)

2 tablespoons snipped fresh basil

Fresh basil leaves (optional)

1. Remove pits from 2 unpeeled peaches; chop. Set remaining whole peaches aside.

2. In a medium saucepan combine the chopped peaches, the wine, the torn basil, and, if desired, sugar to sweeten. Bring to boiling; reduce heat. Simmer, uncovered, for 12 to 15 minutes or until sauce is slightly thickened.

3. Remove and discard the torn basil. Pour remaining peach mixture into a food processor or blender; cover and process or blend until smooth. Chill until ready to serve.

4. Halve the remaining peaches; remove pits. Cut each half into 4 slices. Arrange 6 peach slices on each of 4 plates; sprinkle snipped basil. If desired, garnish with fresh basil leaves.

PER SERVING *205 cal., 1 g total fat (0 g sat. fat), 0 mg chol., 5 mg sodium, 35 g carbo., 5 g fiber, 2 g pro.*

KITCHEN TIP

For best results in this recipe, choose one of these sweet white wines:

- Sauterne
- Tokay
- Riesling
- Gewürztraminer

Watermelon Sherbet

PREP: 25 MINUTES FREEZE: 8 HOURS MAKES: 8 SERVINGS

THIS REFRESHING AFTER-DINNER TREAT IS A WELCOME CHANGE FROM FAT-LADEN ICE CREAM AND IS JUST THE THING TO SCOOP AFTER A HEAVY MEAL.

4 cups cubed, seeded watermelon

½ cup sugar

⅓ cup cranberry juice

1 envelope unflavored gelatin

1. Place watermelon cubes in a food processor or blender. Cover and process or blend until smooth (should have 3 cups pureed watermelon). Stir in sugar.

2. In a small saucepan combine cranberry juice and gelatin. Let mixture stand for 5 minutes. Stir mixture over low heat until gelatin is dissolved.

3. Stir the gelatin mixture into the melon mixture. Pour into an 8×8×2-inch baking pan. Cover and freeze about 2 hours or until firm.

4. Break up frozen mixture and place in a large chilled mixer bowl. Beat with an electric mixer on medium to high until mixture is fluffy. Return to pan. Cover and freeze about 6 hours or until firm.

PER SERVING *83 cal., 0 g total fat, 0 mg chol., 3 mg sodium, 20 g carbo., 0 g fiber, 1 g pro.*

FAST FLAVOR
Prosciutto wrapped around slices of ripe cantaloupe is a classic Italian appetizer. The combination of salt and sweet makes it so delicious. For a twist on this theme, try small chunks of ripe watermelon with shaved Parmigiano-Reggiano cheese on top—and a few drizzles of fig balsamic vinegar.

FOR INFORMATION ON SELECTING AND STORING WATERMELON, SEE PAGE 33.

Raspberry Trifle

PREP: 1 HOUR CHILL: 4 HOURS PLUS OVERNIGHT MAKES: 16 TO 20 SERVINGS

THE BRITISH LOVE TRIFLES. NOT ONLY BECAUSE OF THE GREAT BEAUTY AND CREAMY RICHNESS BUT ALSO BECAUSE THEY ARE AN ENCHANTING CHOICE FOR MAKE-AHEAD DESSERTS.

4 cups milk

1⅓ cups whipping cream

1⅓ cups sugar

12 eggs, beaten

½ teaspoon vanilla

½ teaspoon almond extract

10 to 12 ounces packaged Italian savoiardi biscuits (crisp ladyfingers)

4 cups fresh raspberries

2 cups whipping cream

⅓ cup sugar

2 tablespoons sliced almonds, toasted

1. In a large heavy saucepan combine milk and 1⅓ cups whipping cream; stir in 1⅓ cups sugar. Cook and stir over medium heat just until mixture begins to simmer. Remove from heat. Gradually stir about 2 cups of the warm milk mixture into the eggs. Add egg mixture to milk mixture in saucepan.

2. Cook and stir over medium heat until mixture coats the back of metal spoon. Remove from heat and quickly cool by placing the saucepan in a sink or bowl filled with ice water for 2 minutes, stirring constantly. Stir in vanilla and almond extract. Pour into a large glass bowl or dish; cover surface of custard with plastic wrap. Chill for 4 to 24 hours.

3. Spread one-third (about 2⅔ cups) of the chilled custard in a 4- to 5-quart clear glass bowl or trifle dish (or use 2 smaller dishes). Layer half the ladyfingers side-by-side over custard, breaking to fit and stacking if necessary. Sprinkle 1½ cups of the raspberries over ladyfingers. Repeat layers. Top with remaining custard. Cover and chill overnight.

4. In a large mixing bowl beat remaining 2 cups whipping cream and ⅓ cup sugar with an electric mixer on medium until stiff peaks form. Spread whipped cream over custard. Sprinkle remaining raspberries over whipped cream; sprinkle with almonds. Serve at once.

PER SERVING *438 cal., 26 g total fat (14 g sat. fat), 232 mg chol., 166 mg sodium, 43 g carbo., 2 g fiber, 10 g pro.*

FAST FLAVOR

Should your berries be less than ripe or lacking in flavor—or even if they're perfect and you wish to accentuate their flavor, drizzle the berries with Chambord, France's wonderfully intense black raspberry liqueur.

FOR INFORMATION ON SELECTING AND STORING BLACKBERRIES, SEE PAGE 28.

Blackberry Floating Island

PREP: 30 MINUTES STAND: 30 MINUTES CHILL: 2 HOURS BAKE: 15 MINUTES OVEN: 300F°
MAKES: 6 SERVINGS

IT TAKES A BIT OF TIME AND EFFORT TO MAKE THIS OLD-FASHIONED DESSERT, BUT JUST ONE BITE OF
THE CREAMY CUSTARD AND ETHEREAL MERINGUE MAKES IT WORTH EVERY MINUTE.

5 eggs, separated

1 cup sugar

¼ teaspoon salt

2 cups half-and-half or light cream

1 teaspoon vanilla

½ teaspoon finely shredded lemon peel

½ teaspoon ground ginger

2 cups fresh blackberries, raspberries,
and/or blueberries

3 tablespoons sliced almonds, toasted

1. Let egg yolks stand at room temperature
30 minutes (cover and chill whites).
2. For custard, in a medium bowl whisk
together egg yolks, ½ cup of the sugar, and salt.
In a medium heavy saucepan heat half-and-half
until tiny bubbles just begin to break at edge of
pan. Gradually whisk about 1 cup of the warm
half-and-half into yolk mixture. Gradually
whisk yolk mixture back into remaining
half-and-half in saucepan. Cook, stirring
constantly, until mixture thickens enough to
coat the back of a spoon, about 5 minutes.
Strain custard through a sieve into a bowl. Stir
in vanilla and lemon peel. Place bowl in a larger
bowl filled with ice water; stir about 5 minutes
or until cool. Cover surface with plastic wrap;
chill for 2 to 24 hours.
3. Meanwhile, for meringues, let egg whites
stand at room temperature for 30 minutes.
Preheat oven to 300°F. Position a rack in middle
of oven. Line a baking sheet with parchment
paper; set aside. In a medium bowl stir together
remaining ½ cup sugar and ginger. In a large
mixing bowl beat egg whites on medium about
2 minutes or until soft peaks form (tips curl).
Gradually add sugar mixture, about
2 tablespoons at a time, beating on high until
stiff, glossy peaks form (tips stand straight), and
sugar dissolves. Divide egg white mixture into
6 mounds on prepared baking sheet. Shape
mounds by pulling some meringue up with the
back of a spoon. Bake 15 minutes or until set
and very lightly browned.
4. To serve, spoon custard into 6 shallow
serving bowls. Scatter berries over custards.
Using a large spatula, transfer a meringue to
each dish. Sprinkle with almonds. Serve
immediately or chill, uncovered, up to 1 hour.
PER SERVING *336 cal., 15 g total fat (7 g sat. fat),
206 mg chol., 188 mg sodium, 44 g carbo., 2 g fiber,
9 g pro.*

FAST FLAVOR
When you don't have time to make custard and
meringues, here's a quick, easy (and healthful)
dessert featuring fresh berries: Gently fold fresh
berries into low-fat vanilla yogurt and spoon into
dessert dishes. In a microwave or double boiler
melt semisweet chocolate chips or dark chocolate.
Drizzle the warm chocolate sauce over the yogurt
and berries and serve immediately.

Index

Numbers in bold indicate photo pages for finished dishes.

Numbers in bold indicate photo pages for finished dishes.

Q-R

Numbers in bold indicate photo pages for finished dishes.

Metric Information

PRODUCT DIFFERENCES

Most of the ingredients called for in the recipes in this book are available in most countries. However, some are known by different names. Here are some common American ingredients and their possible counterparts:

■ Sugar (white) is granulated, fine granulated, or castor sugar.

■ Powdered sugar is icing sugar.

■ All-purpose flour is enriched, bleached or unbleached white household flour. When self-rising flour is used in place of all-purpose flour in a recipe that calls for leavening, omit the leavening agent (baking soda or baking powder) and salt.

■ Light-color corn syrup is golden syrup.

■ Cornstarch is cornflour.

■ Baking soda is bicarbonate of soda.

■ Vanilla or vanilla extract is vanilla essence.

■ Green, red, or yellow sweet peppers are capsicums or bell peppers.

■ Golden raisins are sultanas.

VOLUME AND WEIGHT

The United States traditionally uses cup measures for liquid and solid ingredients. The chart (above right) shows the approximate imperial and metric equivalents. If you are accustomed to weighing solid ingredients, the following approximate equivalents will be helpful.

■ 1 cup butter, castor sugar, or rice = 8 ounces = ½ pound = 250 grams

■ 1 cup flour = 4 ounces = ¼ pound = 125 grams

■ 1 cup icing sugar = 5 ounces = 150 grams

■ Canadian and U.S. volume for a cup measure is 8 fluid ounces (237 ml), but the standard metric equivalent is 250 ml.

■ 1 British imperial cup is 10 fluid ounces.

■ In Australia, 1 tablespoon equals 20 ml, and there are 4 teaspoons in the Australian tablespoon.

■ Spoon measures are used for smaller amounts of ingredients. Although the size of the tablespoon varies slightly in different countries, for practical purposes and for recipes in this book, a straight substitution is all that's necessary. Measurements made using cups or spoons always should be level unless stated otherwise.

COMMON WEIGHT RANGE REPLACEMENTS

Imperial / U.S.	Metric
½ ounce	15 g
1 ounce	25 g or 30 g
4 ounces (¼ pound)	115 g or 125 g
8 ounces (½ pound)	225 g or 250 g
16 ounces (1 pound)	450 g or 500 g
1¼ pounds	625 g
1½ pounds	750 g
2 pounds or 2¼ pounds	1,000 g or 1 Kg

OVEN TEMPERATURE EQUIVALENTS

Fahrenheit Setting	Celsius Setting	Gas Setting
300°F	150°C	Gas Mark 2 (very low)
325°F	160°C	Gas Mark 3 (low)
350°F	180°C	Gas Mark 4 (moderate)
375°F	190°C	Gas Mark 5 (moderate)
400°F	200°C	Gas Mark 6 (hot)
425°F	220°C	Gas Mark 7 (hot)
450°F	230°C	Gas Mark 8 (very hot)
475°F	240°C	Gas Mark 9 (very hot)
500°F	260°C	Gas Mark 10 (extremely hot)
Broil	Broil	Grill

*Electric and gas ovens may be calibrated using celsius. However, for an electric oven, increase celsius setting 10 to 20 degrees when cooking above 160°C. For convection or forced air ovens (gas or electric), lower the temperature setting 25°F/10°C when cooking at all heat levels.

BAKING PAN SIZES

Imperial / U.S.	Metric
9×1½-inch round cake pan	22- or 23×4-cm (1.5 L)
9×1½-inch pie plate	22- or 23×4-cm (1 L)
8×8×2-inch square cake pan	20×5-cm (2 L)
9×9×2-inch square cake pan	22- or 23×4.5-cm (2.5 L)
11×7×1½-inch baking pan	28×17×4-cm (2 L)
2-quart rectangular baking pan	30×19×4.5-cm (3 L)
13×9×2-inch baking pan	34×22×4.5-cm (3.5 L)
15×10×1-inch jelly roll pan	40×25×2-cm
9×5×3-inch loaf pan	23×13×8-cm (2 L)
2-quart casserole	2 L

U.S./STANDARD METRIC EQUIVALENTS

⅛ teaspoon = 0.5 ml	
¼ teaspoon = 1 ml	
½ teaspoon = 2 ml	
1 teaspoon = 5 ml	
1 tablespoon = 15 ml	
2 tablespoons = 25 ml	
¼ cup = 2 fluid ounces = 50 ml	
⅓ cup = 3 fluid ounces = 75 ml	
½ cup = 4 fluid ounces = 125 ml	
⅔ cup = 5 fluid ounces = 150 ml	
¾ cup = 6 fluid ounces = 175 ml	
1 cup = 8 fluid ounces = 250 ml	
2 cups = 1 pint = 500 ml	
1 quart = 1 litre	